The Ends of Rhetoric

Contributors

JOHN BENDER

SACVAN BERCOVITCH

MIKKEL BORCH-JACOBSEN

JONATHAN GOLDBERG

NEIL HERTZ

GREGORY NAGY

PATRICIA PARKER

RICHARD SENNETT

DAN SPERBER

DAVID E. WELLBERY

DEIRDRE WILSON

WALTHER CH. ZIMMERLI

The Ends of Rhetoric

History, Theory, Practice

EDITED BY JOHN BENDER AND
DAVID E. WELLBERY

STANFORD UNIVERSITY PRESS

Stanford, California 1990

Stanford University Press, Stanford, California

© 1990 by the Board of Trustees of the Leland Stanford Junior University

Printed in the United States of America

CIP data appear at the end of the book

Contents

Preface vii

Contributors xiii

Part I   Rhetoric Today

Rhetoricality: On the Modernist Return of Rhetoric
JOHN BENDER AND DAVID E. WELLBERY 3

Part II   The Rhetoric of Tradition

The Crisis of Performance
GREGORY NAGY 43

Metaphor and Catachresis
PATRICIA PARKER 60

Part III   Rhetoric, Reading, Writing

On the One Hand . . .
JONATHAN GOLDBERG 77

Lurid Figures
NEIL HERTZ 100

Contents

Part IV The Analytic of Rhetoric

Analytic Speech: From Restricted to General Rhetoric
  MIKKEL BORCH-JACOBSEN   127

Rhetoric and Relevance
  DAN SPERBER AND DEIRDRE WILSON   140

The Emancipation of Rhetorical Elements in Art: From
Postmodernity to the Technological Era
  WALTHER CH. ZIMMERLI   156

Part V Rhetoric and Interaction in America

The Ends of American Puritan Rhetoric
  SACVAN BERCOVITCH   171

The Rhetoric of Ethnic Identity
  RICHARD SENNETT   191

Notes   209

Index   235

Preface

The essays gathered here address questions of rhetoric: its history, theory, and practice. With two exceptions, they were presented at a conference entitled "The Ends of Rhetoric," held at Stanford University in February 1987 under the sponsorship of the Department of Comparative Literature. At that time Comparative Literature at Stanford was negotiating the transition from programmatic to departmental status; that is, from an informal association of interested scholars and teachers to a circumscribed and self-regulating faculty. This conference promised to articulate some of the intellectual reasons for such an institutional change.

The conference held this potential because, for one thing, the theme fit well with the traditional sense of comparative literature as crossing national and linguistic boundaries. Since rhetoric is a universal of literary production and reception, the classics of comparatist study (e.g., the works of Erich Auerbach, Ernst Robert Curtius, and Leo Spitzer) are all concerned with questions of rhetoric. Indeed, one might argue that the academic discipline of comparative literature is the successor in the world of the post-Humboldtian university to the tradition of rhetorical doctrine and education that dominated literary study in Europe prior to the emergence of the national philologies.

But there is a second and for us more urgent sense in which the theme of rhetoric prompts reflection on the intellectual substance of our field. Following the "theory wave" of the past two decades, comparative literature has increasingly become a discipline in which the conceptual foundations of literary study itself are being redrawn. The modifier "comparative" has therefore taken on a new meaning, referring no longer solely to the international dimension of the enterprise, but also to its interdisciplinary and metacritical character. To pursue comparative literature today is in part to explore the connections that link literature to other fields of knowledge. Rhetoric is a domain where these connections become especially salient. Rhetorical inquiry, as it is thought and practiced today, occurs in an interdisciplinary matrix that touches on such fields as philosophy, linguistics, communication studies, psychoanalysis, cognitive science, sociology, anthropology, and political theory. The problematic of rhetoric, then, enables criticism to position itself within the contemporary epistemological landscape.

This volume embodies the interdisciplinary character of rhetoric. The contributors represent not only different national traditions of literary study but also different academic disciplines, and the individual essays draw on the conceptual resources of several fields. Furthermore, the essays combine historical, theoretical, and practical points of view. From a synoptic perspective, therefore—and despite the order imposed by this preface—the book reveals a structure of interlacing and diverging paths of inquiry, a network without a clearly defined beginning or end, and certainly without a preformulated systematic order or chronological sequence. No doubt this is an index of the intellectual ferment characteristic of rhetorical inquiry today: an area of study without accepted certainties, a territory not yet parceled into topical subdivisions, a mode of discourse that adheres to no fixed protocols. It is a noisy field in the cybernetic sense of the term: a fertile ground for creative innovation.

One of the oldest rhetorical insights has it that, in the domain of the uncertain, things overlap and shade into one another and that to commence and deploy a discourse bearing on that domain is, consequently, a radically contingent act. Moreover, such contingency is unavoidable: language leaves us no choice but to choose. We stress this point in order to signal that the order and grouping of essays we have selected here might be different. Other arrangements are possible. Readers will do well to test some of these out and thereby to actualize other connections.

Our opening essay situates modern rhetorical inquiry in a broadly delineated historical and theoretical context. We argue that the discontinuities marking the history of rhetoric are an important component in its contemporary redefinition. In order to ac-

centuate the rift separating rhetoric today from its classical ante-
cedents, we hazard the coinage of a new term: "rhetoricality." We
forge this neologism, bearing in mind Kenneth Burke's notion of
entitlement as a kind of abbreviated program, an invitation to conceptual or narrative development.

The essays by Gregory Nagy and Patricia Parker are yoked together in the book's second part because they both involve reread-
ings of the rhetorical tradition in its classical form. Nagy's contribution examines the inner tensions present in the fact and idea of
performance and the modes of accommodation with which texts
respond to these tensions. His contribution proposes a rethinking of
the concept of tradition as a form of crisis management that involves
selective memory, willful forgetting, and the constitution of authorial identity. Parker, too, engages the theme of "carrying over"
that the notion of tradition implies, but she pursues this theme in
terms of the transfer of meaning characterizing the tropes of metaphor and catachresis. Here also something of a crisis emerges, a crisis that threatens the possibility of clearly distinguishing literal
and figurative meanings and thereby of establishing rhetorical theory as a rigorous discipline. Thus, the tradition of rhetorical theory
from Quintilian to Blair and Fontanier is shown to repress system-
atically the unsettling issues that that same body of theoretical
work raises.

A third group of essays investigates rhetorical intricacies in the
work of exemplary thinkers. Jonathan Goldberg's discussion of
Barthes, Heidegger, and Freud reveals that the materials and gestures of writing are richly laced with erotic and metaphysical investments, that the instruments of script, as dreamt and described
by their users, enact a phantasmatic rhetoric of sameness and difference, origin and repetition, wholeness and division. His detailed
analysis of this "rhetoric of the hand" is all the more compelling
because it attends to writers whose overall theoretical positions
urge the critical dismantling of the scenarios they themselves re-
hearse. Neil Hertz takes up the work of Paul de Man, a critic who
has, perhaps more effectively than any other, insisted on the centrality of rhetorical concepts in literary studies. But rather than repeat
de Man's theoretical insistence on rhetoric, Hertz discloses the rhetorical—and especially figural—operations at work in de Man's
own prose. His essay traces out the sinuous path of de Man's itiner-
ary of reading.

Whereas the essays by Goldberg and Hertz attend closely to the texture of specific works, those gathered in the fourth part are principally concerned with the conceptualization of rhetoric. Mikkel Borch-Jacobsen's argument develops an alternative to the Lacanian version of a psychoanalytic rhetoric. Lacan, of course, had focused on the tropes of metaphor and metonymy, in which, following Roman Jakobson, he discovered rhetorical counterparts to Freud's notions of condensation and displacement. Borch-Jacobsen, however, draws on a different stratum of Freud's work: the question of one's affectability by an other, which is central to such phenomena as hypnotism, the transference, and the formation of social bonds. For Borch-Jacobsen, the real importance of rhetoric to psychoanalysis (and vice versa) lies in the mystery of pathos and persuasion. Dan Sperber and Deirdre Wilson pursue the analytic of rhetoric within the framework of a theory of cognitive processes. Drawing on their earlier modification of Paul Grice's conversational logic in terms of the concept of relevance, Sperber and Wilson show how the figures and strategies (e.g., metaphor and irony) conceived by traditional rhetoric as deviations from a norm in fact represent communicational moves continuous with normal linguistic practice. Their method casts many cherished notions (including those of trope and figurative meaning) by the wayside and opens up new possibilities for rhetorical study. This section's final contributor, Walther Zimmerli, approaches rhetoric from the standpoint of contemporary philosophical discussions bearing on the definition of modernity and postmodernity. Starting from Hans-Georg Gadamer's claim for the universality of hermeneutics, Zimmerli argues that the universality of rhetoric is a necessary corollary of that claim. Zimmerli's analysis of postmodern cultural production, especially architecture, shows how this universality comes to historical light in the liberation of rhetorical elements from functional and representational concerns. Postmodern culture is the culture of a thoroughgoing rhetoric, a rhetoric practiced not as a means to ulterior ends, but rather as an autonomous exercise.

Sacvan Bercovitch and Richard Sennett, in the volume's last part, discuss the peculiarly American deployment of rhetoric in the nation's colonial past and in its urban present. Both consider rhetorical mystification as a means of empowerment, and both notice the violence worked by the arts of persuasion (the most potent form of which may be unconscious *self-persuasion*). Bercovitch investigates the imagery of New England Puritan thought about the bicentennial of Columbus's voyage to the Americas in relation to the paradoxical fusion of sainthood and statehood in federalist rhetoric. The idea of personal or communal spiritual election was elided over time, under the pressure of historical events, into nationalist imagery that assigned to the federal model a mission in visionary history. Sennett suggests ways in which strategies of narrative rupture in James Baldwin's writings might be used in the modern city to break off the alienating rhetoric of ethnicity, which is founded upon narratives of origin in and departure from an idealized past, and to replace it with the shared experience of rupture and fresh arrival in the present that is characteristic of the inhabitants of modern cities.

A book such as this does not come into existence without the support of many individuals and institutions. In planning the conference "The Ends of Rhetoric" the editors were joined by Russell Berman, Elizabeth Heckendorn Cook, Jeffrey Schnapp, Elizabeth Statmore, and William Mills Todd III. Funding was provided through a generous grant from the Andrew W. Mellon Foundation. We are grateful to Bliss Carnochan, Morton Sosna, and the staff of the Stanford Humanities Center for their continuous assistance. Barbara Mendelsohn's artwork captured our theme in striking visual terms. Hayden White and Steven Mailloux offered valuable advice on the shaping of the book. Steven Brown provided essential assistance at every level from the smallest detail to the largest conceptual matters. The editors are especially grateful to Karen Rezendes, who from the beginning contributed so much to the completion of the project. Finally, we thank Helen Tartar of Stanford University Press for her unremitting support.

J.B.
D.E.W.

Contributors

JOHN BENDER is Professor of English and Comparative Literature at Stanford University. He is the author of *Spenser and Literary Pictorialism* and *Imagining the Penitentiary: Fiction and the Architecture of Mind in Eighteenth-Century England,* and coeditor of the forthcoming *Chronotypes: The Construction of Time.*

DAVID E. WELLBERY is Professor of German Studies and Comparative Literature at Stanford University. He is the author of *Lessing's Laocoön* and has edited *Positionen der Literaturwissenschaft* and coedited *Reconstructing Individualism* and the forthcoming *Chronotypes: The Construction of Time.*

SACVAN BERCOVITCH is Charles H. Carswell Professor of English and American Literature at Harvard University. He is the author of, among other books, *The Puritan Origins of the American Self* and *The American Jeremiad,* and is General Editor of the forthcoming multivolume *Cambridge History of American Literature.*

MIKKEL BORCH-JACOBSEN is Associate Professor of French at the University of Washington. He is the author of *The Freudian Subject* and the coauthor, with Jean-Luc Nancy and Eric Michaud, of *Hypnoses.* He is also the coeditor, with Léon Chertok, of *Hypnose et psychanalyse,* and is currently preparing a book entitled *Lacan, the Absolute Master.*

JONATHAN GOLDBERG is the Sir William Osler Professor of English Literature at The Johns Hopkins University. His most recent book is *Writing Matter: From the Hands of the English Renaissance,* from which the essay in this volume is drawn. His edition of Milton, coedited with Stephen Orgel, will be appearing soon.

NEIL HERTZ is Professor in the Humanities Center of The Johns Hopkins University. He is the author of *The End of the Line.*

GREGORY NAGY is the Francis Jones Professor of Classical Greek Literature and Professor of Comparative Literature at Harvard University. He is the author of *The Best of the Achaeans: Concepts of the Hero in Archaic Greek Poetry,* which won the Goodwin Award of Merit, American Philological Association, in 1982. Other publications include *Comparative Studies in Greek and Indic Meter, Greek Mythology and Poetics,* and *Pindar's Homer: The Lyric Possession of an Epic Past.*

PATRICIA PARKER, Professor of English and Comparative Literature at Stanford University, is the author of *Inescapable Romance* and the coeditor of a number of volumes of criticism and theory, including *Shakespeare and the Question of Theory, Lyric Poetry: Beyond New Criticism,* and *Literary Theory/Renaissance Texts.* Her most recent book is *Literary Fat Ladies: Rhetoric, Gender, Property.*

RICHARD SENNETT is Professor of Sociology and University Professor of the Humanities at New York University. He is a social critic and a novelist. This essay is adapted from his new book entitled *Conscience of the Eye.*

DAN SPERBER is a senior scholar at the Centre de Recherche en Epistémologie Appliquée (Ecole Polytechnique and C.N.R.S., Paris). He is the author of *Rethinking Symbolism, On Anthropological Knowledge,* and, with Deirdre Wilson, *Relevance: Communication and Cognition.*

DEIRDRE WILSON is Reader in Linguistics at University College, London. She is the author of *Presuppositions and Non-Truth-Conditional Semantics,* and the coauthor, with Neil Smith, of *Modern Linguistics: The Results of Chomsky's Revolution,* and, with Dan Sperber, of *Relevance: Communication and Cognition.*

WALTHER CH. ZIMMERLI is Professor of Philosophy at the University of Bamberg and Co-Director of the Institute of Society and Science at the University of Erlangen-Nürnberg. He is the author or editor of some 250 publications, including *Die Frage nach der Philosophie, Technologisches Zeitalter oder Postmoderne, Geist und Natur,* and *Wider die "Zwei Kulturen."*

PART I

Rhetoric Today

Rhetoricality:
On the Modernist Return of Rhetoric

JOHN BENDER AND DAVID E. WELLBERY

Roman architects employed materials and methods of construction utterly alien to the Greeks. Instead of the static post and
lintel system that stood behind virtually all Greek architecture,
the Romans used concrete and brick to enclose space in dynamic
membranes based upon circular and spherical forms: the arch, the
dome, the vault. At the same time, the Romans brilliantly inte-
grated into their immense structures the Hellenistic system of co-
lumnar orders—orders that seemed to manifest proportions fundamental to geometry, to the human body, and to nature itself. Using
the orders as visual analogies to human scale, the Romans anchored vast edifices within the same perceptual framework as the
observer. The Pantheon's gorgeously encrusted marble interior testifies that the Romans employed the orders in a full, coherent, and
systematic way as part of a figurative vocabulary, as devices to
communicate the relationship of human proportion to monumen-
tal space.

Greek and Roman societies were differently constituted yet
bound together in a visual tradition that continued deep into the
Middle Ages. Once powerfully reformulated during the Italian Renaissance, this same tradition defined European architecture until
eclecticism, historicism, and exoticism emerged during the later
Enlightenment and Romantic periods. From this point onward,
Greek and Roman classicism came increasingly to be viewed as
regional or historical styles—like the Egyptian, the Chinese, the
Persian—from among which architectural choices might be made.
Classicism ceased to be *the* style and became *a* style. Even though
residual, and often highly prestigious, use of the orders continued

in the nineteenth- and early twentieth-century official architecture associated with the École des Beaux Arts, the introduction of new structural materials such as cast iron and, above all, the prodigious increase of scale that typifies buildings of the industrial era ultimately toppled the orders. Their isolated revival as token elements in today's so-called postmodern architecture merely calls attention to the fact of their demise. When classical architectural forms return on the contemporary scene, their mode of existence is fundamentally different—despite outward similarities of appearance—from that which characterized them in antiquity and in premodern Europe. Only a formalism blinded by its own abstractness could overlook this historical transformation.

In this essay, we shall make an analogous argument regarding rhetoric as a tradition of discursive architecture and adornment, which, like the Greco-Roman paradigms of spatial organization, dominated the production, interpretation, teaching, and transmission of speech and writing in Europe from antiquity to the Enlightenment and the Romantic period. Even more clearly than in postmodernist citations of classical architectural forms, one can observe today a *return* of rhetorical inquiry, a resurgence of intellectual interest in the issues treated by classical and postclassical theoreticians of rhetoric. But returns and repetitions, as Kierkegaard and Gilles Deleuze have shown, are not reproductions of the same.[1] A temporal hiatus separates and distinguishes them from their original instance or reference. The contemporary return of rhetoric presupposes, through its very structure as return, an end of rhetoric, a discontinuity within tradition, and an alteration that renders the second version of rhetoric, its modernist-postmodernist redaction, a new form of cultural practice and mode of analysis. To understand the significance of rhetoric today is to understand why and in what ways it is discontinuous with its past.[2]

Although classical rhetoric followed a historical course different in myriad details from that of architectural orders, the broad outlines correlate. The discipline of rhetoric—adapted through a wide range of reformulations to the specific requirements of Greek, Roman, Medieval, and Renaissance societies—dominated European education and discourse, whether public or private, for more than two thousand years. We can merely glance at the rhetorical conduct of thought and speech during this protracted epoch. We shall concentrate instead on the two-phased period—the phases

4

styled here in drastic abbreviation as those of the Enlightenment and Romanticism—that brought about the end of classical rhetoric as the dominant system of education and communication. We locate the factors determining rhetoric's demise in a bundle of social and cultural transformations that occurred, roughly speaking, between the seventeenth and nineteenth centuries. The various factors that caused, or accompanied, the demise of rhetoric merged into two major historical trends: the first banished rhetoric from the domain of theoretical and practical discourse; the second, from that of imaginative or aesthetic discourse.

We begin by outlining the historical factors that contributed to the end of rhetoric. This historical construction then points us to a thesis delineating rhetoric's modernist return. The specific shape of this return—and thus the specific mode of existence of the new rhetoric—can be grasped only with reference to the end that preceded it. In fact, the rebirth of rhetoric can take place only when those factors that conditioned its cultural death are themselves eliminated. Modernism presents a cultural frame that, by contrast with those of the Enlightenment and Romanticism, is hospitable to, and even requires, a reinvigoration of the rhetorical. But, as compared with its classical antecedent, this rhetoric is radically altered. These alterations we explore in a concluding survey of the premises of some exemplary modern disciplines. The return of rhetoric is a return with a difference, a difference that resonates to the foundations of discursive practice.

The End of Rhetoric: A Historical Sketch

In tracing the demise of rhetoric, or rather in highlighting some of its essential features, we distinguish two large phases of historical development, the Enlightenment and Romanticism. These epochal concepts designate major tendencies in the post-Renaissance world of European culture that exploded the hegemony of the classical rhetorical tradition and created the historical gap following which a return or repetition of rhetoric—not its continuation—becomes possible. Our use of the terms "Enlightenment" and "Romanticism" should not be taken to imply a typology of cultural epochs nor to suggest an all-too-linear logic of succession. On the contrary, the various cultural developments we shall collect beneath these two familiar terms are complexly interlocked, and their effects are visible up to the present day. This point holds also for what we term the classical rhetorical tradition. Although we argue that this tradition effectively ceased, we of course notice that rhetoric maintained itself in numerous residual forms throughout the very centuries that emptied it of cultural centrality.

Classical rhetoric survives today in strangely contracted form as a subject taught in universities. It is contracted because so much of the terrain over which it held absolute sway during the two millennia between Aristotle and Bacon has now been appropriated by other disciplines: linguistics, information theory, stylistics, literary criticism, sociology, communications, marketing, public relations. From its earliest appearance in Grecian Sicily to its residual influence on secondary curricula of the nineteenth and twentieth centuries, the discipline of rhetoric attended to the compilation of instructional synopses often entitled "The Art of Rhetoric." At first, rhetoricians dealt with the performative units of discourse— with such parts of an orator's presentation as his exordium, his relation of facts, his argumentation, his digressive illustration of proof, his conclusion. Later, in imitation of poetics, they treated the local phenomena of sentence structure and style, describing the schemes of thought and the figures of speech that might be employed as devices of persuasion. Plato and Aristotle broadened the discipline to include the psychology, sociology, and ethics of communication and, above all, extended its descriptive typology to embrace the immense range of protological and quasilogical formulations that characterize language use in public spaces. Thus, to classical rhetoric eventually belonged the description and theorization of all aspects of discourse not comprehended by the more delimited formulations of grammar and logic, the other two divisions of the so-called trivium within which knowledge about discursive practice was distributed.

Rhetoric began as a codification of oratorical usage. It survived as an extraordinarily long-lived theory of verbal action in part because it worked to account for behavior in the vast, contingent realm of human dialogue. No less importantly, the early institutionalization of rhetoric within the educational curriculum assured that the ability to perform according to its principles in council chambers or legislatures, in legal disputes, or in public oratory aimed at praise and blame (later to include sermons in church) served as a marker of authority and social standing. The "over-

6

coding" that Umberto Eco finds characteristic of rhetorical speech may signify, for instance, the seriousness of a topic, an occasion, or a cause.[3] But this overcoding points, above all, to the speaker's capacity to employ it. Rhetorical speech marks, and is marked by, social hierarchy.

Rhetorical speech adheres to power and property. Indeed, Cicero tells us that Aristotle traced the origin of codified rhetoric to a time, following the expulsion of the tyrants (467 B.C.), when confusion over the title to confiscated property formerly held by returning exiles led the claimants to employ the expert assistance of Corax and Tisias. These Sicilians no doubt wrote speeches for their clients to memorize but also devised general rules of practice that Corax set down in his, the first known, handbook or "art" of rhetoric.[4] As a specialized system of knowledge acquired, through formal education, in order to maintain property and negotiate social interaction, the art of rhetoric discriminates among audiences according to rank, education, and social character. The orator will address equals in the legislature or judges in the court of law differently from the crowd in the forum.

Rhetoric is an art of positionality in address. Audiences are characterized by status, age, temperament, education, and so forth. Speakers are impersonators who adapt themselves to occasions in order to gain or maintain position. Thus the bond of classical rhetoric to speech itself, as opposed to writing, betokens the place of rhetoric in the physically demonstrative social systems that so powerfully institutionalized its doctrines: city-state democracy and its republican redactions, as well as aristocracy. The cultural hegemony of rhetoric as a practice of discourse, as a doctrine codifying that practice, and as a vehicle of cultural memory, is grounded in the social structures of the premodern world. Conceived in its broadest terms, then, the demise of rhetoric coincides with that long and arduous historical process that is often termed modernization: the replacement of a symbolic-religious organization of social and cultural life by rationalized forms, the gradual shift from a stratificational differentiation of society to one that operates along functional axes.[5]

The antirhetorical bent of modernization shows itself first of all in the Enlightenment. The general feature of Enlightenment that contravenes inherited rhetorical tradition is the development, in various domains, of a mode of discourse conceived as neutral,

7

nonpositional, and transparent. Nowhere is this tendency more apparent than in the emergence of science, the most powerful innovation of the post-Renaissance world, a force that has transformed with dizzying rapidity and thoroughness the shape of life in Europe and, more recently, beyond. From its beginnings, science relied on the convention of a putatively true and undistorted—that is, arhetorical—depiction of natural states of affairs. Bacon's *Novum organum*, one of the foundational texts for modern scientific thinking, variously attacks the practices of rhetoric. The critique of the *idoli fori*, the idols of the marketplace, betrays in particular this aspect of Bacon's program: his denunciation of the illusions of a discourse that is measured only by its persuasive appeal within the shifting contexts of popular whims, antagonisms, and power ploys. His polemic mirrors central features of Plato's (or Socrates') attack on the Sophists, those purveyors of rhetorical tricks and marketeers of semblance, power, and prestige. But whereas Plato establishes dialectical ascent to the realm of suprasensible ideas as the alternative to rhetoric, Bacon envisions an arhetorical discourse that would ground itself in the empirical givens of nature. "The true end, scope or office of knowledge," he writes in *Valerius Terminus, or the Interpretation of Nature*, "consist[s] not in any plausible, delectable, reverend or admired discourse, or any satisfactory arguments, but in effecting and working, and in discovery of particulars not revealed before." This adherence to observable givens leads to "the happy match between the mind of man and the nature of things."[6]

The new science envisioned by Bacon bespeaks a shift in the relationships of power that define discourse. Scientific discourse is no longer embedded within the array of relative power positions that characterizes a stratified or hierarchical social structure; it withdraws from this interpersonal fray and takes as its opposite nature itself, over which it endeavors to establish a total command.[7] The subject who holds this new form of power is no longer an individual leader or hegemonic group, but rather mankind in general, a neutral or abstracted subject, a role that can be represented by whoever attains to the neutrality requisite for exercising it. Not until the twentieth century would this universal subject of inquiry be reparticularized as an amalgam of theoretical paradigms, scientific institutions, and sociopolitical positionality.

8

The withdrawal of scientific discourse from the rhetorical fray of feudal society is strikingly exemplified in the work of Bacon's Italian counterpart Galileo, the founder of the mathematical strand of scientific inquiry that dominates the modern world. Galileo's life has been mythologized as the heroic battle of the scientific spirit against religious dogma and oppression, the tragic encounter of the old world with the new. Although this has proved a persuasive legitimating myth, we know today that Galileo operated as a skillful strategist within a complex network of political and religious alliances. But this very strategic endeavor—realized, inevitably, through the tactics of rhetoric—allows us to measure the gulf that came to separate the rhetorical tradition from the discourse of modern science. In 1610, Galileo published, under the protection of his ruler, the *Sidereus Nuncius* (*Starry Messenger*), in which he announced his construction of a telescope and reported on some of the research conducted with that instrument. The text contains two parts, a dedication to Galileo's patron, Cosimo II de Medici, and the actual account of the scientific observations. Here is a brief passage from the dedication:

> Indeed, the Maker of the stars himself has seemed by clear indications to direct that I assign to these new planets Your Highness's famous name in preference to all others. For just as these stars, like children worthy of their sire, never leave the side of Jupiter by any appreciable distance, so (as indeed who does not know?) clemency, kindness of heart, gentleness of manner, splendour of royal blood, nobility in public affairs, and excellency of authority and rule have all fixed their abode and habitation in Your Highness. And who, I ask once more, does not know that all these virtues emanate from the benign star of Jupiter, next after God as the source of all good things. Jupiter; Jupiter, I say, at the instant of Your Highness's birth, having already emerged from the turbid mists of the horizon and occupied the midst of the heavens, illuminating the eastern sky from his own royal house, looked out from that exalted throne upon your auspicious birth and poured forth all his splendor and majesty in order that your tender body and your mind (already adorned by God with the most noble ornaments) might imbibe with your first breath that universal influence and power.[8]

The dedication reflects and refers to a hierarchical situation—a vertical chain of power positions—and treats this distribution of powers as its sole and complete reality. Within this utterly social and particular frame (everything hinges on the proper name of

9

Cosimo), the text situates itself and performs its operation by employing all the strategies of classical epideictic rhetoric. In order to praise it simulates a drama of praise enacted across a chain of eloquent figurations that draw on astrology, classical mythology, and Christianity, and that even refashion the stars (that is, the moons of Jupiter whose discovery the report will announce) as tokens within this game of suasion.

When we turn to the properly scientific portion of Galileo's text, however, we find no such rhetorical saturation, no overcoding of the discourse. A new mode of address has emerged here that differs from the old in far more than tone:

> The most easterly star was seven minutes from Jupiter and thirty seconds from its neighbor; the western one was two minutes away from Jupiter. The end stars were very bright and were larger than that in the middle, which appeared very small. The most easterly star appeared a little elevated toward the north from the straight line through the other planets and Jupiter. The fixed star previously mentioned was eight minutes from the western planet along the line drawn from it perpendicularly to the straight line through all the planets, as shown above. [Galileo here refers to a diagram that precedes this passage.]
>
> I have reported these relations of Jupiter and its companions with the fixed star so that anyone may comprehend that the progress of those planets, both in longitude and latitude, agrees exactly with the movements derived from planetary tables.
>
> (*Discoveries and Opinions*, p. 56.)

In scientific reporting, the author (clearly a *writer* now since there is no simulation of oral speech) and reader communicate without awareness of differential social rank. On the contrary, their positions are mutually interchangeable: the reader is addressed as the potential observer of what the writer recounts as having himself observed. Perhaps we can even take the telescope as the emblem of this derhetoricized situation. It is an instrument of vision, not of persuasion; it creates an abstract or asocial standpoint that can be assumed by anyone, and, as a matter of scientific convention, everyone who assumes that standpoint is functionally the "same" generalized observer, the same eye and I. Finally, the data the telescope supplies provide an absolute standard against which any discourse purporting to describe them can be checked and, if necessary, corrected. The "message" of the *Sidereus Nuncius* appears to come not from a personal speaker but from the stars themselves. Scientific discourse is arhetorical not merely because it is stylistically spare, unencumbered by the figures of eloquence, but more essentially because it incarnates a pragmatics that is entirely foreign to that of the hierarchized and relativized social field. Inevitably, therefore, once this discourse becomes culturally established, it draws in its wake a severe critique of the doctrine, practice, and institutions of rhetoric.

Such a critique gains full voice in Descartes, the founder, it is often said, of modern philosophy and a fascinated follower of Galileo's ups and downs. The autobiographical portion of the *Discourse on Method* unfolds a conversion narrative that frees the inquiring mind—the "I" of Descartes's text—from the errors and confusions of the past and opens up a futurity for the acquisition of certain knowledge. Part of the aberrant past Descartes repudiates is the institutionalization of knowledge as *eruditio* and the traditional form of schooling, which, among other things, rested on the teaching of rhetorical skills:

> I esteemed Eloquence most highly and I was enamoured of Poesy, but I thought that both were gifts of the mind rather than fruits of study. Those who have the strongest power of reasoning, and who most skillfully arrange their thoughts in order to render them clear and intelligible, have the best power of persuasion even if they can but speak the language of Lower Brittany and have never learned Rhetoric. And those who have the most delightful original ideas and who know how to express them with the maximum of style and suavity, would not fail to be the best poets even if the art of Poetry were unknown to them.[9]

Note here that Descartes rejects as useless and empty not only the doctrine and practice of rhetoric, but also the teaching of poetry as a rhetorical skill. His notion that poetic talent and imagination dwell solely within the inwardness of the subject anticipated by one hundred and fifty years the Romantic elimination of rhetoric as the basis of poetic theory. There is a reason for this historical prolepsis: the Cartesian cogito inaugurated the subject-centered philosophical and cultural discourse that would find its culmination in Romantic thought (Kant's transcendental synthesis of apperception, Fichte's self-positing Absolute Ego, Hegel's notion of substance as subject). Perhaps we can grasp here the affinity between the Enlightenment and Romantic destructions of rhetoric. The cogito, the unshakable foundation of certainty, generates at once the impersonal or abstracted subject of science and the creative, self-forming subject of Romanticism. Once these subjective functions took command over the field of discourse and representation, rhetoric could no longer maintain its cultural predominance. Foundational subjectivity—be it the subject as *res cogitans* or as creative origin, as unique individual personality or as disinterested free agent within the political sphere—erodes the ideological premises of rhetoric.

The transformations we have been describing with reference to Galileo and Descartes had, by the mid-eighteenth century, extended beyond the reaches of speculative thought into the daily conduct of affairs temporal and spiritual. In England, for example, not only had legal theorists increasingly embraced probabilistic, broadly Cartesian thinking about questions of proof, but trial courts were also making practical changes, such as the admission of counsel for the defense, that presaged the development of those impersonal rules of evidence and consistently specified burdens of proof that distinguish modern criminal procedure. Previously, the English criminal trial had been what Sir Thomas Smith once called an "altercation." Accused and accuser confronted one another personally, without benefit of counsel for the prosecution or defense. Judges, unhampered by rules, freely intervened. The parties to the trial occupied rhetorical positions delineated in their own words according to whatever structuring principles they might choose to adopt. Evidence, too, was personal and rhetorically structured since direct testimony (including confession) was the chief basis of proof. Circumstantial evidence, including even inference based upon physical fact, was not fully probative. By the eighteenth century, legal theorists already had begun to embrace the kind of thinking that would lead nineteenth-century jurists actually to prefer circumstantial and inferential evidence over direct testimony. Increasingly, from the mid–eighteenth through the nineteenth centuries, English trials changed from personal, rhetorically governed exchanges to procedures in which plantiff, defendant, judge, and counsel occupied impersonal, rule-governed positions. We still think of trials as places for high rhetoric, but the ancient forensic speech in fact holds little more than a residual place in the modern Anglo-American trial, almost as if to validate our exacting, impersonal trial procedures by the token inclusion of symbolic gestures that connect contemporary juridical practice with a venerable tradition. Precisely because they are rhetorical, the modern counsel's opening and closing statements (so significant in courtroom melodrama) are not structural features of the modern trial.[10]

Interestingly, as Alexander Welsh has shown, the discourses of law and natural religion embraced virtually identical forms of probabilistic thinking during the period when the changes just described were occurring in trial procedure. Matters of religion and of the spirit became subject to impersonal categories of proof. If, says Bishop Butler, we conduct every other aspect of our lives on the basis of probable inference, as in the wake of scientific empiricism perforce we must, why should we not found upon inference a belief in God as secure as our confidence in the existence of matter or of our own personal being? Is inference from circumstance not more persuasive than personal testimony of miraculous experience or scriptural revelation?[11]

These arhetorical tendencies in science, philosophy, religion, and _law_ can be taken as emblematic of the Enlightenment as a whole. They bespeak a general movement toward representational neutrality that could be traced as well in such domains as theory of government, historiography, and psychology. In all these areas, especially across the eighteenth century, a model of critical communication emerged that stresses the neutrality and transparency of discourse and that, in consequence, throws off the rhetorical tradition. Discourse in the Enlightenment, we might say with Michel Foucault, took on a new existence. The effects of this massive cultural transformation can still be felt today. The thinkers of the Enlightenment, however, not only practiced this new discourse, but also developed its theory, a theory that in many cases coincided with the conception of Enlightenment itself. We have already mentioned Descartes, whose philosophy served as the foundation of the first major antirhetorical theory of language, the *Port-Royal Logic* of Arnauld and Nicole. In England, the temporal threshold is drawn somewhat later. Hobbes, the last great philosopher of absolutism, could still, despite his indebtedness to Descartes, compose an *Art of Rhetorick* whose every page reveals itself tributary to the classical tradition.[12]

This was no longer possible, however, for Locke. Not only does the founder of modern empiricism unleash, in the fourth book ("On Words") of his *Essay Concerning Human Understanding*, one of the most virulent antirhetorical tirades on record, he also presents there a "semiotics," or theory of language as sign, that is designed to eliminate the deceptions of rhetoric and to guarantee the transparency of discourse. Locke's was not the first but certainly one of the most influential in a long series of attempts to free language and thought from the confoundments of rhetoric. In Germany, the Enlightenment ideal of linguistic transparency, of a purely neutral representational medium, emerged in Leibniz's project of an *ars characteristica*, a philosophical calculus that would leave the deflections of human language behind in order to reproduce the language of things themselves. This dream, which in a variety of forms obsessed the entire eighteenth century, perhaps most fully exemplifies the removal of discourse from what we referred to above as the rhetorical fray. For, as Leibniz and later Herder well understood, such a perfected sign system would coincide exactly with the absolutely nonpositional mind of God.

Kant brought together the theory of Enlightenment and the theory of discourse. Enlightenment, in Kant's view, is a process of critical communication that unfolds within a free public sphere, a sphere of discourse separated from the particularist interests and pressures of political and religious institutions and authority. Here the subject speaks (more accurately, writes and publishes) as a "scholar," a free inquirer whose only guide is the light of impartial reason and whose addressee is the ideal person "mankind." Within this sphere, ideas are circulated and submitted to criticism, to a kind of winnowing process that removes the chaff of error and in the end leaves nothing but the golden wheat of truth. Kant envisioned, in fact, a kind of intellectual market, but no longer the market of false opinion, varying whims, delusions, and conflicts in which the Sophists and rhetoricians were thought to perform their manipulations. Rather, this is the marketplace of Adam Smith, ordered by an invisible hand that inevitably makes the right selections, or, as in Kant, ordered by a transcendental reason that is everyone's and no one's: that is positionless and therefore arhetorical.[13]

The vehicle that carried Kant's public sphere toward its future of perpetual improvement was the institution of publishing, without which Enlightenment is unthinkable. One need only consider the great publishing enterprises of the period—foremost of all perhaps the *Encyclopédie* of d'Alembert and Diderot—or the expansion of literacy that occurred across the eighteenth century, with its proliferation not only of books but of learned and moral jour-

nals.[14] Practical and theoretical knowledge, not to speak of literature, were no longer tied to a situation of oratorical exchange,
no longer simulated the scene of face-to-face contact. From mid-
century on print established itself as the dominant medium of
linguistic communication, reading became the passion of the age,
and publishing statistics for the first time caught up with and sur-
passed the post-Gutenberg boom of the sixteenth century. This is
another feature of Enlightenment that caused rhetoric's demise, for
rhetoric took its point of departure from the direct and oral encounters of classical civic life, and even as it maintained itself across the
manuscript culture of the Middle Ages and into the first phase of
modern print culture, it inevitably referred back to a face-to-face
oratorical situation. All this disappeared with the Enlightenment,
the first epoch to constitute itself as a culture of print. Rhetoric
drowned in a sea of ink.

What the Enlightenment accomplished in the domains of theoretical and practical discourse, Romanticism achieved in the aesthetic domain. Only with Romanticism was rhetoric finally and
thoroughly evacuated from the realm of imaginative expression. In
fact, this very phrase—"imaginative expression"—reveals the im-
pact of the Romantic revolution. Prior to the last decades of the
eighteenth century, the concept of literature covered virtually all of
writing; the breadth of its application was made possible by the
overriding unity of rhetorical doctrine, which governed all of verbal
production. With Romanticism, however, the concept of literature
emerged that still today shapes the organization of disciplines
within the university. Literature became imaginative literature, an
autonomous field of discourse endowed with its unique inner laws
and history.[15] Romanticism, in other words, set the paradigm for
the postrhetorical production, interpretation, and historiography of
literature, and in this sense brought on the second death of rhetoric.

One consequence of this cultural transformation is legible in
Ernst Robert Curtius's elegiac monument, *European Literature
and the Latin Middle Ages*.[16] The elaborate system of topoi this
book describes did not fall into desuetude, as Curtius notes, until
the last third of the eighteenth century. In other words, the evacua-
tion from cultural memory of the topoi—those dense and finely
branched semantic clusters that had since antiquity governed discursive invention—coincided exactly with the emergence of Ro-

manticism. The Romantic destruction of rhetoric altered the temporal framework of literary production, replacing rememorative conservation (*traditio*) with an insistence on originality.

This shift can be delineated in other ways. One major Romantic innovation was the full articulation of the concept of "author" as the productive origin of the text, as the subjective source that, in bringing its unique position to expression, constitutes a "work" ineluctably its own. Subjectivity and not adherence to a generic type or reference to an esteemed predecessor or topical paradigm now gave a work its identity. This insistence on the principle of authorship—still today one of the most compelling assumptions of literary studies and the very organizing principle of our libraries—does not flow merely from the nature of things. As Foucault has suggested in a powerful essay, authorship is a function, one that varies both historically and among disciplines. Romanticism produced the author function in its modern form.[17]

Legal history makes this perfectly clear. The English Copyright Law of 1709 still did not protect the author against reproduction of his work. Its point of reference was the book itself, over which it gave the first publisher command for fourteen years (a limitation of previous practice) and the author for twenty-eight, the same duration as for a patent. The practice of royal privileges still remained common, and the universities held onto certain special exemptions. Only in 1774, after a tangled history of legal disputes, did the author receive an exclusive right over his work. In 1814 this authorial right was specified as holding for a period of twenty-eight years after first publication or, should the author outlive this duration, until the end of his life. In France, the old system of royal privileges and permissions held until the Revolution. Then, in its meeting of July 19, 1793, the National Assembly granted exclusive rights over reproduction to the authors themselves. This right held until ten years after the author's death. Finally, in the German-speaking countries the Universal Prussian National Law of 1794, which instituted from above so many of the reforms that in France had come into being with the Revolution, based the right of publication in a contract between author and publisher, with the publisher-seller, however, still the most important figure. Only in 1810, with the National Law of Baden, was the author finally accorded exclusive rights over "his" work. As these dates reveal, the years arrayed around the turn of the nineteenth century witnessed the full

emergence of the author as the decisive factor in assigning proprietary status to printed language. This legal transformation is one
institutional counterpart to the Romantic reconceptualization of
literature.[18]

The same period revised educational practices bearing on literature. The Latin schools that had emerged across post-Renaissance
Europe initiated their pupils into discourse by leading them through
the rhetorical constructions of exemplary classical texts. This education culminated with imitative exercises in which the student
produced speeches and poems in the manner of one of the great authorities. But by the end of the eighteenth century this rhetorical
pedagogy was experienced as moribund. Reviewing a treatise on
the cultivation of taste in the public schools, the young Goethe,
destined to become one of the major figures of European Romanticism, wrote in 1772: "We, however, hate all the imitation that
the author recommends at the end. We know there are many whose
claim to fame is that they write like Cicero or Tacitus, but it always demonstrates a lack of genius when they fall into this misfor-
tune."[19] Genius is the vital term here, the name of subjective originality and the antithesis of rhetorical *inventio*. Goethe's complaint
was soon to see results as new methods of pedagogy entered the
schools, methods that sought to disclose and cultivate the personal
uniqueness of the pupils by teaching "free" expression. The medium of this expression was no longer the public oratorical performance in which the pupil demonstrated his mastery of standard
techniques, but rather a written product that articulated his own
individual point of view.[20] A similar change occurred in the universities. Whereas the study of the classical authors had traditionally
meant memorizing, translating, and imitating the loci classici, the
new discipline of philology encouraged an interpretive grasp of the
animating authorial intention out of which the entire work was
produced. These academic institutes of philology, the most famous
of which was established by Christian Gottlob Heyne at the University of Göttingen during the 1770's, institutionalized Romantic
hermeneutics as the methodology of modern literary understanding. Since then literary education has lent support to the antinomy
between creative self-expression on the one hand and interpretation on the other.[21]

Of course, the Enlightenment had already begun to dismantle
rhetorical doctrine as the organizing matrix of literary production.

On the level of theory the late Enlightenment witnessed the birth of philosophical aesthetics, a discipline whose emergence marked a decisive cultural relocation of art and literature. Alexander Baumgarten's *Aesthetica* (1750–55), the foundational treatise of the new discipline, was still based on the traditional rhetorical triad of *inventio, dispositio,* and *elocutio,* but one nevertheless notes a shift in the significance of the terms. Aesthetics is not a theory of the production of effective or persuasive discourse; it is a theory of "sensate cognitions" and of the signs that convey them. Its frame of reference is not a notion of social interaction within a hierarchical space, but the soul conceived as a faculty of representation. Art retreats from the *cour et ville* of aristocratic society and takes up residence within the mental immanence of a universalized "mankind."[22] As Michael Fried has shown, a similar development took place in French painting and art criticism during the same period: the shift from a paradigm of "theatricality" to one of "absorption" amounted to a derhetorization, an abandonment of oratorical gesturality.[23] Finally, at the brink of Romanticism, Kant made the obsolescence of rhetoric explicit, banishing it in a famous paragraph of his *Critique of Judgement* not only from poetry but also from the legal courts, the chambers of government, and the pulpits of the church. His condemnation of rhetoric so thoroughly epitomizes the developments we have tried to sketch here that it is worth citing it at length:

> Rhetoric, in so far as this means the art of persuasion, i.e. of deceiving by a beautiful show (*ars oratoria*), and not mere elegance of speech (eloquence and style), is a dialectic which borrows from poetry only so much as is needful to win minds to the side of the orator before they have formed a judgement and to deprive them of their freedom; it cannot therefore be recommended either for the law courts or for the pulpit. For if we are dealing with civil law, with the rights of individual persons, or with lasting instruction and determination of people's minds to an accurate knowledge and a conscientious observance of their duty, it is unworthy of so important a business to allow a trace of any luxuriance of wit and imagination to appear, and still less any trace of the art of talking people over and of captivating them for the advantage of any chance person. For although this art may sometimes be directed to legitimate and praiseworthy designs, it becomes objectionable when in this way maxims and dispositions are spoiled in a subjective point of view, though the action may objectively be lawful. It is not enough to do what is right; we should practice it solely on the ground that it is right.[24]

18

Kant's *Critique of Judgement* not only assembles in this passage and elsewhere the accusatory motifs typical of all antirhetorical polemics (deception, unfreedom, luxuriant excess, demagogic manipulation), it also clearly reveals why rhetoric becomes irrelevant to the literary arts. For art, in Kant's view, has its source in genius, in the subjective instance of creativity that derives the rules of its productive action not from any cultural code, but from nature itself (*Critique of Judgement*, pp. 150–51). This attachment of art to expressive subjectivity led directly into the Romantic reconceptualization of the aesthetic, after which rhetoric lost its centrality to the production and interpretation of poetry. In Descartes initially, and then in Kant and the Romantics, we find this rule everywhere confirmed: the insistence on the originating power of subjectivity is incompatible with rhetorical doctrine. This is why Romanticism represents the final destruction of the classical rhetorical tradition.

Indicative literary genres appeared in tandem with characteristic refusals of rhetoric during the Enlightenment and Romantic stages even though the rhetorical model of production continued to prevail in officially sanctioned literature throughout the seventeenth and well into the eighteenth centuries. However, both the seeming inability of European writers to sustain the ancient tradition of epic poetry (except through translation and mock heroic) and, during the Enlightenment, a relative decline of lyric poetry in favor of satire and didactic-descriptive verse (those closest to prose among traditional forms) evince the incursion of prosaic rationalism.

The eighteenth-century emergence of the extra-official "new" novel is still more significant. The novel is the genre of writing par excellence. As Mikhail Bakhtin argues, all of the traditional literary genres, "or in any case their defining features, are considerably older than written language and the book, and to the present day they retain their ancient oral and auditory characteristics. Of all the major genres only the novel is younger than writing and the book: it alone is organically receptive to new forms of mute perception, that is, to reading."[25] Even if Bakhtin overstates the case— even if residues of orality may be found in certain earlier novels— the marked consolidation during the later eighteenth century of a novelistic technique such as free indirect discourse (*style indirect libre*), which has no counterpart outside of written narrative, validates for our period the point about reading and mute perception.[26] The novel's peculiar gravitation toward a neutral transparency of style (the opposite of rhetorical overcoding) participates in the genre's conventional pretense to reportorial accuracy of the kind possible only in writing. In other respects as well the eighteenth-century novel operates within the Enlightenment model of critical communication. The novels of Defoe, Richardson, and Fielding, for example, not only pretend to offer densely particular, virtually evidentiary accounts of the physical and mental circumstances that actuate their characters and motivate the causal sequences of their plots, but also attempt, with greater or lesser consistency, to frame the subjectivity of their characters within editorial (Defoe and Richardson) or narratorial (Fielding) objectivity. In point of both thematic exposition and narrative strategy, these novels force readers into the position of neutral observers arriving, probabilistically, at judgments based upon available facts and reasonable inferences. Although these novels in truth continue to echo plot forms and incidents traditional to the fantastical romances their prefaces ritually condemn, the concern expressed by these novelists to distinguish their enterprise from that of earlier prose fiction indicates from our point of view the urgent significance of the generic reformulation then in progress.

If the emergent novel demarcates a generic space within which the impersonality of the modern subject position may be exercised, the Romantic lyric exhibits the creative, self-forming aspect of the subject. Though the novel's opposite in so many other respects, the genre of the Romantic lyric not only shares the novel's use of natural, unadorned language, but also aggressively deprecates rhetorical speech as disingenuous. The earlier lyric tradition had displayed the ancient rhetorical forms of praise and blame, as well as the schemes and tropes designed to persuade a particular kind of person, in some specified situation, to act in some precise way. The Romantic lyric affirms individual personal identity by delineating a specific epiphanic moment in the history of a single speaking subject. Some of the most remarkable examples go so far as to efface entirely the scene of rhetorical speech by incorporating into the lyric another equally specific subject who uniquely shares the epiphany. Wordsworth's *Tintern Abbey* places his sister Dorothy in this empathetic role, while Coleridge's *This Lime Tree Bower My Prison* reflects upon a specific occasion when the absence of friends provoked meditations that might have been shared but would, of course, have been altered had the friends been present. Similar developments can be traced on the Continent, where, as in England, the model of folk poetry became the chief paradigm of lyric song. Already in the 1770's the young Goethe had begun to produce lyric texts that cleave to the inner movements of subjectivity and that redefine orality as the inner voice of emotion rather than as public-oriented oratorical communication. The lyrics of Goethe and his romantic successors are, in fact, a kind of verbal music that eventually could fuse seamlessly with the melodies of Schubert, Schumann, and Wolf.

Romanticism brought with it one final cultural transformation that worked to institutionalize the devolution of rhetoric. The rhetorical paradigm was international in character, tied to the Latin language, which dominated the higher schools and universities throughout Europe, and to the classical treatises and authorities that enjoyed universal recognition. Rhetoric was the foundation of an international intellectual community, the *res publica litteraria*, and the vehicle of a unified tradition. This quintessentially international character of classical rhetoric came to an end in the period of Romanticism because the Romantic destruction of rhetoric was linked to the rise of the modern nation-state. National identity was grounded in the linguistic identity of the *Volk*; the national languages replaced the international Latin koine, cutting off civic and cultural consciousness from its Roman roots. The universality of the *res publica litteraria* was shattered by the proliferation of vernacular reading publics, and the classical *traditio* ceded its preeminence to national historical traditions.[27] Perhaps the anxious territorialism so common today in university departments of literary study is a last desperate defense of the Romantic organization of the world of letters along national historical lines.

The linguistic character of the nation-state worked to bring on the end of rhetoric, but an equally important factor was the political structure—the form of sovereignty and political participation—that the nation-state developed. Within the context of national civic organization rhetorical performance was restricted to specialized legislative venues and ceremonial occasions. Citizenship came to reside in the relation of an individual to a collectively willed body of law; governmental participation and legal practice became professionalized and increasingly print-bound; and the scene of po-

21

litical action, which had previously possessed the concrete reality of a forum or court, was dispersed. The citizen, thoroughly privatized, was thus no longer distinguished by oratorical talent, as his Roman ancestor had been, and therefore no longer required rhetorical training. The nation-state is not a sphere of face-to-face encounter, but an ideal entity to which one relates abstractly through the internalization of its laws and concretely through its various bureaucratic apparatuses.

The Modernist Return of Rhetoric: A Thesis

Such were the manifold developments that, during the Enlightenment and Romanticism, brought the classical tradition of rhetoric to its end. Our procedure in sketching these developments has been to highlight individual cases and local events exemplifying the fact of rhetoric's demise. But these particular instances also have opened a view onto structural features of bourgeois culture that dethroned rhetoric from its position of supremacy much as the French Revolution dethroned the king as the symbol of traditional hierarchical order in European society. In other words, our historical narrative has led us to formulate a thesis specifying the constellation of forces that brought about rhetoric's end. Reversing the Kantian formula, we may call these ideological and institutional forces the *conditions of impossibility* of rhetoric: cultural presuppositions that, by relocating and reshaping discourse within society, rendered the traditional practice and doctrine of rhetoric obsolete. Five factors seem especially prominent:

1. "Transparency" and "neutrality" emerged as the leading values of theoretical and practical discourse—scientific discourse became anchored in "objectivity."

2. The values of "authorship" and "individual expression" came to define the literary domain—imaginative discourse became anchored in "subjectivity."

3. Liberal political discourse emerged as the language of communal exchange.

4. The oratorical model of communication was replaced by print and publishing—Europe was alphabetized.

5. The nation-state became the central political unit, and standardized national languages emerged as the linguistic sphere of reference for cultural production and understanding.

Where these conditions obtain, rhetoric can occupy only the place of a memory, an anachronistic and ritualized practice, or a dusty academic specialization. Once it becomes estranged from both cultural production and the most advanced forms of inquiry, associations of mendacity, empty scholasticism, and false artfulness attach themselves to its name. And this is what the Enlightenment and Romanticism accomplished: they altered the conditions of discursive action along the lines of the five tendencies listed here and thereby rendered irrelevant the rhetorical tradition that had for centuries been the organizing matrix of communication in Europe.

But rhetoric has returned. Throughout the course of this century it has acquired renewed theoretical and practical importance, and more recently it has become an explicit focus of inquiry in a variety of domains. How is this possible? How can rhetoric return after having been so thoroughly displaced from our cultural horizon? We contend, centrally, that this repetition of the rhetorical tradition within modernism comes about when the five conditions of rhetoric's impossibility are themselves eliminated, when a new cultural and discursive space is fashioned that is no longer defined by objectivism, subjectivism, liberalism, literacy, and nationalism. The modernist cultural transformation, in other words, is accompanied by a return of rhetoric precisely because it explodes the cultural predominance of these five tendencies. From this perspective, modernism (construed as a broad sociocultural epoch) presents a reverse image of the antirhetorical cultural premises that increasingly organized the production of discourse from the seventeenth century onward:

1. From the paradoxes of Heisenberg and Gödel to the demotion of truth in the epistemology of Nelson Goodman, modernism has witnessed the crumbling of the ideal of scientific objectivity and the loss of faith in the neutrality of scientific and practical discourse. Modernism no longer possesses a reliable standard of representational transparency; even so-called observation sentences are recognized as theory-laden; and the history of science itself has come to be viewed less as a progressive discovery of the facts than as a series of constructions accomplished within the framework of governing conceptual paradigms.

2. Modernism has eroded as well the value of founding subjectivity, which, starting from Descartes and continuing through Ro-

23

manticism, had contributed so powerfully to the decline of rhetoric. From Baudelaire's relegation of authorship to an anachronism and Mallarmé's elimination from poetic writing of the elocutionary subject to the automatic writing of the surrealists, the willed anonymity of Kafka, Beckett, and Blanchot, and the collective compositions of the Renga poets, modernist literary production has dismantled the values of individual authorship and creativity. Freudian psychoanalysis has decentered the subject, while disciplines such as linguistics and sociology have disclosed impersonal patterns and forces at work in human agency. Far from forming a world out of itself, the modernist subject, as Heidegger suggests, is "thrown" into the world, split by an alterity that can never be recuperated into a homogeneous and sovereign self-mastery. Rimbaud's line is emblematic of this condition: "Je est un autre."

3. Modernism, arising in tandem with mass society and its forms of exchange, explodes the liberal Enlightenment model of communication, in which individual rational subjects contribute disinterestedly to political debate within the public sphere. In both the modern political arena and the modern marketplace rhetorical manipulation becomes the rule. Advertising, marketing, propaganda, and public relations stir the cauldron of public opinion; politics, as Walter Benjamin noted, is aestheticized; and art, which Romanticism had enclosed within its own autonomous sphere, becomes one discursive force among others: impure, tendentious, a reflection on its own inadequacy.

4. Modernism is marked by the dethroning of print. Of course, the graphic word continues to infiltrate the other media at innumerable points, yet we no longer live in the world of newspaper and book. Print has given way to film and television, to phonographic reproduction and to the various forms of telecommunication. Literacy, far from being the sole access to culture, is merely one form of information processing, and a highly restricted one at that.

5. Finally, modernism has destroyed the model of a national language, which had served as the supervening form of Enlightenment and Romantic cultural production and self-understanding. The urbanistic marketplace of the twentieth century is irreducibly polyglottal; dialects, sociolects, and idiolects proliferate and clash; disciplines develop and dwell within their respective jargons. Translation is the universal state of affairs. This dispersion of the national language, the language of the people, is accompanied by an

unraveling of national tradition: modernism fosters an inrush of the archaic into the scene of culture, the shattering of the idea of national uniqueness and of an individual national history. The frame of national culture, which had displaced the internationalism of the rhetorical tradition, collapses.

These modernist cultural tendencies have created, then, the conditions for a renaissance of rhetoric, which today is asserting itself in all fields of intellectual endeavor and cultural production. But the new rhetoric is no longer that of the classical tradition; it is attuned to the specific structures of modernist culture; its fundamental categories are markedly new. Rhetoric today is neither a unified doctrine nor a coherent set of discursive practices. Rather, it is a transdisciplinary field of practice and intellectual concern, a field that draws on conceptual resources of a radically heterogeneous nature and does not assume the stable shape of a system or method of education. The rhetoric that, with the ruin of Enlightenment-Romantic culture, now increasingly asserts itself, shares with its classical predecessor little more than a name.

Our historical thesis leads us to this conclusion: *Modernism is an age not of rhetoric, but of rhetoricality,* the age, that is, of a generalized rhetoric that penetrates to the deepest levels of human experience. The classical rhetorical tradition rarified speech and fixed it within a gridwork of limitations: it was a rule-governed domain whose procedures themselves were delimited by the institutions that organized interaction and domination in traditional European society. Rhetoricality, by contrast, is bound to no specific set of institutions. It manifests the groundless, infinitely ramifying character of discourse in the modern world. For this reason, it allows for no explanatory metadiscourse that is not already itself rhetorical. Rhetoric is no longer the title of a doctrine and a practice, nor a form of cultural memory; it becomes instead something like the condition of our existence.

We have proposed that the modernist return of rhetoric be conceived in relation to a complex set of historical factors. The social, scientific, technological, and experiential formations of modern life have altered the conditions of discourse. These formations are co-extensive with a cultural frame in which language becomes detached from the supports created for it by the Enlightenment and Romanticism. Rhetoricality names the new conditions of discourse in the modern world and, thus, the fundamental category

25

of every inquiry that seeks to describe the nature of discursive action and exchange. Rhetoricality may be considered as a name for the underlying features both of modern practice and of the theories that seek to account for it. In the modernist phase these structural features, on the whole, had to be inferred from symptomatic social, cultural, and disciplinary phenomena. More recently, in the episode—or episteme—now designated by the term "postmodernism," new forms of rhetorical inquiry are emerging that explicitly recognize and analyze features we designate under the term "rhetoricality."

Nowhere is the modernist shift in the meaning of rhetoric—the shift from rhetoric to what we are calling rhetoricality—more forcefully evident than in Nietzsche, the paradigmatic philosopher of modernity and postmodernity. Acutely aware of the condition of language in mass culture, Nietzsche set the agenda for the modernist reconceptualization of rhetoric and opened that general field within which the diverse forms of rhetorical inquiry on the contemporary scene formulate their individual programs.

As a professor of classics at the University of Basel, the young Nietzsche offered a course in rhetoric, which, as Philippe Lacoue-Labarthe has shown, was of fundamental importance to his mature thought.[28] The early text by Nietzsche that sets the groundwork for all his thinking about language—"On Truth and Lie in an Extra-Moral Sense"—insists especially on the essential rhetoricity of language and on the human "drive to form metaphors" as the basis of our rendering of the world. The inherited concept of figures of speech here undergoes a decisive reinterpretation: the figures are no longer devices of an *elocutio* that adorns and presents the invented thoughts of the speaker, but mobile, shifting categories that are always at work in every encounter with the world. During this same early phase of his career Nietzsche developed the notion that truth itself is the product of a certain "pathos," that it is an affectively invested figure able to claim no legitimacy beyond the urgency with which it is affirmed. This conceptual move tears the underpinnings from the notion of an arhetorical language of observation: the truth claims of science, in Nietzsche's reading, are themselves merely one rhetoric among others.

The later Nietzsche promotes the category of "appearance" (*Schein*) to universal status: appearance is not the opposite of truth, but rather includes truth as one of its varieties. Nietzsche's insistence on the concept of power is similarly motivated: if all language is rhetorical, if even objectivity is the product of a certain strategy, then discourses are no longer to be measured in terms of their adequacy to an objective standard (which Nietzsche's perspectivism exposes as a myth) but rather to be analyzed in terms of their strategic placement within a clash of competing forces themselves constituted in and through the very rhetorical dissimulations they employ. In this sense, Nietzsche's philosophy can be characterized as the thought of a generalized rhetoricality, of a play of transformation and dissimulation, that is the condition of possibility of truth and of subjectivity. Rhetoric returns in Nietzsche, not as a doctrine governing the production and analysis of texts, not as a procedure to be employed within specific situations toward determinable ends, but rather as a kind of immemorial process—an a priori that thought can never bring under its control precisely because thought itself is one of the effects of that process. Rhetoric loses in Nietzsche its instrumental character and becomes the name for the rootlessness of our being.[29]

Rhetoricality and Contemporary Styles of Knowledge: A Survey

The field of inquiry that Nietzsche's thought discloses is at once vast and diverse. Its conceptual repertoire resists synopsis, for its unity is as diffuse as modern knowledge itself. Thus, it would be impossible to provide a précis of modernist rhetoric such as that sketched out for the classical tradition with such precision and economy by Roland Barthes.[30] And even an encyclopedic account patterned after Heinrich Lausberg's compendious handbook of classical rhetoric would be incapable of absorbing contemporary rhetorical practice into a sharply delineated structure.[31] The best one can do at this point is to list some of the major disciplinary approaches to rhetorical questions and to chart their congruences and divergences.

The New Rhetoric of Science. One of the most fascinating areas of contemporary rhetorical inquiry—although it does not always go by that name—is concerned with the discourse of the sciences. As we have mentioned, the ideal of scientific objectivity, that is, of a neutral and standpoint-free language of description, has come to an end in the twentieth century. The last gasp of this ideal was in all likelihood the neopositivist notion of the protocol sentence, a linguistic formulation that was thought to present in propositional form the raw data generated by experiment. But the notion did not hold up to scrutiny, and the ideal of neutrality was dismantled from within the neopositivist school itself. The paradigmatic instance of this turn in scientific metatheory is Thomas Kuhn's book *The Structure of Scientific Revolutions*, written as a contribution to the neopositivist-inspired *Encyclopedia of Unified Science*.[32] Despite the criticism and controversy the book has encountered since its publication, Kuhn's basic argument to the effect that scientific inquiry rests on research paradigms themselves not derivable from observed data or from axiomatic statements still enjoys a general consensus. And Kuhn's historical approach has spawned an entire body of research bearing on the extrascientific forces at work in the formation of scientific knowledge. For example, in *Against Method* Paul Feyerabend, the prophetic voice of anti-objectivism, reviews with extreme care the scientific work of Galileo, discovering there not the untarnished presentation of facts, but a complex strategic-rhetorical operation of persuasion.[33] In a similar, if less jubilantly radical vein, Ian Hacking has shown how scientific instruments, far from being the neutral devices that Galileo's telescope appeared to be, in fact participate in the "creation of phenomena," in what we could would like to call a scientific *inventio*.[34] Finally—and still remaining within the postanalytic tradition—according to Nelson Goodman's *Ways of Worldmaking*, no one world exists that we strive to represent as neutrally as possible, but rather there are a host of world-versions, themselves functions of divergent representational or symbolic systems.[35]

In this plurality of worlds, rhetoric, albeit in a nonclassical version, finds its place once again. At issue in this new form of metascientific analysis is the essential rhetoricality of the scientific enterprise: its procedures of legitimation; its institutional context; its dependence on overriding convictions or presuppositions on the part of its practitioners.[36] The same interest in rhetoricality also has penetrated the social and human sciences. Hayden White, for example, has elaborated a rhetoric of classical historiography that undermines any claims of impartiality and objectivity that discipline might proffer.[37] Likewise, Clifford Geertz has examined the production of anthropological knowledge as an intrinsically rhetorical operation and his explorations will soon be followed by others that explore the rhetoric of neighboring human sciences.[38]

Perhaps above all, Foucault's work, with its insistence on both the institutional embeddedness and the cultural productivity of discourses, sets the standard for any inquiry that seeks to lay bare the rhetoricality of what we anachronistically call our positive knowledge.

Rhetoric and Modern Linguistics. The Romantic concept of language essentially banned rhetoric from the field of language study, replacing it with stylistics conceived as the analysis of individual or national expressive forms. Indeed, if we recall the work of the last great avatars of Romantic linguistics, the neo-idealists Charles Bally and Karl Vossler, it becomes clear that stylistics is not merely a branch of Romantic language study, but rather its culmination. With the Saussurean breakthrough, a return of rhetorical analysis became possible, and once again this return of the rhetorical tradition assumed the form of a differential repetition.

No doubt the privileged—the most famous and influential—site of this return is Roman Jakobson's 1956 article "Two Aspects of Language and Two Types of Aphasic Disturbances."[39] What Jakobson accomplished in this piece can be described as a reorganization of the rhetorical field, or, to be precise, of the rhetorical subfield traditionally denoted *elocutio*. By using the term "reorganization" we want to emphasize the idea of creative change and transformation, the idea of a reconstitution of the object of rhetorical study. How does this occur? Through the projection of the categorical pair paradigm/syntagm from post-Saussurean linguistic theory (Saussure himself used the term "association" rather than "paradigm") onto the domain of the rhetorical figures. And since the terms of this categorical pair are juxtaposed within structuralist theory as are "similarity" and "contiguity," the projection yields within the rhetorical domain a fundamental bifurcation into two semantic-figural processes, operating along the paths of similarity relations on the one hand and contiguity relations on the other. In Jakobson's terminology, these processes carry the names, familiar from the rhetorical tradition, of "metaphor" and "metonymy." Thus, a powerful homology emerges into view: in the domain of language "paradigmatic" is to "syntagmatic" as in the domain of semantic-discursive processes "metaphor" is to "metonymy."

Jakobson's homology has engendered various confusions, among them that the terms "metaphor" and "metonymy," as he uses them, are held to be equivalent to those same terms within the rhetorical tradition. This is clearly not the case. Within the traditional doctrine of *elocutio*, metaphor and metonymy are two figures among a host of others; they are, we might say, particularistically conceived, pertaining to individual instances of discourse. Jakobson means something quite different: for him the terms designate two (and, in his view, the only two) general processes of semantic production; they are class terms that subsume the entire field of the traditionally defined figures, dividing it into two basic groups. Thus, when Jakobson suggests that Romanticism and Symbolism are predominantly metaphorical, Realism predominantly metonymical, he is not saying that in these literary movements either metaphors or metonymies are exclusively used, but rather that the large-scale tendencies of semantic production within these movements follow the paths of similarity and contiguity respectively. What we find in Jakobson's inquiry, then, is a fundamental displacement that affects the traditional terminology of rhetoric, a generalization of certain items within that terminology and a wholesale abandonment of other items. Certain old rhetorical terms have come to designate general processes that are at work, in their juxtapositional interplay, across the entire field of discourse, that are anterior to any instrumental choices a writer might make, and that even govern such transindividual phenomena as the succession of period styles. Exactly this shift in the theoretical function and significance of concepts is what we are calling the move from rhetoric to rhetoricality.

Of course, post-Saussurean linguistics has spawned efforts to rethink in detail the utterly specific categories of traditional *elocutio*. Two examples of this research program are the *Rhétorique génerale* of the Belgian *Groupe mu*, and Paolo Valesio's *Novantiqua*.[40] But even in these cases, where the inherited taxonomies of rhetorical theory are respected in their specificity, the displacement of tradition is nonetheless perceptible. For what such analyses show is that the traditional classifications of the tropes and figures are crude; terms such as "metaphor" or "synecdoche" designate not at all simple and homogeneous operations, but rather bundles of phonological, syntactical, and semantic processes so complex in their intertwining that they must be deemed inaccessible to the reflective manipulation of the speaker. What the rhetorical tradition conceived as a set of tactics available to the strategic intentions of the speaker has been displaced into that same unconscious knowl-

30

edge in which linguistic theory locates our ability to speak and write. Rhetorical competence, to adapt Noam Chomsky's terminology, is a theoretical fiction, the product of a reconstructive process that deploys a reticulated repertoire of theoretical concepts. The object of study here, as in a different way in the case of Jakobson, is no longer rhetoric but rather rhetoricality.

Rhetoric and Psychoanalysis. Correlative with the modernist alteration of the object of study in linguistics from evident to unconscious patterns, from national syntax to universal structure, and from commonsensical to counterintuitive evaluation is Freud's inferential psychology of the unconscious. In psychoanalysis the mechanisms of an otherwise hidden mental world are revealed in the figurations of language. Verbal patterns, metaphors, replacements, and similar tropes that classical rhetoric might have described in terms of surface ornamentation and effect upon an audience become outward, consciously unintended manifestations of wishes and fears, desires and terrors that have been driven inward. Thus, in tandem with his discovery of the revelatory condensations and displacements operative in dreams, Freud also probed "figures" such as jokes, spoonerisms, and puns as symptoms of unconscious operations. Particular content may vary with each individual, but the structure of the unconscious—its ways of proceeding and the strategies of containment whereby it is held in check—are constant. The manifest content of dreams or slips of the tongue may be specific to the individual's history, but the mechanisms are impersonal and function without reference to subjective choice. The old figures of speech and thought are depersonalized and transformed into general conditions of existence rather than remaining, as in classical rhetoric, part of a lexicon or repertory from among which speakers make deliberate choices according to occasion. At least in retrospect, Lacan's famous dictum that the unconscious is structured like a language seems to follow inevitably from the juxtaposition of Freud's treatises on dreams and jokes with Jakobson's specification of metaphor and metonymy as the basic mechanisms of discourse production, since these figures, as Jakobson notices, are the rhetorical equivalents of condensation and displacement—the fundamental processes of Freud's "dream work." Furthermore, the rhetoric employed in current psychoanalytic theory is not limited to expressive phenomena. As Jean Laplanche has suggested, the very processes of ego formation are rhetorical in nature, following paths of contiguity and similarity.[41] Indeed, psychoanalysis itself, as Nicolas Abraham has argued, is a rhetorical enterprise, its terminology a figurative shell that refers to kernels of psychic meaning without being able to grasp them directly.[42] The metatheory that endeavors to chart psychic processes is imbued, in other words, with the dynamic of rhetoricality that characterizes those processes themselves.

Rhetoric and Mass Communication. As the forms of communication characteristic of mass society have been extended and consolidated during the twentieth century, the classical liberal model in which individual free subjects contribute disinterestedly to open, unconstrained political exchange has become no more than heuristic. Images and slogans replace the ideas and expository discourse by which exchange in the public sphere was defined. Although the basic technology of movable type was developed during the Renaissance, print as a medium (especially newspapers, periodicals, and cheap books) and the growth in literacy that it ultimately fostered were distinctive to the Englightenment and to the bourgeois culture of nineteenth- and earlier twentieth-century industrial Europe. But, while the graphic word continues to play a significant role in cultural life, the structure of literacy has undergone decisive alterations. Print has given way to film and television, to phonographic reproduction, and the digital inscription of language itself in computers. The collation of image and sound in the mechanical media, even where oral language is concerned, recalls but does not reconstitute the face-to-face speech and physiognomic and gestural performances of classical rhetoric. For images and sounds may now be synthesized: the voice, like that of our current telephone information "operators," may be no more than a mechanical function, the opposite of an impersonation.

Advertising, in particular, works by condensation and montage to shatter those sequences of cause and effect integral to the construction, representation, and comprehension of personal identity. Like other forms of mass communication, advertising rehabilitates—indeed renders virtually universal—a rhetoricality at once akin to and utterly divorced from classical persuasion. The fixed traits of celebrity replace the classical orator's varied impersonations. Metonymic substitution and juxtaposition supplant that imitation of the logical connectedness of philosophical discourse so central to Aristotle's conception of rhetoric. Thus, the forms of

communication operative in contemporary life lie closer to the figurative formations described by Freud and Lacan than to the manifest processes of a traditional forum.

The depersonalizing tendencies of modern rhetoricality find illustration in the conjunction, so characteristic of mass society, of
advertising and fashion. The mimicry endemic to the selection of
clothing is now directed toward personality functions concocted
and circulated by the media. In perhaps the ultimate extension of
this principle, the names of celebrities known as designers are inscribed on clothing and other accessories in place of the personal
monograms that once discreetly marked attire as individual. The
designer, in turn, need not be alive, or even a real person, since the
creative personality marked by the famous name is often itself
produced artificially by a corporation—or at least by a corporate
design team. The putatively individual name works metonymi-
cally to screen collectivity.

Collective effort on a huge scale is the reality of which individ-
uality has become the imaginary or fantastic representation. This
phenomenon, in which audiences are manipulated by the delusion
that products are the result of individual creative effort, replaces
the old forms of persuasion. And, incidentally, any real human beings who happen to occupy the position of metonymic celebrity—
be they Calvin Klein or Ronald Reagan—become virtually mecha-
nized ciphers acting out the script of their own renown, themselves
as much manipulated as the audience they manipulate. The recent
presence of a professional film actor in the White House merely
made self-evident the contemporary truth that the performative
force of presidential elocution lies not with the seeming individual
who happens to be in office but with the impersonal corporate
state.

Rhetoric and Pragmatics. Not only in the metatheory of science, linguistics, mass communication, and psychoanalysis are we
the inheritors of Nietzsche's legacy, but also in what might be
termed the sphere of everyday life. The concept of rhetoricality bespeaks the universality of the rhetorical condition, its nonrestric-
tion to the specialized circumstances of formal communication
and persuasion. It is a characteristic of modernism that the sphere
of everyday life—the domain of utterly trivial activities and inter-
changes through which we daily pass—has increasingly become an
object of scientific inquiry. To cite just two examples from philoso-

[handwritten margin note: NPR news as rhetorical analysis]

33

phy, both the early Heidegger with his hermeneutics of *Dasein* in its *Alltäglichkeit* (everydayness) and the British school of ordinary language philosophy that developed out of the later Wittgenstein's work are oriented toward this most secularized and elusive of domains, the nexus of our normality. And it is no accident that what inquiry finds in this domain (Wittgenstein's concept of language game tells us as much) is a web of rhetorical operations. In other words, precisely that sea of invisible communicative transactions that the tradition of classical rhetoric did not and could not take into account becomes in the modernist environment a privileged object of study. Just as the modernist return of rhetoric displaces the rhetorical operations to an unconscious sphere in such fields as linguistics and psychoanalysis, so too in the area of what might be termed "pragmatic" studies modernist rhetoric finds its theme in the impersonal domain of what occurs among us, unnoticed and without deliberation or grandeur.

The displacement of rhetoric from the classical trivium to the dense tangle of our triviality can be illustrated through reference to a plethora of research programs that have emerged within various disciplines but nevertheless share a concern for the *pragmata* of everydayness. What else, for example, is ethnomethodology (despite its insistence on a phenomenological grounding) but a sociological rhetoric of normal doings? Within the disciplinary limits of sociology, one could also refer to the illustrious example of Erving Goffmann, whose major works bear titles like *Forms of Talk* and *The Presentation of Self in Everyday Life*.[43] Linguistics also has addressed itself with increasing sophistication to this domain. One thinks in this connection of the recent boom in pragmatic studies, an example of which is Dan Sperber and Deirdre Wilson's book *Relevance*, a study of "communication and cognition" that endeavors to formalize the rules of conversational exchange and that develops along its way a reconceptualization of such rhetorical tactics as metaphor and irony. Indeed, Sperber and Wilson's argument in this portion of their study exactly confirms our thesis regarding the shift from rhetoric to rhetoricality insofar as it demonstrates that metaphor and the other tropes "are simply creative exploitations of a perfectly general dimension of language use."[44] That is to say, the figures of language can no longer be treated as a specialized domain, as a limited set of elocutionary options. Rather, they make up the very fiber of every communicative transaction.

34

One could further document the new rhetoric of everyday life through reference to other fields. For instance, cognitive science and artificial intelligence stand, in our view, to inherit and radically reformulate the heuristics of classical rhetoric. Marvin Minsky's "frames," for example, or Roger Shank's "scripts" are schemata of practical knowledge that can be regarded as redactions of the classical theory of topoi.[45] Even asking for ketchup at a hamburger joint can prove to be a rhetorical operation of astonishing complexity, accomplished by recalling and modifying a "restaurant frame" or schema of typical restaurant behavior to which no single eatery conforms in every detail. George Lakoff and Mark Johnson's book *Metaphors We Live By* demonstrates even in its title that from the perspective of cognitive science rhetoricality has become the condition of modern life.[46]

Rhetoric and Literary Criticism. During the period when classical rhetoric governed the analysis and production of discourse, the aspects of the discipline now called literary criticism not comprehended by rhetorical categories were treated under the subheading "poetics." Later, after the Enlightenment and Romantic demolitions of rhetoric, criticism of literature could be found in association with the new, often nationalistic, disciplines of aesthetics, philology, and positivistic history. Traditions derived from these disciplines have enjoyed surprising longevity among Western literary scholars of the twentieth century, as have survivals and revivals of the ancient rhetorical scholia. The Anglo-American movement known as "new criticism," springing initially from William Empson, I. A. Richards, and Allen Tate, may be considered, for example, as a nostalgic attempt to fuse the organicist presumptions of Romantic aesthetics with the formal, figural analysis characteristic of classical rhetoric. Also nostalgically present in the new criticism was the presumption of a shared community of literate and tasteful gentlemen who, though writing for publication, took the forms of conversation as their stylistic ideal. Their obsession with the figures of irony, paradox, and ambiguity derives at once from the contradictions inherent in their project and from their virtually oratorical impersonation of the detached stance of the disinterested man of letters.

The revivalist aspect of new criticism—so deeply entrenched in British and American academic departments of literature—may help to account for the shock that greeted the arrival of structuralist and poststructuralist methods from Europe during the late 1960's and early 1970's. These methods, based upon characteristic modernist developments in linguistics and philosophy, worked from utterly different principles. Consider, for example, the difference between the contained, localized irony of the new critic and the deep-structural irony of Derrida or de Man. In these writers, irony is no longer a figure of speech or an educated habit of mind; it is the fundamental condition of language production. Since there is no such thing as a first, original, or direct statement, they view every utterance as intrinsically figural, unstable, and haunted by implications that militate against its overt claims. Poetry is no longer a privileged kind of discourse but a specific case illustrating the general instance of language itself. In the structuralist— and now poststructuralist—frame of reference, every human endeavor, including fundamental social and cultural institutions, must be understood as discursively constituted and therefore subject to the foundational irony disclosed by analyses such as Derrida's. As the rhetoricality of twentieth-century culture becomes ever more apparent, both survivals of classical rhetorical analysis and revivalist methods like the new criticism appear terribly restricted in scope. It is not surprising, therefore, that prestructuralist Anglo-American critics who attempted large typologies of discourse, such as Kenneth Burke and Northrop Frye, have fared better than many others.

Burke's work presents an especially forceful illustration of our argument bearing on rhetoricality. Even where the focus of his ruminations is a specific literary text, as for example in his famous analysis of Keats's "Ode on a Graecian Urn" or his speculations on Goethe's *Faust*,[47] Burke characteristically directs his inquiry not at meaning in a hermeneutic sense, nor at the cooperation of formal and thematic components in the manner of the new criticism, but rather at the text's symbolic labor, its suasive operations. Thus, his analyses are rhetorical in their basic orientation; it is indicative that two of his books carry the term "rhetoric" in their titles.[48] Although Burke himself named his method "dramatism," a term that signals his abiding concern for the place of language in human action and interaction, the rhetorical thrust of his wide-ranging inquiry is evident on every page. Much of Burke's vocabulary can be taken as the lexicon for a modernist rhetoric: terministic screen, entitlement, representative anecdote, strategies of motivation, master tropes, scene-act ratio, god-term, temporizing of essence. More-over, Burke's work illustrates many features we take to be charac-teristic of rhetorical inquiry under the conditions of modernity. It is resolutely interdisciplinary, drawing on sociology, anthropology, psychoanalysis, philosophy, and poetics; it is recursive in struc-ture, applying its categories to itself as a strategy of argument and inquiry; its range of objects (one might better say: occasions) crosses disciplinary boundaries and includes philosophical schools, political tracts, everyday life, ritual and religion, economic and for-eign policy, literary works, and bodily practices, to mention just a few. Its final ground is an anthropology that comes close to the Nietzschean definition of man as the imperfect animal, as a being whose only nature is the unremitting nonnaturalness of his sym-bolic-rhetorical self-constitution.[49]

Rhetoricality pervades even methods that, viewed superficial-ly, might seem to continue formalistic traditions. Julia Kristeva's concept of "intertextuality," for instance, could easily be misun-derstood as a reinscription of the old rhetoric.[50] But whereas the new critics considered the formal boundaries of the poem, story, or other verbal construct to delimit a universe with its own rules and self-referentiality, Kristeva's intertextuality reveals how every seemingly closed, evidently personal or otherwise situational utter-ance actually consists of all-but-infinite interlocking networks of reference, quotation, and paraquotation. Every text merges without boundary into every other, just as for Bakhtin—Kristeva's font of inspiration during the period when she worked out her ideas about intertextuality—every word abides in, and itself contains, countless intersecting ideological contexts. For Bakhtin every utterance is many utterances; every speaker is many speakers; and every seem-ingly rhetorical context encodes many other occasions. Bakhtin's works, deeply influenced by those of Nietzsche, could be read as virtual treatises on the nature and functioning of rhetoricality.

Why, then, does contemporary literary research continue to draw on the terminology of the inherited rhetorical tradition? Is there not a fundamental continuity that knits past and present to-gether? Especially in literary studies, a field often deeply troubled by the rifts of history and by the fear of cultural oblivion, one en-counters projects that anxiously work to reconstitute for the pres-ent a unity of tradition and doctrine that no longer exists. This sug-gests that in those cases where the rhetorical tradition is invoked, what is really being accomplished is the satisfaction of a nostalgia or the legitimation of one's enterprise of inquiry through a venerable genealogy. Of course, overriding constants may be posited in order to construct a history of rhetoric from, say, Aristotle to the present, and thus to attribute contemporary value to ancient rhetorical theory in the manner of the Chicago neo-Aristotelians.[51] But such continuities will be largely terminological or so abstract in nature (e.g., rhetoric has always been concerned with language in action) that their cognitive value will be minimal. In either case, the categorical displacements that have occurred behind the apparent stability of signifiers such as "metaphor" or "irony" will be suppressed. Rhetorical study has been able to vitalize literary research today precisely because it is no longer what it used to be. To get clear on this point, moreover, seems to us a prerequisite for the continued vitality of that research. Once rhetoricality is understood as the fundamental condition under which any contemporary literary criticism must proceed, the discipline itself will be transformed because its boundaries will be redrawn.

In general, then, what are we to conclude about the shape of rhetoric today, following its return? This question elicits a double answer, both parts of which point to the decisive transformations that rhetoric has undergone. First, the very object of rhetorical analyses and theories has changed. We are dealing no longer with a specialized technique of instrumental communication, but rather with a general condition of human experience and action. We have designated as "rhetoricality" this new category—the category that opens the field of modern rhetorical research. Second, there can be no single contemporary rhetorical theory: rhetoricality cannot be the object of a homogeneous discipline. Modernist (and postmodernist) rhetorical study is irreducibly multidisciplinary; one cannot study rhetoric *tout court*, but only linguistic, sociological, psychoanalytic, cognitive, communicational, medial, or literary rhetorics.

Note that these two aspects of rhetoric in its modernist return fit together: for if rhetoricality is our condition and if it names the irreducible, a priori character of rhetorical processes, then it also implies the impossibility of a single governing discourse that could know that condition. No single theory can detach itself from the limits set to knowledge and representation by rhetoricality; and every version of theory bearing on rhetoricality itself partakes of the rhetorical processes it endeavors to map. Rhetoric, we mentioned at the outset, originated in disputes regarding property, and has been concerned throughout its tradition with ensuring the identification of the proper. But rhetoricality designates the thoroughgoing impropriety of language and action and therefore cannot be captured in the net of a single form of knowledge. This is not to say that the different disciplines that address themselves to questions of rhetoric are entirely insulated from one another. On the contrary, interdisciplinary translations are not only possible but necessary. Such translations, however, fruitful and provocative as they are, can never culminate in a totalizing theory of rhetoric such as the classical tradition possessed. Modern rhetorical research must be an open-ended series of translations and transformations. It is irrevocably dispersed because of the nature of its foundational category. Rhetoricality, then, also designates the partial and provisional character of every attempt to know it.

PART II

The Rhetoric of Tradition

The Crisis of Performance

GREGORY NAGY

The point of departure for this presentation is a fundamental insight of Albert Lord, in the context of his studies of oral traditions in epic poetry: that composition and performance are aspects of the same process.[1] Building on this insight, I turn to various attested patterns of differentiation between composer and performer in oral traditions, as most succinctly illustrated by the incipient semantic split of *trobador* as 'composer' and *joglar* as 'performer' in Old Provençal usage. Such patterns of differentiation, I shall argue, reflect a fundamental state of crisis in the very process of performance.

Here we may bring into play J. L. Austin's notion of a *performative* utterance or *speech act*, where the antithesis of word and action is neutralized in that the word *is* the action.[2] I invoke also Barbara Johnson's application of Austin's notion of speech act to poetry—an application that Austin himself resisted—and her insistence on the self-referential quality of the performative: "The performative, then, acts like a 'shifter' in that it takes on meaning only by referring to the instance of its utterance."[3] Johnson adds her own translation of Emile Benveniste's formulation: "An utterance is performative insofar as it *names* the act performed. . . . The utterance *is* the act; the utterer performs the act by naming it."[4]

If indeed the performative "takes on meaning only by referring to the instance of its utterance," then this instance, this occasion, must be the basis for the intent of the utterance, for its rhetoric. If, further, the occasion should ever be lost or removed, then the intent of the utterance is destabilized. We may say that the very notion of genre serves as compensation for the lost occasion.

43

I take it, then, that questions of meaning in oral poetry and song cannot be settled in terms of composition alone: we must keep in mind what the composition says about its performance or potential performance, and what that says about whoever is the composer, whoever is the performer. Only this way can we begin to do justice to questions of authorship and even of authority. Such questions, it perhaps goes without saying, extend to written as well as oral traditions.

In treating the differentiation between composer and performer as a reflection of the crisis of performance, I propose to begin with Homer. From the standpoint of the *rhapsōidoi* 'rhapsodes', those who perform Homeric poetry, the notion of 'composer' is drastically retrojected to a proto-poet whose poetry is reproduced by an unbroken succession of performers; Socrates can thus envisage the rhapsode Ion as the last in a chain of magnetized metal rings connected by the force of the original poet Homer.[5] More accurately, we may say that Ion is the next to last in the chain with relation to his audience, who would be the last link from the standpoint of the performance (Plato, *Ion* 536a). By implication, the magnetic force of the poetic composition becomes weaker and weaker with each successive performer. Ion, then, by virtue of being the last or at least the latest reproducer of Homer, would also be the weakest.

By contrast, in phases of a given tradition where both composition and performance can be "owned" by the same person at a given occasion, the advantage of the immediate composer-performer, as conferred by the occasion at hand, can be conventionally contrasted with the relative disadvantage of his predecessors, who are at this point of course deprived of their own occasion. Such an attitude is expressed as follows in one particular Eskimo song: "All songs have been exhausted. He picks up some of all and adds his own and makes a new song."[6] Note here the oral performance's reference to the "newness" of its composition. It would be deceptive, here as elsewhere in oral traditions, to equate such "newness" with our own general notions of "innovation." We must be on guard against projecting into oral traditions an anxious modernist vision of the creative self, which can lapse all too easily into romantic scenarios of creation out of self-contained genius.[7]

Or again, we may note the juxtaposition made by Ferdowsi, poet of the *Shāhnāma*, with his predecessor Daqiqi: "In transmitting, his [Daqiqi's] words became weak. Ancient times were not renewed by him."[8] Again I draw attention to the "renewal" claimed by the composer. A variant in the same passage reads: "Now I will tell what he [Daqiqi] has told. For I am alive and he has become united with the dust." The poet here is presenting himself as owning the composition on the grounds that it is now he, and not his predecessors, who has access to the occasion, which is stylized as performances before assemblies: "These stories, grown old, will be renewed by me in all assemblies."[9] Note again the notion of "renewal."

In the case of Plato's *Ion*, the mythmaking retrojection of Homeric composition back to the strongest proto-poet of course belies the evolutionary progression of a Tradition wherein the aspect of recomposition gradually diminishes in the process of diffusion entailed by performance in an ever-widening circle of listeners. The wider the diffusion, the deeper the Tradition has to reach within itself: the least common denominator is also the oldest, in that a synthesis of distinct but related traditions would tend to recover the oldest aspects of these traditions. Given the ever-increasing social mobility of the poet,[10] who is teleologically evolving into the rhapsode, his cumulative exposure to a multiformity of traditions in a plurality of places is analogous to the experience of an ethnographer who attempts to reconstruct back to a prototype the distinct but cognate versions of traditions in different but neighboring locales. A synthetic Tradition is like a prototype of variant traditions, and the diachrony of its evolution thus becomes its own synchrony. Homeric synchrony, to take the clearest example, is like this: it operates on the diachronically oldest recoverable aspects of its own traditons.

The synthetic Tradition, in order to survive, must prevail over the countless variant traditions from which it was constituted. And in order to prevail, the Tradition must be performed. To understand that performance is essential, we may turn to the observation of Claude Lévi-Strauss in his book on masks:[11] each performance of a myth, he notes, entails a re-creation of that myth, so that the latest version of the myth, in the context of its performance in the here and now, takes precedence over all previous versions. The latest performance is by necessity a crisis point for the traditions of myth, in that the latest performance will determine what continues to be transmitted and what does not. Or, at the very least, the latest performance will determine what is highlighted and

45

what is shaded over, with the ever-present possibility that the shading-over will lapse, with the passage of time, into total darkness.

In this evolutionary vision of change in oral traditions, I have deliberately used the imagery of light in order to bring home a point that is actually made by the poetic traditions of Greek myth-making, although there the view is episodic, not evolutionary: the poetic power of *mnēmosunē* 'remembering' is traditionally represented as light, which is in conflict with the darkness of *lēthē* 'forgetting'. What is illuminated or obscured by poetry is what is respectively preserved or lost in the tradition.

The concept of *lēthē* 'forgetting', however, is not only negative. That is, *lēthē* is not only the opposite of *mnēmosunē* 'remembering': it can also be an aspect of *mnēmosunē*. For example, the goddess *Mnēmosunē* is described in the *Theogony* of Hesiod as giving birth to the Muses, divine personifications of the poet's power, so that they, through their poetry, may provide *lēsmosunē* 'forgetting' of sadnesses and of worries for humankind (*Theogony* 53–55); whoever hears the Muses no longer *memnētai* 'remembers' his own ills (*Theogony* 103).[12] By implication, the highlighting of the glory of poetry is achieved by shading over anything that detracts from it. A bright light needs a background of darkness.

Such a concept of *mnēmosunē* can only be achieved through an ever-present awareness of its opposite, *lēthē*. Without the obliteration of what need not be remembered, there cannot be memory—at least, from the standpoint of archaic Greek poetics.

Let us reformulate these thought patterns in terms of an opposition between "unmarked" and "marked" categories, as formulated by Roman Jakobson. These terms have been defined as follows: "The general meaning of a marked category states the presence of a certain (whether positive or negative) property A; the general meaning of the corresponding unmarked category states nothing about the presence of A."[13] The unmarked category is the general category, which can include the marked category, whereas the reverse situation cannot hold.[14] For example, in an opposition of the English words 'long' and 'short', the unmarked member of the opposition is 'long' because it can be used not only as the opposite of 'short' but also as the general category. 'Long' is the opposite of 'short' when we say "This is long, not short." 'Long' is just a general category, however, when we say "How long is this?" Such a question does not judge whether something is long or short,

46

whereas "How short is this?" does. In an opposition of *mnē-* 're-member' and *lēth-* 'forget', *mnē-* would be the unmarked member and *lēth-* the marked, in that *lēth-* can be included by *mnē-* as an aspect of *mnē-*. Besides the passage that we have just considered from the *Theogony*, I cite another striking illustration, from a different source: in the ritual of incubation connected with the cult of Trophonios, the initiate has to drink from the springs of both *Lēthē* and *Mnēmosunē*; this way, the undesired mental state can be shaded over while the desired mental state is highlighted (Pausanias, *Description of Greece* 9.39.8).

To pursue the subject of these thought patterns even further, I cite another example of unmarked/marked opposition in the English language. In an opposition of the pronouns 'he' and 'she', the former is the unmarked member and the latter the marked, in that 'she' is included by 'he' as the feminine aspect of being 'he'. The masculine aspect of being 'he', by contrast, has to be achieved through an ever-present negation of the feminine. We may say something like "This is not a she but a he!" Otherwise, 'he' does not, of and by itself, convey a masculine aspect. In generalizing statements, for example, 'he' can stand for both 'he' and 'she', as in "Everyone may interpret as he chooses." Where the unmarked member excludes the marked member through a negation of the marked, the unmarked member receives a *minus-interpretation*; where the unmarked member includes the marked, it receives a *zero-interpretation*.

These relationships can be conceived as a larger circle of *mnēmosunē* that includes an inner area of *lēthē* surrounding a smaller circle of specialized *mnēmosunē* that excludes the outer area of *lēthē*. The area of forgetting is visualized as the ongoing erasure of things not worth remembering, erasure by way of *lēthē*; the smaller circle of remembering, within the larger circle, is highlighted by the area of darkness surrounding it, the area of forgetting. In fact, there is a special word in the diction of archaic Greek poetry that formalizes this specialized and exclusive kind of remembering: that word is *alētheia*, normally glossed in English as 'truth'. The *alētheia* of the poet is the nonerasure of the poetic glory that is his to confer. The same concept is evident in the periphrastic expression *oude me / se / he lēthei* 'it does not escape my/your/his-her mind', which conventionally reinforces injunctions to be *memnēmenos* 'mindful, remembering'.[15]

47

Besides contrasting with negative thoughts about human ills[16] or erroneous thoughts that lead to injustice, the *alētheia* of Greek poetry, I submit, tends to contrast with the multiformity of poetic versions in the process of achieving a uniform version acceptable to all Hellenes. This brings us back to the observation of Lévi-Strauss to the effect that the latest performance of myth is in principle an occasion for selecting from and thereby potentially erasing versions available from countless previous performances. In what survives of archaic Greek poetry—and now I am using the word "poetry" in the broadest sense—what we keep finding is the ultimate extension of this principle—to the point where the latest version becomes the last version, a canonization that brings to a final state of crystallization what had been becoming an ever less fluid state of variation in performance.[17] And I attribute this canonization not to the phenomenon of incipient literacy but to the broader social phenomenon of Panhellenization.[18] As we shall see, this phenomenon is relative from the standpoint of an outsider to the tradition, in that some compositions will be more Panhellenic in scope than others. From the standpoint of the insider to the tradition, however, in the here and now of performance, the Panhellenic perspective is the absolutist perspective of *alētheia* 'truth'.[19]

This notion of "canonization," as I have just outlined it,[20] is analogous to a concept used by scholars associated with the Museum housing the great library of Alexandria.[21] This concept is *krisis*, in the sense of separating, discriminating, judging (verb *krīnō*) those works and those authors that are worthy of special recognition and those that are not.[22] The Alexandrian scholars who inherited the legacy of this process of separation, discrimination, judgment, were the *kritikoi* 'critics',[23] while the classical authors who were recognized as the survivors of this process of *krisis* were called the *enkrithentes*,[24] a term that corresponds to the Roman concept of the classics, the *classici*, who are authors of the 'first class', *primae classis*.[25] The *krisis* of the *enkrithentes*, however, starts not with the Alexandrian scholars, nor even with the likes of Aristotle.[26] The "crisis" of this *krisis* is already underway in the archaic period of Greece. We must remind ourselves that songs and poetry were traditionally performed in a context of competition. A striking example is the tradition of dramatic festivals at Athens, with the *krisis* 'judgment' of winners by *kritai* 'judges'.[27] But the *criteria* of the *crisis* are different. In the archaic period, what is at stake is the survival or nonsurvival not merely of specific works or specific authors but of tradition itself. What must be preserved and what may be lost is decided by an ideology that can be reduced to a basic question: what is Panhellenic, *alētheia*, and what is not?

For illustration, I offer seven carefully selected passages concerning the concept of *alētheia* as a Panhellenic truth-value. This truth-value, as we shall see, is associated not just with poetry in the narrower sense but also with song, as in the lyric poetry of Pindar, and even with prose, as in the *History* of Herodotus. The seven passages that follow, then, are selected from the widest possible range of Greek verbal art, ranging all the way from song to prose.

Let us begin with the "Days" part of the *Works and Days* of Hesiod:

> Take care to mark the days[28] [of the month],
> which come from Zeus, giving each day its due.
> (Hesiod, *Works and Days* 765)

The very first day-of-the-month to be mentioned is a crisis point for the Panhellenic perspective, since it is the day when each *polis* is most idiosyncratic, with local traditions prevailing:

> Do this for your laborers. The thirtieth day of
> the month is best
> for inspecting different kinds of work that have
> to be done and for apportioning food-supplies.
> This is the day that people spend by sorting out
> [*krīnō*] what is truth [*alētheia*] and what is not.
> (Hesiod, *Works and Days* 766–68)

A commentator on the *Works and Days* remarks: "Civil calendars often fell out of step with the moon . . . and it was on the 30th that errors arose. Each month had to be allowed either 29 or 30 days, but the last day was called *triakas* (or in Athens *henē kai neā* [meaning 'the old and the new']) in either case, the preceding day (?) being omitted in a 'hollow' month. So it was always a question of when to have the 30th."[29] In other words, each *polis* had its own traditions about the calendar. At the time of the thirtieth, then, there is a crisis about arriving at a Panhellenic norm from the standpoint of each *polis*. This norm is conveyed here by the notion of *alētheia* 'truth', which, I have argued, is the criterion of Panhellenism. Then the poet embarks on a catalogue of those days of the month that share the highest degree of consensus in local traditions, with the catalogue proceeding in a descending order of consensus. The thirtieth may be a crisis point, varying from *polis* to *polis*, but the crisis leads to a shared Panhellenic perspective. The poet has blotted over the differences, simply noting that *alētheia* is being sorted out (i.e., is in a crisis: to repeat, the verb is *krīnō*) on the thirtieth. After the thirtieth, it is possible to arrive at a fixed sequence of given days traditionally spent in given ways by all Hellenes.[30] The poet will now highlight this fixed sequence, which is the Panhellenic perspective. Zeus, as the god who is the planner of the universe, is an appropriate symbol for the organizing principle that underlies the Panhellenic perspective, and it is with Zeus that the poet begins the catalogue:

> For what I now tell you are the days of Zeus the
>   Planner.
> 770 To begin with, the first,[31] fourth,[32] and
>   the seventh[33] are each a holy day
> (it was on the seventh that Leto gave birth to
>   Apollo of the golden sword).
> So too the eighth[34] and the ninth.[35] And
>   yet, these two days of the waxing part of the
>   month
> are particularly good for various kinds of work
>   by mortals.[36]
> 775 The eleventh and the twelfth are both good
>   for shearing sheep and for gathering the
>   benign grain.
> But the twelfth is much better than the
>   eleventh.
> It is on that day that the spider, levitating in
>   the air, spins its web
> in full day,[37] while the Knowledgeable One[38]
>   amasses her pile.
> On that day a woman should set up her loom and
>   get on with her work.
> 780 Avoid the thirteenth day of the waxing part of
>   the month
> for beginning to sow. But it is the best day for
>   getting your plants bedded in.
> The sixth day of the middle of the month is very
>   unfavorable for plants,
> but it is good for giving birth to male
>   descendants. As for females, it is not at all
>   favorable
> either to be born at all on that day or to get
>   married.

785 Nor is the first sixth day an appropriate one for
    a girl to be born.
But, for gelding kid goats and sheep
    it is a kindly day. Also for making an enclosure for
    the sheep.
It is good for the birth of a boy, but such a
    child will grow up liking to utter words of
    mocking reproach,
which are lies, crafty words, and stealthy
    relations.[39]
790 On the eighth day of the month geld the boar and
    the loud-roaring bull.
Do the same with the work-enduring asses on the
    twelfth.
On the Great Twentieth, a full day,[40] a
    knowledgeable man
should be born.[41] Such a man is very sound in
    his mind [*noos*].
The tenth is favorable for a boy to be born; for
    a girl, it is the fourth
795 of the mid-month. On that day, sheep and
    shambling horned oxen,
as well as the sharp-toothed dog and
    work-enduring asses,
are to be tamed to the touch of the hand. But
    take care in your mind [*thūmos*]
to avoid the fourth of the beginning and ending
    of the month.
Do not have your heart eaten away with troubles
    on this day, which is very much a day when the
    gods bring things to fulfillment.
800 On the fourth of the month bring home your wedded
    wife,
having sorted out the bird-omens, which are best
    for doing this.
Avoid fifth days. They are harsh and ominous.
For they say that it was on the fifth that the
    Erinyes assisted
at the birth of Horkos (Oath), to whom Eris
    (Strife) gave birth, to be a pain to those who
    break an oath.
805 On the seventh of the mid-month cast the sacred
    grain of Demeter
upon the smoothed-over threshing floor, looking
    carefully about you.
Have the woodman cut beams for the rooms in your
    house
and plenty of ship-timbers which are suitable for
    ships.

On the fourth, begin to build sleek ships.
810 The ninth of the mid-month is better when evening
approaches.
But the first ninth is the most painless for
humans.
It is good for conception and for being born
for man and woman alike. It is never a
completely bad day.
Or again, few people know that the thrice-nine of
the month is best
815 for opening a wine-jar and for putting yokes on
the necks
of oxen, mules, and swift-footed horses,
or for hauling a swift ship with many oars down
to the wine-colored sea.
Few give it its true [alēthēs][42] name.
Open your jar on the fourth. The fourth of the
mid-month is the most holy of them all.
820 Again, few do it [i.e., give it its true
name].[43] I mean the after-twenty [i.e., the
twenty-first][44] which is best
when dawn comes. As evening approaches, it is less good.
These, then, are the days, a great blessing for
earth-bound men.
The others fall in between. There is no doom
attached to them, and they bring nothing.
Different people praise different days,[45] but
few really know.[46]
825 Sometimes the day is a step-mother, and sometimes
it is a mother.[47]
With respect to all of these days, fortunate and
blissful is he who knows all these things as he
works the land,
without being responsible to the immortals for
any evil deed,
as he sorts out [verb krīnō] the bird-omens, and
as he avoids any acts of transgression.
(Hesiod, *Works and Days* 769–828)

In the following passage, the Muses promise to teach Hesiod to speak in a mode that they describe as the absolute truth, the noun for which is *alētheia*.

We know how to say many false things that are
just like real things.
But we know also, whenever we are willing, how to
announce things that are true [alēthea].[48]
(Hesiod, *Theogony* 27–28)

The ideology of Panhellenism in archaic Greece is a relative one, though it presents itself as absolute: to be Panhellenic, a given composition must highlight those aspects of Greek tradition that are shared by *most* Greek locales, while all along shading over those aspects that vary from locale to locale.[49] In the process of aiming at a consensus, such an ideology is clearly relative; still, in claiming that it represents *all* Greek locales, it is presenting itself as absolute.[50] To "announce things that are true [*alēthea*]" is a model for the evolution of a unique Panhellenic theogony out of an untold number of local theogonies, which are here set apart as a plethora of falsehoods.[51]

> Indeed there are many wondrous things. And yet, the words that men tell, myths [*mūthoi*] embellished by varying falsehoods, beyond wording that is true [*alēthēs*], are deceptive. But Kharis,[52] which makes everything pleasurable for mortals, has brought it about, by way of conferring honor, that even the *untrustworthy* [*apiston*] oftentimes becomes *trustworthy* [*piston*].
>
> (Pindar, *Olympian* 1.28–32)

Here we see the juxtaposition of what purports to be a unique and true Panhellenic version with a plethora of false versions, described as *mūthoi* 'myths'. The *mūthoi* are the "outer core," containing traditions that are *apista* 'untrustworthy'. In referring to itself, the *alētheia* of Panhellenic poetics represents *mūthoi* as if they were additions to the "kernel of truth."[53] It is as if *mūthoi* were additions to the kernel of truth as formulated by *alētheia*. I would argue, however, that the *mūthoi* are in fact the outer core of epichoric myths as differentiated from the inner core of Panhellenic myths.

> But the *kharis* of the past is asleep, and mortals are *unaware* [negative of *mnē-*] of anything except for that one thing, that cresting blossom of poetic art, which emerges wedded to the glory-bringing streams of poetic words.
>
> (Pindar, *Isthmian* 7.16–19)

The tradition that informs this poem is realized only in the here and now of performance, which is visualized as blossoming from the irrigating "streams" of the tradition. The '*kharis* of the past' is the cumulative response to all other potential realizations of the tradition, with the adjective *palaio-* 'of the past' implicitly drawing a contrast with the present performance. In the diction of Pindar, the present performance is conventionally described as *neo-* or *nearo-* 'new', which refers not to the novelty of a theme but to the ad hoc application of a myth to the here and now of those who attend and are the occasion of performance.[54]

> Men would most rather give glory [*kleos*] to that song
> which is the newest for its listeners.
>
> (Homer, *Odyssey* 1.351–52)

Telemachus says this to his mother, Penelope, who had tried to stop the singer Phemios from singing what is described as the *nostos* 'homecoming' of the Achaeans (1.326).[55] Here too, as in the diction of Pindar, the concept *neo-* 'new' refers to the appropriateness of the myth to the situation in the here and now.[56] In this case, of course, Odysseus both is already a prime figure in the myth and is about to become a prime figure in the here and now being narrated by the poem. His *nostos* is literally in the making, which is precisely the subject of the singer. Naturally, the Panhellenic *nostos* of Odysseus in the *Odyssey* is one to end all *nostoi*.[57]

> About the other kings, they [the Egyptian priests] had no public state-
> ment [*apodeixis*] to tell, since there was nothing distinguished
> [literally, "bright"], except for the last [king].
>
> (Herodotus, *History* 2.101.1)

The word *apodeixis* 'public display' refers to the medium for performing what we see written in Herodotus.[58] Since this medium makes public the deeds of men, what men do is also *apodeixis*, in that their deeds are being publicly witnessed. In this case, the *apodeixis* of the priests—and of Herodotus, in turn—erases the deeds of all kings except one. To put it in terms of the passage itself, the making public of a tradition by way of performance—or at least by way of a written record that simulates performance—highlights the deeds of an exceptional figure as it darkens over the deeds of other figures.

> This is the public display [noun *apodeixis*] of the inquiry [*historiā*] of
> Herodotus of Halikarnassos, with the purpose of bringing it about (a)
> that whatever results from men may not, with the passage of time,
> become evanescent, and (b) that great and wondrous deeds—some of
> them *publicly performed* [verb *apodeiknumai*] by Hellenes, others by
> barbarians—may not become *akleā* [without *kleos* 'glory']. In particu-
> lar, [this *apodeixis* of this *historiā* concerns] why [i.e., of what *aitiā*
> 'cause'] they came into conflict with each other.
>
> (Herodotus, *History prooemium*)

54

The prose of Herodotus, in the *prooemium* to the *History*, is presenting itself as an extension of the poetry of Homer. In Homeric poetry, we find that *kleos* means not only 'fame' or 'glory' but also, more specifically, *the fame or glory that is conferred by the medium of poetry*.[59] In the *prooemium* of Herodotus, it is implied that *kleos* is *the fame or glory that is conferred by the medium of poetry or prose*. Thus the prose of Herodotus does not differentiate itself, in self-reference, from the poetry of Homer.

The medium of Herodotus, in calling itself *apodeixis*, is *public*. By contrast, Thucydides presents his writings as a *private* possession, a *ktēma*, of permanent value ("*ktēma . . . es aiei*"[60]— something that is not the product of a *competitive public performance, meant to be heard and intended merely for the here and now* ("*agōnisma es to parakhrēma akouein*," 1.22.4). The word here for "competitive public performance" is *agōnisma*, derived from *agōn*, 'assembly, contest'. This concept of *agōn* is crucial for understanding the archaic Greek performance traditions of prose, poetry, and song.

One of the clearest examples is the great *agōn* between Aeschylus and Euripides in Hades, as dramatized by Aristophanes in the *Frogs*, first performed in 405 B.C. That tragedy is the *tekhnē* 'craft' of poetry par excellence—and this concept recurs frequently[61]—is the one given that is held in respect by both sides in the contest.[62] What is at issue is the superiority or inferiority of the old and current ways of practicing that craft, as represented by Aeschylus and Euripides respectively.

The fundamental reason for Euripides' loss to Aeschylus in the *Frogs*, and in general for his being singled out as a special target for the comedy of Aristophanes, is that his poetics are *current*. The definitive statement on what is current in the poetics of tragedy is treated as a foil by the poetics of comedy.[63] That it is Aeschylus who wins the contest in the *Frogs*, thus winning the chance to be brought back to the contemporary world of the living by the god of theater himself, is the wish fulfillment of a nostalgia for the undifferentiated Dionysiac essence of Drama.

The contest of Aeschylus and Euripides in the *Frogs* takes the form, to repeat, of an *agōn*, and this word is actually used in self-references.[64] The very format of the *agōn* is indicative of an undifferentiated phase of drama as it must have existed before the differentiation of the City Dionysia. It has been argued that the

functional part of comedy known as the *agōn* consists of two an-
tagonistic *antikhoria*, "each combining the aggressive entrance of
the parodos with primitive features of the parabasis: self-presenta-
tion and self-praise, invocation and invective, 'literary' polemics."[65]

Ironically, however, the very notion of *agōn* as "contest" is the
basis for the ongoing differentiation of poetics in the theater. The
agōn of a poetic contest requires a judgment, the word for which is
krisis, and the two words actually occur together at a crucial point
in the *Frogs*.[66]

At the very beginning, we observed that the Alexandrian concept of *krisis*, in the sense of *separating, discriminating, judging*
(verb *krīnō*) those works and those authors that are to be preserved
and those that are not, was crucial to the concept of "canon" in the
classical world. The Alexandrian scholars who were in charge of
this process of separation, discrimination, judgment, were the *kritikoi* 'critics', while the classical authors who were meant to survive the *krisis* were called the *enkrithentes*. We also observed that
the *krisis* of the *enkrithentes* started not with the Alexandrian
scholars, nor even with the likes of Aristotle: the "crisis" of this
krisis was already under way in the archaic and classical periods of
Greece, where songs and poetry were traditionally performed in a
context of competition. I stressed the premier example of such
competition, namely, the tradition of dramatic festivals at Athens,
with the *krisis* 'judgment' of winners by *kritai* 'judges'.[67] What we
see in the *agōn* of the *Frogs* of Aristophanes is a dramatization of
that competition between drama and drama, and this time the
competition is happening *within* drama. This way, the ontogeny of
drama is recapitulating its own phylogeny as a competitive medium, an *agōn* calling for the *krisis* of selection.

Given that the Theater of Dionysus at Athens is the primary
context for the evolution of drama, specifically, for the eventual
differentiation of choral dramatic contests into the separate categories of tragedy, comedy, dithyramb, and satyr drama, we may look
for other references to such evolution within drama itself. The ritual essence of Greek drama as a choral performance that takes
place at a seasonally recurring festival is highlighted by the *Bacchae* of Euripides, a tragedy performed some time shortly after the
death of the poet in 406 B.C., which represents the actions concerning the god Dionysus and the hero Pentheus as a sort of proto-

festival, a primitive version of the Feast of the City Dionysia in Athens.[68] "If," it has been argued, "the tradition that Thespis produced a *Pentheus* as one of the earliest Greek dramas was current in Euripides' time, the choice of subject of Dionysus' introduction of a primitive drama into Thebes would be particularly appropriate."[69] In the *Bacchae* we witness a scene where a herdsman is telling how he and his companions, *boukoloi* 'cowherds' and *poimenes* 'shepherds', had come together for a contest of words in describing the wondrous things performed by the devotees of Bacchus (*Bacchae* 714–16). Concerning later traditions of dancing by *boukoloi* in worship of Dionysus, it has been observed that such dances "may well have had their *aition* in such stories as the herdsman tells here."[70] In other words, the myth of Dionysus and Pentheus is referring to itself as the motivation, or, to put it in Greek, the *aition* 'cause', of the ritual complex known as the Feast of the City Dionysia, as represented by the *Bacchae*.[71] Moreover, this *aition*, telling of *boukoloi* and *poimenes* who *come together* (*Bacchae* 714) to compete in describing the wonders of Bacchus, reenacts the very etymology of the crucial word *agōn*, apparently derived from the root *ag-* of *agō*, as in *sunagō* 'bring together, assemble, gather'.[72] The notion of 'assemble' is intrinsic to the general sense of *agōn*, that is, 'assembly'.[73] But the word can also specifically mean 'contest'.[74] Thus *agōn* conveys not only the social setting for an activity, to wit, an *assembly* of people, but also the activity itself, to wit, a *contest*. The notion of competition built into *agōn* is admirably reflected in the English borrowing "antagonism."[75] Moreover, *agōn* can designate a festival of contests in poetry.[76] The ritual aspect of these activities is suggested by attestations of the derivative word *agōniā* in the sense of 'agony'.[77]

A semantic parallel is the English usage of "trial" in the sense of "ordeal," and we may also note that the etymological cognate of the English "ordeal" in German is *Urteil*. In the *Bacchae* of Euripides, Dionysus himself describes the upcoming ordeal of Pentheus—in which he will be dismembered by the god's devotees—as a great *agōn* (975). At the moment, Pentheus may interpret *agōn* on the surface, as it were, in the mere sense of a 'contest' with adversaries against whom Pentheus expects to win (*Bacchae* 964, 975); but the real winner will be Dionysus, while Pentheus will undergo an *agōn* in the deeper sense of the ultimate 'agony' of an ultimate 'ordeal' (ibid.). From this latter perspective, the competition of the herdsmen who come together to tell of the wonders of Dionysus *is* the ordeal of Pentheus.

In having just offered this sketch of traditions in composition and performance, I should close by stressing that I do not deny the notion of "poets within a tradition."[78] I am aware that the oral composer, in the context of performance, can execute considerable refinements in the act of recomposition. As we have seen, he can even appropriate the recomposition as his own composition, as if it emanated exclusively from his own authority: "This is my song." But I maintain that the gradual replacement of multiformity in local oral traditions by uniformity in Panhellenic oral tradition led to an internal idealization of the very concept of the composer. If indeed Panhellenization gradually eliminated opportunities for recomposition-in-performance, we should then expect a commensurate elimination of opportunities for successive generations of performers to identify themselves as composers. I am therefore not arguing generally that tradition creates the poet.[79] Rather, I am arguing specifically that the Panhellenic tradition of oral poetry appropriates the poet, potentially transforming even historical figures into generic ones who merely represent the traditional functions of their poetry. To put it another way: the poet, by virtue of being a transmitter of tradition, can become absorbed by the tradition.

The appropriation of a historical person by the poetic tradition in which he or she is composing can be visualized hypothetically in the following general schema of progressive phases, which have been constructed from specific examples of performance conventions taken from a variety of societies:

1. At a phase of the tradition where each performance still entails an act of at least partial recomposition, performer L publicly appropriates a given recomposition-in-performance as his or her own composition.[80]

2. At a later phase of the tradition, performer M stops appropriating the recomposition of the recomposition as his or her own composition and instead attributes it to the predecessor L; this attribution is then continued by the successors N, O, P, Q, and so forth.[81]

3. In the process of successive recompositions by $N, O, P, Q \ldots$, the self-identification of L is itself recomposed often

enough to eliminate the historical aspects of L's identity and to preserve only the generic aspects (that is, the aspects of the poet as defined by the poet's traditional activity as a poet or by his being the ancestor of those who continue in the tradition).[82]

The key to loss of identity as a composer is lack of control over performance. Once the factor of performance slips out of the poet's control, even if the performers of the poet's poetry have a tradition about what to say about the poet as a composer, nevertheless, the poet becomes a myth. More accurately, the poet becomes part of a myth, and the mythmaking structure will appropriate his or her identity.

Metaphor and Catachresis

PATRICIA PARKER

The first thing that strikes one in the history of the terms "metaphor" and "catachresis" is the apparently unnecessary confusion of the two, since the difference between them was clearly defined as early as Quintilian's discussion of catachresis in the *Institutio oratoria*. Catachresis (*abusio*, or abuse) is defined there as "the practice of adapting the nearest available term to describe something for which no actual [i.e., proper] term exists."[1] The lack of an original proper term—the lexical gap or lacuna—is in this passage the clear basis for Quintilian's distinction between catachresis, or *abusio*, and metaphor, or *translatio*: catachresis is a transfer of terms from one place to another employed when no proper word exists, while metaphor is a transfer or substitution employed when a proper term does already exist and is displaced by a term transferred from another place to a place not its own.

The terms of Quintilian's clear distinction are repeated through the centuries wherever the differentiation founded on the prior existence or nonexistence of a proper term is made. Joannes Susenbrotus, in the sixteenth century, defines catachresis—in an almost exact echo of Quintilian—as "the practice of adapting the nearest available term to describe something for which no proper term exists," thus differentiating it from "a metaphor, which changes the proper term into another one."[2] Yet in spite of the best efforts and frequent reiteration of this tradition of clear and logical distinction, the confusion of the two terms persists with a remarkable tenacity right up to the present. The *Rhetorica ad Herennium*, for example, thought for centuries to be Ciceronian and re-

60

ceived with the authority of Cicero, muddies the clear waters of logical distinction by defining catachresis (*abusio*) as "the inexact use of a like and kindred word in place of the precise and proper one." The abuse in *abusio* is here instead an abuse of metaphor, the wrong or inexact use of it as a substitution for the proper term. And the alternative term *audacia* for catachresis joins *abusio* as another highly charged pejorative, with potential application to an "audacious" metaphor.

This confusion, or more precisely the identification of catachresis with an abuse of metaphorical transfers (especially in the variety known as "farfetched" metaphor), continues not only into the Renaissance but even into contemporary attempts at definition. Richard Lanham, in his *Handlist of Rhetorical Terms*, gives two definitions for catachresis: (a) "implied metaphor, using words *wrenched* from common usage" (my emphasis) and (b) "a second definition which seems slightly different but perhaps is not: an extravagant, unexpected, far-fetched metaphor, as when a weeping woman's eyes become Niagara Falls."[3] Northrop Frye writes in *Anatomy of Criticism* of "the unexpected or violent metaphor that is called catachresis," while the *Princeton Encyclopedia* defines catachresis almost exclusively in terms of a strained, farfetched, or mixed metaphor, with no mention whatsoever of the long-standing distinction on the basis of the presence or absence of an original proper term.[4]

What we may be even more surprised to find, however, is that the confusion or breaking down of this clear and logical distinction between metaphor as *translatio* and catachresis as the figure of "abuse" inhabits the discourse of Quintilian himself, in the very sentences juxtaposed in his definition of catachresis as *abusio*. The clear boundary we have already remarked is initiated in this sentence: "We must be careful to distinguish between abuse [*abusio*] and metaphor [*translatio*], since the former is employed where there is no proper term available, and the latter when there is another term available" (*Institutio* 8.6.35). But then, immediately afterward, the distinction breaks down in a single reference to poetic practice: "As for poets, they indulge in the abuse of words even in cases where proper terms do exist, and substitute words of somewhat similar meaning [*Nam poetae solent abusive etiam in his rebus, quibus nomina sua sunt, vicinis potius uti*]." The preference

61

of poets for the metaphorical, for an alien rather than a proper term, even when a proper term already exists, here also becomes a form of "abuse."

Even more revealing than this local juxtaposition is the combination of catachresis and metaphor within Quintilian's earlier discussion of metaphor itself. For if the *Institutio* is the source of the clear distinction between the two—in its discussion of catachresis as a separate form—it is also one of the sources, along with Cicero and the *Rhetorica*, of the blurring of boundaries that subverts subsequent attempts at ordered definition. At the beginning of his discussion of metaphor, Quintilian remarks that it "adds to the copiousness of language by the interchange of words and by borrowing, and finally succeeds in accomplishing the supremely difficult task of providing a name for everything" (8.6). *Metaphora* or *translatio*, then, is related to a primitive lack in language—a lack that the later description of catachresis will associate exclusively with it—and contributes to extending the empire of names. The description of metaphor that follows mixes alternately the features of both kinds of transfer—those in which a proper term already exists and those in which one is lacking:

> A noun or a verb is transferred from the place where it properly belongs to another where there is either no proper term or the transferred term is better than the literal. We do this either because it is necessary or to make our meaning clearer or; as I have already said, to produce a decorative effect. When it secures none of these results, our metaphor will be out of place [*improprium*]. (8.6.6)

The definition here is the *Institutio*'s initial description of metaphor. And yet the definition includes in its very comprehensiveness both what will later be called "catachresis" and what will be distinguished from it as "metaphor" in a more specific sense. The definition's first sentence includes both of the transfers that will only subsequently be separated out—the catachretic ("where there is . . . no proper term") and the metaphorical (where "the transferred term is better than the literal" and the transfer is instituted by preference rather than compelled by lack). The conflation continues: "We do this either because it is necessary" (catachresis), "or to make our meaning clearer" (both?), "or . . . to produce a decorative effect" (metaphor).

What follows in this dense, contradictorily packed, and immensely influential passage from Quintilian are examples of transfers "by necessity" and transfers for the purpose of "ornament." The distinction between what the text will eventually term *abusio* (catachresis) and *translatio* (metaphor) is thus first introduced as a distinction between "necessity" and "decoration"—depending on whether a prior "proper" term exists. But both are included within the discussion of metaphor as the transfer of a term from one place to a place "not its own," and both are therefore at least potentially "out of place." The signal importance of "place" becomes even clearer where the text observes, in speaking of metaphor, that it "should always either occupy a place already vacant"—which is to say, it should be what will later be termed "catachresis"—"or if it fills the room of something else" (that is, if it is metaphor as distinguished from catachresis), "it should be more impressive than that which it displaces" (8.6.18). The notion of a vacant "room" occupied by a transferred term that then becomes indistinguishable from the lacking "proper" term (catachresis) or of a room already occupied by a term whose place is instead usurped (metaphor) brings to mind the underlying figures of *oikos* and *oikonomia*, which structure this whole neoclassical discourse on tropes and figures as moving from place to place and which give us, in a later writer like César Dumarsais, a reiteration of the definition of metaphor as occupying a "borrowed home" (*demeure empruntée*).[5] Catachresis, in Quintilian, involves a lack that the term transferred must fill; *suppléer* is the term used later by both Dumarsais and Pierre Fontanier. The notion of the "room" or "house" is joined in this economics of language and figure by a motif, and motive, of lack and "supply."

Even in Quintilian, then—the very source of the clear division between catachresis and metaphor—both are subsumed within the larger category of metaphorical transfer, the movement of a term from its original place to another place. Not surprisingly, the subsequent history of attempts to distinguish them is a history of the breakdown of boundaries even as they are erected. In the Renaissance, George Puttenham, for instance, moves from a description of metaphor into a counterdefinition of catachresis that is careful to separate the "figure of TRANSPORTE," or metaphor, from catachresis as the "figure of ABUSE." But the very boundaries he sets up

to distinguish them are elided, since the examples he offers of catachresis could be as readily exchanged for instances of metaphor.
Exempla here undermine the mutual inviolability of the very categories they are set up to exemplify. Metaphor and catachresis are
placed side by side, but the dividing line between them is in the
process transgressed and blurred. As with Quintilian, whom he follows at times so closely as to miss the logical fissures this imports
into his own attempts at distinction, Puttenham includes what
he will subsequently call catachresis as one of the "three kinds
of metaphor"—metaphor used "for *necessity* or want of a better
word."[6]

This blurring of the distinction between metaphor and catachresis persisted into the eighteenth century, in Dumarsais's *Les
tropes* (1729). In fact, it is precisely this confusion of the two that
Fontanier, both in the *Commentaire raisonné* (1818) and in *Les figures du discours* (1821–27),[7] is at such pains to correct. Catachresis, in Dumarsais, comes strikingly where most other discussions of rhetoric place metaphor—as the first of all the tropes—and
its prior placement puts it in a position of priority in his text. The
placing also reflects the historical priority of catachresis at the origin of figurative language, in that original lack of proper terms that
it is the function of catachretic transfers to supply. Dumarsais
states: "The richest languages have not a large enough number of
words to express every particular idea by a term which would be
only the proper sign of this idea; thus one is often obliged to borrow
the proper name of an idea, one which is most closely related to
that idea one wants to express."[8] As Dumarsais's description proceeds, however, the distinction between catachresis and metaphor
becomes more and more difficult to maintain until, when he arrives at the application of the verb *avoir*, he no longer knows by
which term to call it and speaks, therefore, about a transfer "by
metaphor and by abuse." The more common the word, the more
difficult it becomes to maintain the boundary line. And *avoir*, like
other such words, finishes as an instance of a figure so customary,
and hence with usage so buried in the familiarity of everyday
speech, that it is not even recognized as a figure. Catachresis—
what Fontanier will later define as a kind of intermediary proper
term[9]—becomes indistinguishable from "dead" metaphor.

It is the conclusion of Dumarsais's entire discussion of catachresis, however, which elides the boundaries so completely that catachresis becomes literally the master trope, reigning over all of figurative language ("Elle règne en quelque sorte sur toutes les autres figures," 1:75). Children, those notorious perpetrators of catachreses, because they lack or are unaware of the "proper" term, transport meanings away from their original places to places "not their own," and language itself eludes the ordering attempts of any legislation that would keep it within carefully regulated bounds. Catachresis reigns not only over the other figures but finally, in this resonant conclusion, over language itself. It has in *Les tropes* both priority and pride of place, even before the text comes to what appears in contrast to be the more conscious and deliberate transfer involved in metaphor, conducted according to the principles of actively perceived comparison and resemblance.

Dumarsais's vision of catachresis as reigning in some fashion over all other figures, and finally over all of language, may suggest why Fontanier is so obsessed with bringing order back to the distinction. For if Fontanier's attempt to correct a master presented as disordered and naive because he classes both metaphor and catachresis indiscriminately among the "figures" of discourse is a signal mark of his revisionist rhetorical enterprise, Fontanier's own assertion of a firm distinction might also be seen as repressing the glimpse in Dumarsais of the invasion of all language by catachresis, neither figurative nor proper but occupying an uncertain realm between the two.

What precisely, we need to ask, is at stake in the distinction between catachresis and metaphor, in preserving boundaries that are so easily transgressed and that threaten so persistently to break down? For Jacques Derrida, in a now familiar essay, catachresis threatens the very distinction between proper and figurative on which the understanding of metaphor as something secondary and deviational—in relation to a "proper" meaning—characteristically relied.[10] For Dumarsais and others in the eighteenth century—to focus on the historical juncture most revealing in this respect—the relation between catachresis and metaphor is central because it is inseparable from the origins of language itself and hence from a sense of historical as well as of linguistic progress.

In this particular combination of trope and history, eighteenth-century discussions routinely reiterate a single densely packed passage from Cicero, which begins the discussion of metaphor as the beginning of tropes by providing first a little historical progress narrative:

> Metaphor [*modus transferendi verbi*] . . . sprang from necessity [*necessitas*] due to the pressure of poverty and deficiency [*inopia . . . angustiis*], but it has been subsequently made popular by its agreeable and entertaining quality. For just as clothes were first invented to protect us against cold and afterwards began to be used for the sake of adornment [*ad ornatum*] and dignity as well, so the metaphorical employment of words [*verbi translatio*] was begun because of poverty [*inopiae*], but was brought into common use for the sake of entertainment [*delectationis*].[11]

The temporal narrative presented here moves from "poverty" to "adornment," from a situation of lack and the constraints of "necessity" to the delights of "entertainment." Metaphor, in other words, *begins* in this little progress narrative *as* catachresis—as a transfer necessitated first by the lack of a sufficient supply of proper terms. What is crucial for subsequent discussions—not just in Dumarsais near the beginning of the eighteenth century but as late as Fontanier—is the historical narrative contained within the Ciceronian "later," or *post*: metaphor as clothing adopted not by necessity but for adornment is only a later, more advanced stage, in which transfers originally dictated by poverty and lack become a matter of taste or choice. The difference, as Cicero's discussion later suggests, is between the "compulsion" involved in transfers by "necessity" (where "necessity compels one to borrow what one has not got," *necessitas cogit quod non habeas*) and the delight in one's own cleverness (*ingenii*) in being "led to something else . . . without going astray" (*De oratore* 3.39.159–60).

This discussion in Cicero also underlines the need to control the extremes of metaphor, so that voluntary "delight" does not turn into violence or abuse. Here, as later in Quintilian, what is crucial is not just the more logical conception of metaphor as a condensed simile, based on the active perception of resemblance by one who employs it deliberately, but also the notion of proper place and careful control: "A metaphor is a short form of simile, contracted into one word; this word is put in a position not belonging to it as if it were its own place" (*in alieno loco tanquam in suo*

66

positum, 3.39.157). Its movement into this new place must be carefully monitored, lest its intrusion be too sudden, unexpected, or violent:

> If one is afraid of the metaphor's appearing a little too harsh, it should be softened down with a word of introduction. . . . In fact the metaphor ought to have an apologetic air, so as to look as if it had entered a place that does not belong to it with a proper introduction, not taken it by storm, and as if it had come with permission, not forced its way in. (3.41.165)

It is precisely this more sudden and unexpected intrusion that later reiterations of this passage identify with catachresis, perhaps because both involve a form of constraint, something out of the user's control and therefore less a matter of voluntary "delight." One Renaissance discussion conflates precisely these separated parts of the Ciceronian text—the origin of language in necessity and metaphor's potential for violence:

> The fine maner of wordes is a garnishing of speech, whereby one word is drawn from his first proper signification to another. . . . This changing of words was first found out by necessitie, for the want of words, [and] afterward confirmed by delight, because such wordes are pleasaunt and gracious too the eare. Therefore this change of signification must bee shamefest, and as it were maydenly, that it may seeme rather to be led by the hand to another signification, than to be driven by force unto the same: yet sometimes this fine manner of speech swerveth from this perfection, and then it is . . . the abuse of this fine speech, called KATACHRESIS.[12]

The *abusio* of catachresis is here identified with failure to moderate metaphor's potentially violent intrusions. In another contemporary discussion, the terms of the distinction are similarly charged: "A METAPHOR, or TRANSLATION, is the *friendly* and *neighborly* borrowing of one word to express a thing with more light and better note, though not so directly and properly as the natural name of the thing meant would signify." Catachresis, on the other hand, is "somewhat *more desperate*" than a metaphor.[13]

Cicero's discussion also introduces into the whole neoclassical tradition a thematics of the "naturalness" of metaphor—its employment not just by those schooled in the art of manipulating it but also by peasants (*rustici*) who use phrases such as "jewelled vines" when something "can scarcely be conveyed by the proper term" (*De oratore* 3.38.155). The paradox of something at once learned and natural, primitive and refined, is deepened in Quintilian's description of the metaphor as "elegant" when it is "correctly and appropriately applied" (*Institutio* 8.6.4–5) and yet at the same time so "natural" that it can occur "unconsciously" (*non sentientes*) and in the speech of the "uneducated" (*indocti*). The passage in Quintilian goes on not only to make the distinction between the "necessary" and the "ornamental" that will later become the distinction between catachresis and metaphor, but also to define among "necessary" transfers Cicero's instance of the peasants who call a vinebud a "gem" because they lack any other, proper term (*Institutio* 8.6.6).

We can only begin to sketch here the implications of this influential Ciceronian progress narrative from "necessity" to ornament, primitive to civilized, or its echo in Quintilian's description of transfers that are not "conscious" as distinct from those that result from what Aristotle called the "mastery" of metaphor. But one way of exploring the contradictions they import into a whole subsequent history of discussions of language and figure would be to look at the echoes of Cicero and Quintilian in yet another eighteenth-century text, which echoes Dumarsais and which allows us to glimpse, through its own internal fissures and contradictions, the relation between the forced, or "catachretic," entry of metaphor and the phenomenon of uncanny intrusions into the familiar.

This text, which translates so much of the continental and neoclassical tradition, is Hugh Blair's *Lectures on Rhetoric and Belles Lettres* (1783), whose date puts it between Dumarsais's *Les tropes* (1729) and Fontanier's nineteenth-century revision. In the Ciceronian tradition shared by Blair, the logical distinction between catachresis and metaphor is again inseparable from the question of the origins of language in general and of figurative language in particular. For Blair, since the original creation of tropes was necessitated by the lack of a sufficient supply of proper terms to cover every idea or object, all tropic activity originates in catachresis, which extends the meaning of words to cover the gaps in language resulting from that lack. The subsequent distinguishing of catachresis from metaphor, of compulsion and necessity from something more voluntary and free, is here, as in Cicero, only a later historical development made possible through an increase in the supply of terms now seen as "proper" (though they originated

68

in catachresis)—since metaphor in the definition that distinguishes it from catachresis must displace an already existing "proper" term. The necessity behind catachresis, then, according to this little progress narrative, diminishes with the increase of proper terms, and this progress makes possible the freedom of metaphor as substitution by choice and conscious perception rather than by necessity. Metaphor belongs, in this fundamentally economic model of linguistic progress, to a kind of linguistic leisure class. And both the progress narrative and social discriminations from Cicero and Quintilian recur in Blair's distinction between language as "a rude and imperfect interpreter of men's wants and necessities" and language as "an instrument of the most delicate and refined luxury."[14] But if catachresis (constrained, forced, connected with paucity or poverty) is the poor cousin or primitive precursor of metaphor, this is at least in part because metaphor has successfully dissimulated, or obliterated the memory of, its origins—the time *before* the distinction itself could be made. The later development—what Blair calls the "gradual progress" of language "towards refinement" (*Lectures*, 1: 284)—is accompanied by an erasing of figures, the phenomenon of the habitual or "dead" metaphor whose figurative beginnings are replaced by what becomes the "proper" term.

This historical narrative and its plotting of stages—primitive and refined, primary and secondary—inform contradictions within Blair's text that frequently echo the earlier text of Dumarsais. On the one hand, figures involve a departure or deviation from the plainest and "most simple form of speech," something different from a word's "original and primitive meaning" (1: 275). On the other hand, figures are the most "natural" form of speech, since according to the historical model of progress from figurative to proper, primitive to refined, "all Languages are most figurative in their early state" (1: 283).[15]

Other contradictions in Blair as elsewhere in this neoclassical tradition occur within the repeated image of clothing or ornament. Blair repeats the familiar Ciceronian image of figures as the dress of thought: by implication, metaphors are clothing that, like ornament employed by choice rather than by necessity, can be put on but also taken off at will. But his insistence that figures are natural and that they therefore cannot be "detached from the subject, and . . . *stuck to it*, like lace upon a coat" (my emphasis) belies the contradiction within the very image of ornament and detachability, one compounded when in a contrary echo of his text's own terms he goes on to warn against figures being "*stuck on* to a discourse too profusely" (1: 300). The idea of metaphor as clothing and as the displacement of an already existing proper term distinguishes it from catachresis precisely because it can be taken away or taken off, unlike catachresis, which, because it replaces nothing, presumably sticks. But a transferred term that cannot, or can no longer, be distinguished from the "proper" one can, as Paul de Man has suggested in another context, also become a clinging shirt of Nessus, a clothing that cannot be removed.[16]

Most compelling of all in Blair, however, are the fissures that appear within the very idea of control, which not only rules the distinction between metaphor as a transfer made by choice and catachresis as dictated by necessity or lack but also dominates the Ciceronian and neoclassical conception of metaphor as a form of condensed simile, based on the perception of resemblance by a controlling subject who applies the figure at will. Sometimes the contradiction appears within a single line. Blair writes, for example (1: 301), that figures contribute best to the embellishment of discourse when they are inserted in their "proper place," a description that invokes the tradition of the "mastery" of metaphor. But the very passage in which he describes the mind's delight in its controlled application of figures is inhabited by something beyond control. Just after he has defined metaphor as nothing but a contracted or shorter form of simile, he writes: "There is nothing which delights the fancy more, than this act of comparing things together, discovering resemblances between them, and describing them by their likeness. The mind, thus employed, is exercised without being fatigued; and is gratified with the consciousness of its own ingenuity" (1: 296). The passage directly echoes Cicero's on the willed "ingenuity" (*ingenii*) of wielding metaphor by taste or choice, and underlines, in its "consciousness," Quintilian's sense of transfers distinguished from those that are *non sentientes*, or unconscious. It then, however, moves in the very next sentence to the recognition that "all Language" is "tinctured strongly with Metaphor": "It insinuates itself even into familiar conversation; and, unsought, rises up of its own accord in the mind. The very words which I have casually employed in describing this, are proof of what I say; *tinctured, insinuates, rises up*, are all of them metaphorical expressions. . . ."

The rest of the lecture treats of the "proper management" of metaphor and of the regulation necessary to keep it "in its proper place." But in the observation here that the figure earlier described as novel, unfamiliar, and delightfully strange "insinuates itself even into familiar conversation; and, unsought, rises up of its own accord in the mind," "insinuation" begins to suggest something considerably less under control, the uncanny appearance of the unfamiliar at the very heart of the familiar, within the very discourse with which the speaker, by the process of habit and usage, is at home. The dead metaphors or virtual catachreses of familiar discourse come back to life within Blair's own description of the management of figures and undermine its figure of figuration as a clothing to be put on and taken off at will. If the neoclassical distinction between metaphor and catachresis rests in part on a distinction between choice and necessity, freedom and compulsion, here too the distinction is threatened: the metaphor potentially out of a subject's control precisely because it inhabits the most familiar terms also involves a challenge to that subject's independence and mastery.

Fontanier, in the wake of both Dumarsais and Blair, repeatedly insists that in metaphor as distinct from catachresis, the use of a trope must be deliberate or conscious. Its use by the *indocti*, or uninstructed—the "peasants" (*rustici*) of Cicero that Quintilian goes on to portray as perpetrators of catachreses—leads again in Fontanier to the class distinction that associates catachresis with poverty or constraint and metaphor with refinement, taste, and free choice. Quintilian's remark that metaphor is "so natural a turn of speech that it is often employed unconsciously [*non sentientes*]" and by "uneducated persons" (*Institutio* 8.6.4) stands in the background of the observation, in Dumarsais, that "there are more figures used in the market place in a single day . . . than in several consecutive sessions of the Academy" (1: 5). But it is applied in Fontanier's *Figures du discours* to the involuntary nature of catachresis as distinct from metaphor as a figure wielded "à propos" and "by design" (*Les figures*, pp. 168, 219). And the first part of Quintilian's description—that metaphor is "often employed unconsciously [*non sentientes*]" structures Fontanier's overriding insistence on separating the "forced" transfers of catachresis from the willed applications of metaphor.[17] In his refusal to admit catachresis—as a transfer dictated not by the controlling subject but by

language itself—into the realm of the "figures" on the argument
that there can be no figure in general or trope in particular unless
the speaker is *conscious* of substituting a figurative expression for
the "proper" one, Fontanier never tires of reiterating that "figures"
occur only "by choice, by simple *jeu d'esprit*, and as an ornament
of discourse," as matters of "taste" (*par gout*) rather than necessity
or "force."[18] Tropological meaning is "either *figurative* or purely an
extension [i.e., catachresis], according to whether the new signification . . . was given freely and as if playfully to the word, or
whether it had become a forced, habitual signification, almost as
proper as the primitive signification."[19]

Once again, the distinction is presented in terms of clothing.
Catachresis (in the chapter entitled "Des Tropes comme pures cat-
achrèses, et, par consequent, comme non vraies figures") is a trope
that presents one idea, and that one "naked and without disguise"
(*toute nue et sans déguisement*), unlike the "'tropes figures' that
always present two ideas, present them consciously [*à dessein*],
and the one beneath the image of the other or alongside the other"
(*Les figures*, p. 219). It is the element of freedom in metaphor as opposed to constraint in catachresis that is underscored when the
text speaks of metaphor as the taking of words in a sense that is
"merely borrowed" and "for the moment" only (p. 66). But the distinction breaks down, once more, in the vision of the "naturalness" of tropes, in the fact that even the deliberate and conscious employing of metaphor becomes indistinguishable, through
the fading of usage, from the foundations of language (p. 104), and
hence from the constraint and forced usage identified with catachresis (p. 159): "Having become, at length, familiar, habitual, or
even fixed and invariable, they have finished by losing completely
the sense of having been borrowed, by being regarded as virtually
proper significations."[20] The trope associated with children, sav-
ages, and "ignorans," with poverty and a lack of consciousness,
ends in Fontanier as not just an underlying "langue" but a "langue
maternelle" to which even the most deliberate or consciously
wielded of figures are ultimately reduced.

If metaphor that is beyond conscious manipulation or direction
involves those involuntary and potentially unconscious transfers
that Fontanier insists on limiting to catachresis, then the issue is
finally not just a distinction based on the presence or absence of an
original proper term but the question of conscious control. What is

at stake, finally, is both a psychic hierarchy and a social one. And the stakes in the former are no less than the mastery of language itself, the question of whether its movements control or are controlled by the subject in question. An issue that we might think a peculiarly modern one turns out to have a long Enlightenment history, one that works itself out through discussions of metaphor and catachresis, primitive and civilized, compelled and free. Quintilian's *non sentientes*, the possible unconsciousness as well as primitive origins of metaphors as yet undistinguished from catachreses, joins the little progress narrative in Cicero which moves only secondarily to a later and more "civilized" stage of development, one that might still be undermined by apparently more primitive transfers. And the progress narrative that inhabits the work of Blair and Fontanier also takes us forward chronologically to later developments in the discussion of language and its conscious control. It therefore provides an Enlightenment history, from within what seem at first mere technical discussions of rhetorical terms, for preoccupations that continue to haunt the twentieth century—from the destabilized subject and the language that speaks the speaker rather than the other way around to the linking of psychic and linguistic that inhabits psychoanalysis from its beginning, from Freud's uncanny to the Saussurian legacy of Jacques Lacan. The violent intrusions of catachresis and the possibility of transfers that, unwilled, subvert the very model of the controlling subject, are the gothic underside of the mastery of metaphor, the uncanny other of its will to control. And words' taking on a life of their own not only conflates the abuses of metaphor with the abusio of *catachresis* but informs a potential linguistic return of the repressed, the insinuation of figures into the most "familiar" and apparently "proper" discourse, the *unheimlich* return of the dead or slumbering to life.

PART III

Rhetoric, Reading, Writing

On the One Hand . . .

JONATHAN GOLDBERG

The great epoch (whose technology is marked by paper, pen, the envelope, the individual subject addressee, etc.) and which goes shall we say from Socrates to Freud and Heidegger. . . .   —Jacques Derrida, *The Post Card*

The open hand of eloquence; the closed fist of logic: rhetoric dreams itself a hand. A deconstructive reading of rhetoric would be possible, situating what is said to be in the mouth in the hand. That is not the subject of this essay; rather than the hand of rhetoric, I explore the rhetoric of the hand, following still a Derridean trajectory.

Toward the end of the first part of *Grammatology*, as well as in the concluding paragraphs of "Freud and the Scene of Writing," Derrida considers the possibility of a graphology as the material support for a "science" of grammatology that would escape the metaphysical complicity that a certain view of the history of writing imposes. Included in this "cultural graphology," Derrida writes, would be a consideration of "problems of the articulation of graphic forms and of diverse substances, of the diverse forms of graphic substances . . . or instruments."[1] In short, the new graphology would consider "all the investitures to which a *graphie*, in form and substance, is submitted" (p. 87). In "Freud and the Scene of Writing," four areas are mapped for this new field: "a *psychopathology of everyday life*"; "a *history of writing*"; "a *becoming-literary of the literal*"; and "a new *psychoanalytic graphology*."[2] It is these various itineraries that are followed in this essay, pursuing the rhetoric of the hand writing in texts of Roland Barthes, Martin Heidegger, and Sigmund Freud.

On 27 September 1973 Roland Barthes was interviewed in *Le Monde*, in a series called "how writers work." Others interviewed

A longer version of this essay appears as the last chapter in *Writing Matter: From the Hands of the English Renaissance*, © 1990 by the Board of Trustees of the Leland Stanford Junior University. Reprinted by permission of Stanford University Press.

may well have given in to the lure of that rubric, for the writer to mythologize (to idealize and dematerialize) the activity of writing. Barthes, however (and not surprisingly, considering his relentless unveiling of the mythologies of the modern world), refused such a gambit. Declining to talk about methodology in any metaphysical way, Barthes insisted upon the practices of writing—such things as the instruments he used, his schedule, the layout of his desk. Sounding very much like someone heeding the Derridean call for a new graphology, Barthes decried the lack of concern with practices of writing at their "most material level."[3] Registering the mythological scene of the interview, he describes this material approach to the question of "how writers work" as "anti-mythological," and articulates a desire to reverse "that old myth which continues to present language as the instrument of thought, inwardness, passion, or whatever, and consequently presents writing as a simple instrumental practice" (*Grain*, p. 177). The "old myth" is, of course, what Derrida calls logocentrism; in its reversal, inside and outside change places, and the material practices of writing determine thought and language.

Rather than "a simple instrumental practice," Barthes confesses that his relationship to the scene of writing exhibits "un rapport presque maniaque avec les instruments graphiques," "an almost obsessive relation to writing instruments" (p. 178). Barthes was obsessed by pens. It is this obsession with a writing instrument that I want to analyze. For however wittily aware he was of his own graphic investment, and however brilliantly he analyzed such investments in others, Barthes nonetheless does not quite recognize that what accompanies his response to the lure of the pen—and of the hand writing—is a logocentric complicity.

Barthes's obsession with pens occurs within a hierarchized scheme of types of writing instruments. Testifying to an uncontrollable urge to try all sorts of fountain pens, including those with felt tips, Barthes draws the line at the ballpoint. The Bic is evidence, perhaps, of the Americanization of France, a making-commercial of writing that is epitomized, however, in the typewriter. Barthes explains that although he uses a typewriter to transcribe what has first been written by hand, he doubts that he ever will compose on a typewriter. Nonetheless, he has been practicing his typing technique, partly at the instigation of Philippe Sollers, who has assured him that "writing directly at the typewriter creates a kind of unique

78

spontaneity which has its own beauty" (p. 179). Still, it is not likely that this new regime will replace his old habit of writing by hand, "outmoded and eccentric [*passéiste et individualiste*] though that may be" (p. 179).

The hierarchy in which the fountain pen holds the supreme position thus is historicized: the investment in the pen is old-fashioned. It is antitechnological, and it carries with it an investment in "individualism." Perhaps there is no surprise in finding that a theorist who was obsessed with nineteenth-century texts seems to have been equally at home with nineteenth-century modes of textual production. Indeed, Barthes's willingness to use the typewriter at all only came from the fact that he occasionally needed to make use of a typist to transcribe his handwritten texts; doing so, he found himself in a position that elicited (as he describes it) another scene from the nineteenth century: "an alienated social relationship: a person, the typist, is confined by the master in an activity I would almost call an enslavement, when writing is precisely a field of liberty and desire!" (p. 179). Barthes's terms of analysis are recognizably those of Marx and Hegel; and, so, too, the idealism of writing as "a field of liberty and desire" would seem more apt for the nineteenth century. Indeed, ascribing to Sollers the notion that the typewriter (it is, in fact, an electric typewriter that is in question) carries with it "its own beauty" is yet another sign of the idealizing aestheticism of Barthes's encounter with the instruments of writing. While he may appear to heed Derrida's strictures about the "*becoming-literary of the literal*," that is, recognizing that the instrument is not indifferent to the production of the text but implicated in it, the sign of literariness for Barthes is beauty, a term that seems to efface material production and to supply some transcendental measuring device. This is not entirely surprising; when Barthes summarizes the argument of *Grammatology* in a piece on "Erté, or A la lettre," he says it "sets in opposition to speech a *being of writing*: the letter, in its graphic materiality, then becomes an irreducible ideality, linked to the deepest experiences of humanity."[4]

Barthes's summary is slippery; while it may mean to reduce ideality to materiality, and while its "deepest experiences" may also attempt to resituate a definition of "humanity," the formulation slides in the opposite direction, to a recouping of idealism and humanism in the name of materiality. Much the same could also be said of the rather easy Marxism of Barthes's analysis of the exploitation of the typist. For it appears to allow him to turn his obsession with writing instruments into a seemingly unproblematic (and delighted) form of bourgeois acquisitiveness: "I have far too many pens—I don't know what to do with all of them! And yet, as soon as I see a new one, I start craving it. I cannot keep myself from buying them" (*Grain*, p. 178). This unembarrassed celebration of the joys of surplus value is joined to equally suspect alignments of his writing practices with the "almost religious asceticism" (p. 178) with which Chinese scribes faced the task of writing, or with the habits of monks in medieval monasteries, meditating for a day before they began their task of copying. Evoking such practices, Barthes attempts to purify his urge to acquire new pens, and also to elide the very differences in writing practices that these non-Western and medieval scenes of writing evoke. For one thing, of course, the monks were copyists; yet precisely because the typewriter is only a machine for making copies, Barthes cannot see himself composing on it. Moreover, the invocation of the monks smacks of the medieval revival of the nineteenth century, and the Chinese example, of ethnocentrism.

These would all seem to follow from the way in which Barthes reads Derrida, or from an inescapable logocentrism that can as readily invest itself in writing as in speaking. In the interview in *Le Monde*, one can see lapses of the pen, slips in writing in which Barthes betrays his bourgeois individualism even as he consciously speaks against the bourgeois scene in which he speaks. (To grant an interview to a newspaper is, of course, to commit oneself to being copied beyond the capacities of any typewriter.) And, indeed, there is an unconscious writing in this text, one, in fact, that the illustrator for *Le Monde* had no difficulty discerning (perhaps because he read the mythological Barthes of his own desire). Accompanying the interview is a picture of Barthes at the typewriter. He is all head atop an atrophied body; his miniature torso ends in an exaggerated pair of hands, the two fingers that Barthes claimed to use at the keyboard poised in action. The head, however, looks straight forward. It is the head of Michelangelo's Moses, but instead of horns Barthes sprouts pens. Tucked behind his ears, beneath his hair, these pens seem to come from, or, at the very least, to penetrate his skull. The illustration thus makes visible the metaphysical and psychic investment of the pen, instrument of the mind and of desire. The desire for the pen is a logocentric desire; writing by hand betrays its essentialism; it puts the hand in mind; it transforms the hand into the mind.

This analysis stands, I think, despite those places in the interview where Barthes seems virtually to be citing Derrida, for such citations, as I have suggested, depend upon a reading of Derrida that reidealizes *Grammatology*, one that grants originary value to writing. Barthes's insistence on the material practice of writing is admirable, of course; nonetheless it hovers constantly on the brink of a de-originated origin and an origin that has been reinvested metaphysically. When he tells the interviewer that he prefers to the notion of method the word "protocol," since it is derived etymologically from the scene of writing in which a page is glued onto the beginning of a manuscript, he insists on the scriptive origin of his own vocabulary, and refuses to trace an origin for writing in the mind; nonetheless, this is a return to an origin, not the de-originated origin of the Derridean trace. When he says that writing begins for him with a calligraphic urge and that "desire is invested in a graphic impulse" (*Grain*, p. 179), the hand would appear to have been invested in a writing that precedes the individual act of inscription, or that cannot locate the "individual" except in the pressures of the hand. Yet there is a desire behind or beneath the graphic impulse; the hand-in-writing is attached to the body and its desires, and these do not seem to originate in writing but to find themselves realized there. Scenes of writing seem to require some originary impulse that is not reducible to a calligraphic urge, but to an ideality and a humanity that appears to precede the act of inscription, or to be generated from it.

Hence, the sign insists upon itself, and writing practice is reduced to an idealized semiotics. If the aim in the interview is to focus on what might be regarded as insignificant—the protocols of writing—this is, Barthes insists, because they signify: "Insignificance is the locus of true significance. This should never be forgotten" (p. 177). Here Barthes sounds like Freud. But, if so, his sentences bear witness, as does Freud's *Psychopathology of Everyday Life*, to the forgetting of writing in the very act of making writing significant. It is remarkable, as Derrida notes at the close of "Freud and the Scene of Writing" (p. 230), how inattentive Freud is when he writes about slips of the pen. For what slips from discussion is, precisely, writing.

With Barthes, it is in the very attention to the movement of the hand and the slips of the pen that writing is elided and reinvested in directions that Barthes would, at least at times, not appear to want to go. In *Roland Barthes*, in a section on "Fautes de frappe," typos, Barthes writes of the *lapsus calami*—not of slips of the pen, but rather of typing mistakes. Here, too, the program seems Derridean. For, as "Freud and the Scene of Writing" argues, it is as a writing machine that Freud represents the relationships between the unconscious and consciousness. "Through the machine," Barthes writes, "the unconscious writes much more surely than natural script does, and one can conceive of a *graphanalysis*, much more pertinent than our insipid graphology."[5] But one must notice the part the pen plays in these remarks, as the guarantee of a "natural script"—as if the pen were not itself a machine too. "Manuscript particularities," as Barthes refers to them in this passage, alone would seem able to retain their ability to be "individualiste," while typing would appear to have a privileged relation to the unconscious, as if, one supposes, the unconscious, being itself a machine, would speak more directly, and without an intermediary, when the keys of the typewriter were (mis)struck. Yet even that possibility is denied as Barthes proceeds, for it is only his own unconscious that could be revealed in a typo. The enslaved secretary, the transcriber of the master's text, puts in another appearance. "It is true," Barthes concludes the section on typos, "a good secretary does not make mistakes: she has no unconscious!" (*Barthes*, p. 97).

Barthes here not only repeats the scene that his interview is willing to scrutinize, however banal the terms of his Marxist analysis may be, but now the copyist is also inscribed in another dialectic; not only do we have writer versus copyist, master versus slave, here, it is man versus woman. Not, perhaps, surprising considering Barthes's obsession with pens. For the scene of bourgeois acquisition of numerous pens is also a homosexual scene of cruising. "I've tried everything," Barthes confesses. "When felt-tipped pens first appeared in the stores, I bought a lot of them. (The fact that they were originally from Japan was not, I admit, displeasing to me.) Since then I've gotten tired of them, because the point flattens out too quickly" (*Grain*, p. 178). It is the only admission of disappointment in the text/culture that elsewhere in *Roland Barthes* he claims to be his one entirely successful piece of writing, *The Empire of Signs*, a success that is one of writing and of sexuality; "a happy sexuality doubtless finds its corresponding discourse quite naturally . . . : *in what he writes, each protects his own sexuality,"* (*Barthes,* p. 156). Protects, not projects? (Is that, perhaps, a typo?)[6] Should we recall those Chinese scribes and Christian monks to discover a happy—and *castrated*—sexuality?

It is something like a happy sexuality that Barthes encounters in "Stationery Store" in *The Empire of Signs.* Invidious comparisons are drawn between Western (American and French) and Japanese stationers. The first two are emporia for commerce where "the user experiences no need to invest himself in his writing," and where the quintessential patrons would be "the eternal copyists, Bouvard and Pecuchet."[7] But the Japanese stationery store is otherwise, a place where the numerous papers display their "fibrous origin" and the brush gestures like fingers: "It has the carnal, lubrified flexibility of the hand" (*Empire,* p. 86). The hand invested in (Japanese) writing is a hand playing with itself; felt-tip pens that flatten too easily perhaps allegorize the relationship between West and East. At the origin, which is what Japanese—Oriental—writing would seem to signify for Barthes, the pen apparently never is exhausted. Indeed, for Barthes, even the Japanese typewriter is not, as the machine is in the West, a producer of copies transforming writing "into a mercatile product" (p. 87). For in Japanese typewriters, characters are not lined up in the row that represents the logocentric tyranny of the line; rather they are rolled on a drum, and to strike the key, Barthes contends, would extend the graphic pulsion of the free hand at play on the page.

If this is Barthes in the guise of Pierre Loti, perhaps the only difference in his Orientalism (I use the term advisedly) is its coding of homosexuality. Yet the sexual terms, despite that inversion, are recognizably phallogocentric, and the investment of desire in Japan conforms to the classism of much late nineteenth-century homosexuality (Gide might be cited as an example), while the coding of the text on pens as an erotic text also conforms to the Oriental genre of such writing (it can be found, in fact, as early as Byron).[8] To make my point perversely: the investment in the pen for Barthes produces such forms of desire.

The slips of the pen in these passages from Barthes succumb to the terms of analysis that Derrida suggested at the end of "Freud and the Scene of Writing." For, whatever Barthes's conscious program in these passages, they betray unconsciously their logocentric bias. In so doing they write a small episode in the history of writing (marked by the pen/typewriter antithesis) and offer an instance for "a new *psychoanalytic graphology*," not least because Barthes so recognizably rewrites Rousseau's dangerous supplement—the alliance of writing and masturbation. In short, Barthes's texts reveal, as Derrida suggests must always be the case, the inextricability of Western metaphysics even from a deconstructive text.

The scenario that I have begun to read in Barthes can be found in another set of texts, this time by Heidegger, and indeed the legibility of the problematic of the hand that I read there is indebted to Derrida's work on Heidegger, in particular to two essays on *Geschlecht*, and especially to "*Geschlecht* II: Heidegger's Hand."[9] In the pages that follow, I can do little more than explicate texts in a manner to which Derrida has pointed, extending the argument a bit, and focusing on the rhetoric of the hand.

Heidegger shares a distrust of the typewriter with Barthes, and there are no Japanese exceptions for him. In his 1942–43 lectures on Parmenides, Heidegger inveighs against the typewriter; for him, as for Barthes, it is a copying machine and not a writing machine. "Die Maschinenschrift . . . die Handschrift und damit den Charakter verbirgt. In der Maschinenschrift sehen alle Menschen gleich aus."[10] Type hides the hand, and all men appear the same in type, Heidegger claims here. The sexist marker "Menschen" is worth remarking, for, as with Barthes, the scene of writing is one that betrays phallic desire, although Heidegger does not invest that desire homoerotically; he writes, we might say, after Eve Kosofsky Sedgwick,[11] the homosocial script of Western culture, inflected here, as elsewhere, with the abstractions that would seem to guarantee the equation of universality with masculinity. As Derrida comments in "Geschlecht: Sexual Difference, Ontological Difference," Heidegger's neutralization of questions of sexual difference seems always to be implicated in the binarism that it apparently suppresses. Moreover, as Derrida comments, pursuing the multiplicities of the neutral *Geschlecht* (a word that means genus, sex, and race), Western culture for Heidegger inevitably has a Germanic cast, as much in his hand as the Fraktur that he wrote. "Typewriting . . . hides handwriting and, thereby, character": character, here, may mean both masculinity and national character. Yet, as the word *Charakter* cannot help but remind us, character is, precisely, a scriptive formation. Heidegger does not mark these multiple sexual and national meanings, and in his very silence he attempts to make character mean the human character. The scriptive duplication of terms also goes unremarked; for him, as for Barthes, the handmade mark betrays a nostalgia for the individual. It bears a nostalgia, too, for a style of German transcendental philosophy (and Romantic poetry)—for the human here is essentialized. The typewriter is the machine of a modernity that Heidegger repudiates.

More than nostalgia (as with Barthes's nineteenth-century attachments) is in question; indeed, the investment in the hand in Heidegger carries with it (despite itself) metaphysical and logocentric assumptions. Heidegger proclaims as essentially human the possession of the hand. Whereas for Barthes, the hand is continually invested as natural, and writing as a material practice derives its materiality from the body, the hand for Heidegger is, at once, denaturalized and nonetheless quintessentially human. As he puts it in *Parmenides*:

> Die Hand ist in einem mit dem Wort die Wesensauszeichnung des Menschen. Nur das Seiende, das wie der Mensch das Wort "hat," kann auch und muss "die Hand" haben. . . . Kein Tier hat eine Hand. . . . Der Mensch "hat" nicht Hände, sondern die Hand hat das Wesen des Menschen inne, weil das Wort als der Wesensbereich der Hand der Wesensgrund des Menschen ist. (pp. 118–19)

> The hand is, along with the word, the essential mark of mankind. Only the being that, like man, "has" the word, can and also must have "the hand." . . . No animal has a hand. . . . Man "has" not hands, rather the hand holds [has] the essence of man within, since the word, as the essential domain of the hand, is the essential ground of man.

On the one hand, Heidegger's denaturalization of the hand is a deconstructive gesture, and it is one that speaks powerfully against the "graphic impulse" in Barthes, which seems to come from some notion of the naturalness of the pen and paper. On the other hand, the attempt to define the human against the animal runs the risk of inscribing a transcendental difference in man and the activity of the hand, a biologistic determinism that, as Derrida implies, relates to Heidegger's "nationalism" ("*Geschlecht* II," p. 173). It runs that risk, moreover, since the passage, which makes language and the hand the marks of humanity, effaces the scene of writing implicit in this equation. A powerful repression of writing is at work.

The problematic in these sentences from the lectures on Parmenides can be glossed further with some remarks that appear early in *Was Heisst Denken?*:

> The hand's essence can never be determined, or explained, by its being an organ which can grasp. Apes, too, have organs that can grasp, but they do not have hands. . . . Only a being who can speak, that is, think, can have hands and can be handy in achieving works of handicraft. The hand's gestures run everywhere through language, in their most perfect purity precisely when man speaks by being silent. . . . Every motion of the hand in every one of its works carries itself through the element of thinking. . . . All the work of the hand is rooted in thinking.[12]

This passage is not immediately elucidatory, although it seems clear that Heidegger's gestures here are, once again, antimetaphysical and yet nonetheless metaphysical. They are most significantly materialistic in their association of an essential humanity with the activity of the hand, and sound a bit like Engels in his brief, exploratory essay, "The Part Played by Labour in the Transition from Ape to Man," where Engels argues that the hand played this crucial role in the evolution of primates, and that speaking and thinking only followed the activity instituted by the hand. Heidegger does not situate the material investment of the hand in a history of labor (he regards that history as entangled with Hegelian metaphysics), but within a philosophical conception.

What he means by "works of handicraft" can be understood, I think, by the discourse of the hand that appears in *Being and Time*. (Frank Lentricchia has applauded passages from that work precisely for the way in which whatever is meant by the mind is rooted in the hand and in handiwork, and in the world defined as a workshop, which suggests to him the materialistic and antimetaphysical investment that is carried by the Heideggerian hand.[13]) The hand is fundamental to the vocabulary of *Being and Time*, so much so that questions of being and temporality are constituted through a crucial term that runs through the text, ready-to-hand (*zuhanden*). That term is paired with the term present-at-hand (*vorhanden*), and it is in the relationship between the two terms that the hand of the Parmenides lectures and *Was Heisst Denken?* is clarified.

"Present-at-hand" seems to mean an ordinary mode of being in the world, an unthinking everydayness in which objects seem simply to be there as objects. "Present-at-hand" thus names the object within the dualisms of a Cartesian universe. Heidegger argues, on the contrary, that the mere objective existence of things is a derivative effect, following upon a failure of the ready-to-hand. That is, it is only in the refusal of things simply to be ready-to-hand, whether in their opacity or their unavailability, that an object seems simply to be there, present-at-hand. It arises, that is, in the failure of the ready-to-hand, a failure we might consider a slip of the pen.

What arises at such moments of failure, Heidegger insists, is what is precisely ungraspable, a revelation not of the essential being of the object as divorced from the hand, but that the object *is* only when it is in hand. But that in-handedness of the ready-to-hand is not a function of the hand's ability to grasp. Unlike Hegel, as Derrida observes, Heidegger does not read the hand's grasp and conceptual grasping as on a continuum: "If there is a thought of the hand or a hand of thought, as Heidegger gives us to think, it is not of the order of conceptual grasping" (*"Geschlecht* II," p. 173). As opposed to the Cartesian hand—and to the hand of technology— the Heideggerian hand is not the property of a subject who can master the object. In the double movements of the ready/unready-to-hand, the unveiling and veiling of the object within its essence occurs. Typewriting, and the typewriter, would seem to line up with the present-at-hand. In the Parmenides lectures, the typewriter is said to destroy language on two counts: by removing the hand from script (thereby objectifying writing, and splitting it off from the subject), and by producing letters that are themselves unconnected to each other (thereby destroying a relatedness that defines the Heideggerian notion of essence, a scriptive essence, defined by the connections of the cursive hand).

"The hand is a peculiar thing," Heidegger begins the passage quoted above from *Was Heisst Denken?* (p. 16). "In the common view, the hand is part of our bodily organism." But, as he goes on to say, the hand (assuming that the "peculiar" hand is to be associated with the ready-to-hand) is, however bodily, not organic. Here, then, we can see a sharp contrast with Barthes, who invests so strongly in physicality and nature, as if those were not constructed. If Heidegger demystifies the everyday, and recognizes the constructedness of existence ("Perhaps thinking, too, is just something like building a cabinet," he remarks earlier in this passage), the hand that has been detached from nature, and is distinguished from "paws, claws, or fangs," is denied its definition in the ability to grasp. And that which is ungraspable is the ready-to-hand; indeed, another name for it is thought, for, as Heidegger says throughout *Was Heisst Denken?*, we are not yet thinking, and thinking would seem to lie elsewhere. It is the need for that elsewhere, however much it has been invested materially, which remains metaphysical, even if what is beyond the physical somehow arises from it or is still imagined through it or as it.

But not quite as an it. From the unready-to-hand to the ready-to-hand it is still the hand and the discourse of the hand that carry Heidegger's discourse. If the hand cannot grasp being and if its present is always slipping away, the hand is nonetheless what is "had," and being lies in the hand if not present-at-hand. The contrast between the typewriter and the pen, thus, speaks to the contrast between the ready-to-hand and present-at-hand. If the typewriter facilitates, its facility would seem to stifle thought; it offers the illusion of communication and transparency, opening the entire public sphere that Heidegger relentlessly denounces for its inauthenticity. Yet Heidegger claims that typing *hides* the hand and obscures character; if so, its readiness-to-hand would also seem to have the qualities of unreadiness-to-hand that Heidegger claims to be necessary if one is to have a genuine relationship to the tool. Heidegger designates three modes of unavailability that make the ready-to-hand unready and, therefore, able to read the derivativeness of mere presence-at-hand: "The modes of conspicuousness, obtrusiveness, and obstinacy all have the function of bringing to the fore the characteristic of presence-at-hand in what is ready-to-hand." [14] The typewriter, especially in its definition as that which hides the hand, would seem capable of making the break that Heidegger considers necessary if one is to pass from the present-at-hand to the ready-to-hand. The refusal to grant this capacity to the typewriter thus speaks to ways in which the natural—the hand—remains a metaphysical term in Heidegger. If, then, the typewriter must be denied for the sake of the hand, and the human, and the essential, it is nonetheless the case that Heidegger's own analysis cannot provide terms for that break. For insofar as Heidegger's analysis is also aimed at a denaturalization, the typewriter might serve as an image for the hand on the other side of the break. Putting it that way, we may still be caught in a choice between ideas of the thing and the thing itself, a choice between idealism and empirical objects, which is no choice at all, since they are the same.

And yet, what is pertinent to this discussion is the fact that what lies on the other side of the break, the hand that holds human being within it, is insistently a hand and not, beyond that abstraction, an abstraction, not a Platonic idea (perhaps nothing like an idea at all). Being and writing are entwined, and in ways that deny the metaphysical break that nonetheless seems to function in Heidegger. They meet in language. "The hand's gestures run everywhere through language," Heidegger continues in *Was Heisst Denken?*, "in their most perfect purity precisely when man speaks by being silent." Yet, a page later, Heidegger proclaims Socrates "the purest thinker of the West. . . . He wrote nothing." Once again, as Derrida points out in *"Geschlecht* II (pp. 179–81), Heidegger's text is riddled with double gestures. The hand in language, language that is not speech, could define language as writing, yet the hand cannot, on the other hand, be writing—or, at least, such is the explicit force of this example of Socrates, and there are numerous other passages in *Was Heisst Denken?* that carry on a typical logocentric devaluation of the nonessentiality of writing. Yet the materiality that Heidegger ascribes to the ready-to-hand participates in writing; what else is the path that withdraws and draws?

This inextricable relationship between Being and writing is seen most easily in the explication of a sentence from Parmenides that occupies the second half of *Was Heisst Denken?* Being-in-the-hand is, almost exactly, Heidegger's formulation there. For the master sentence of Parmenides is: "One should both say and think that Being is" (quoted p. 178), and, as Heidegger characteristically pauses over every term in the sentence, he finds the hand everywhere. "One should" means "needful"—it designates a mode of using—and the Greek word, Heidegger says, derives its etymology from the hand (p. 186); the hand of "one should," however, is the hand that leaves alone: "So understood, use itself is the summons which demands that a thing be admitted to its own essence and nature, and that the use keep to it" (p. 187). One should therefore put one's hand into the hand that holds the human within it. If the hand is characteristically human, its humanity is a derivative quality; its essence thus lies elsewhere, in the hand that calls (that calls for thinking, and for the thoughtful handling that lets things lie). "The hand designs and signs, presumably because man is a sign" (p. 16);

the hand therefore points to the essence that points to it, the circulation of the sign (this is "die Wesensauszeichnung" of the Parmenides lectures).

From "one should" in the sentence of Parmenides, Heidegger proceeds to "say," finding that the Greek word here is the cognate of the Latin *legere* (p. 198), a word that means both *lay* and *read*. For what lies before us to be gathered is, in both senses of the word, relation—connection and tale-telling. "Man" is a sign that is already written; his character lies at hand, to be gathered like the letters of the alphabet (p. 208), whose collation constitutes an act of reading that is not simply phonetic transcription. Meaning is not in the sound, but silent. This "originary" script, then, is not phonetic. Gathering is the act of thinking, yet what thinking thinks is the duality between Being and beings, a split, then, in the tautology "Being is."

The duality in tautology is a primordial quality of language for Heidegger. And language, at least in *Was Heisst Denken?*, and despite all disclaimers, is written language, a sentence from Parmenides, glossed, as often as not, by lines of Hölderlin. Heidegger's etymological drive, at least in *Was Heisst Denken?*, arrives repeatedly at scriptive origins, being-in-the-hand. We seem, in other words, to be once again in the nineteenth century, as Heidegger (like Victorian classicists) seeks a moment—for Heidegger it is even before Aristotle and Plato—the originary moment of culture from which the West has strayed.

Although Heidegger and Barthes may not seem ultimately comparable, their attitudes toward the typewriter and their attachment to the handwritten imply similar investments in the hand, similar investments in logocentrism. Both are antitechnological; the typewriter is opposed for the sake of the human. Individual difference cannot be maintained if the hand is not extended by the pen, if the marks are made by the intrusive machine. Yet, as I have been arguing, much in Heidegger should recognize the machine, and the same could be said for Barthes. A logocentric atavism is to be found in their attitude toward the typewriter and in their insistence on the hand. Heidegger, early in *Was Heisst Denken?*, writes explicitly that the search for thought is also the search for the essence of technology (p. 14). But Heidegger cannot locate its essence elsewhere than in Being. Nor, finally, can Barthes. "The machine is dead. It is death," Derrida writes in "Freud and the Scene of Writing" (p. 227), describing finally the mystic writing pad. It is death "not because we risk death in playing with machines" (which could be a way of saying what Heidegger and Barthes fear, the death of man) "but because the origin of machines is the relation to death." And that origin, Derrida goes on to argue, is no other than the origin Freud himself ascribed to life in *Beyond the Pleasure Principle*. Life originates in death; the "being" of the machine (call it the typewriter) is the production of copies, not of originals; the type-written page is not the product of the hand, and in its distance from life and nature it occupies a reproductive position. It is, in a word, the space of representations. It intimates the secondariness of all origins, including the origin of life. "The machine—and, consequently, representation—is death and finitude *within* the psyche," Derrida concludes (p. 228).

Barthes would only put two fingers on it, refusing to allow his hands to be at the service of the machine. Heidegger would not use it at all. For him, the hand is so singular, and so essential, that it is, almost without exception, but one hand. Heidegger's insistence on the singularity of the hand is a mark of its abstract essence. As Derrida has commented, virtually the only time that Heidegger mentions the fact that man has two hands is when he speaks of them locked together in prayer ("*Geschlecht* II," p. 182). Nowhere does Heidegger consider the hand embracing another's hand. Nowhere is the abstract hand gendered save as the hand of man. Yet the hand, in languages that do gender their nouns, is marked as feminine: *die Hand, la main, la mano, manus*. And, as the last two designations might suggest, the gendering of the hand is complex. In Latin and Italian the hand appears, by its ending, to be marked as male, yet it is female in gender. Is this a sign that confirms Heidegger in regarding the hand as primordial, virtually present in all language? Or is it a sign of the neutralization of sexual difference? Or a sign of difference that Heidegger cannot afford to recognize?

Here, with such questions, we seem to pass to psychoanalytic graphology from these brief attempts to locate Heidegger in the history of writing (the history of logocentrism and, in Barthes as well as Heidegger, the attempts, however baffled, to think beyond the closure of Western metaphysics). Freud's unpromising text on slips of the hand therefore calls for attention, if only because it too repeats the problematic of the hand. Like Barthes and Heidegger, Freud's text registers attempts to think beyond the closure; indeed, it offers Derrida terms for his deconstructive strategies. These terms, however, must always be scrutinized since they can succumb to metaphysics—it is for that reason that Derrida borrows the notion of repression from Freud to describe the place of writing in Western philosophy, but cannot simply repeat the Freudian term since it represses writing too. Repression "contains an interior representation" ("Freud and the Scene," p. 196), Derrida writes, for what is repressed is neither forgotten nor remembered. It exists in and as writing, the writing of the machine that at once retraces; repressed memories are remembered, but one must emphasize the "re," both to account for the "original" and always unavailable writing (which is also and always its simultaneous effacement) and for the return to consciousness of the repressed. For consciousness remembers by a further act of reinscription. It does not unearth the repressed. It rewrites it. "Press" in repression is etymologically one with "press" in impression—or in the printing press; repression, even as a word, implicates the scene of writing, and the holding back of the "re" is, at the same time, the duplication of what is inscribed along the facilitating and blocked paths of memory.

All of this, Derrida contends, can be read in Freud; yet, what also can be read is the supposed truth beneath these scenes of inscription—the primal scene, to go no further. And when Freud passes to readings of such sexual scenes, he bypasses the scene of writing that would keep one from ever arriving at the Freudian truth. This, as I mentioned earlier, is precisely the case in *The Psychopathology of Everyday Life*. Whereas texts contemporary with the first edition of the book had begun to regard the unconscious as a rebus (*The Interpretation of Dreams* is the most notable example), and thus to move toward the originary secondary script that Freud finally conceptualizes through the mystic writing pad, the book on parapraxes, rewritten over and again through the same time period, is curiously silent about this development. In each edition subsequent to the first in 1901, chapter 6, on slips of the hand, swelled with new examples. Yet these are never taken to demonstrate anything that might not also be found in a slip of the tongue or in an instance of the forgetting of names. The chapter only comes after those parapraxes have been explored, and slips of the hand even take second place in the chapter they share with mistakes in reading. Thus, although the terms of analysis are important ones for Freud (condensation and displacement, among others), slips of the hand seem only to repeat what has been discovered in slips of the tongue; writing appears to be entirely secondary and instrumental, and the chapter operates in a fairly perfunctory manner, repeating solutions of a type that by then have become standard in the book. However the unconscious is manifest through them—for the slips allow for lapses in repressive mechanisms—the unconscious that is revealed in these slips is, on the whole, remarkably uninteresting, or, at least, uninteresting to Freud as the site for any further revelations. What is, for the purposes of this inquiry, most remarkable is the failure of the scene of writing to intrude itself upon these slips in any overt fashion.

There is apparently no specific graphic discourse. Unlike Barthes or Heidegger, Freud has no invidious comparisons between pen and typewriter organizing the observations of written slips of the hand. Freud's examples come from handwritten letters, but also from newspapers, books, and telegrams. The unconscious considered can be that of the writer or of the copyist, or even of the compositor; no distinctions are made at the level of nationality, class, or gender (although the examples do line up in quite remarkable—and unremarked—ways in terms of gender, and matters of class and nationality also do figure). Still, there is no sense that any particular instrument intrudes itself more readily or speaks more naturally to or for the unconscious. These categorical absences at the theoretical level bespeak a powerful universalizing tendency (and indeed the history of accretions to the text offers a local version of that since it gathers together the testimony of colleagues and even occasional anonymous readers to confirm the truth of the text), and the failure to privilege or hierarchize suggests how endemic slips of the hand are, although nothing marks such slips as distinct from others or as in any way originary. The unconscious, it would appear, is dehistoricized, dematerialized; although Freud recognizes that political conditions of censorship might occasion slips of the pen, these too only can be explained by the unconscious. Any writing practice, in any situation, can reveal its operations. Nonetheless, it is worth pointing out that Freud does not join Barthes and Heidegger in a polemic against technology, and that essential humanity has no fear of the machine as some inhuman domain.

Despite such ecumenism, *The Psychopathology of Everyday Life* is a powerfully repressed text. And, thus, although Freud endorses Wundt's dictum "that we make slips of the pen more readily than slips of the tongue,"[15] he does not follow Wundt in his claim that writing, as a mechanical activity less subject to conscious control, is thereby a less inhibited activity than speaking. Rather, confirming the direction of his thought toward the writing machine, Freud insists that conscious attention has nothing to do with the production of parapraxes; instead, "a *disturbance* of attention by an alien thought" (p. 132) explains all lapses, whether of the tongue or of the hand. That alienation, it seems fair to say, although Freud does not, has to do with the materiality of the signifier. Having insisted on the unconscious, the letter is repressed.

Similarly, when Freud offers personal examples in chapter 6, what they reveal about him seems to have almost nothing to do with lapses of the pen per se; his pen slips, writing "Oct. 20" instead of "Sept. 20" (p. 116)—he desires a female patient to come a month sooner than her next appointment, and the slip is made while he keeps accounts. Elsewhere, there is another slip in writing a number when money has to be withdrawn for an ailing relative. Even if Freud does not go very far in analyzing these scenes, what seems possible to say about them would appear to have little to do with writing, and even as personal revelations they seem quite banal. So, too, for the scene of professional rivalry that dictates the mangling of the name of someone who had written an unfavorable review; perhaps the substitution occurred more readily because it took cover under the identical name of a gynecologist. And when a telegraphist mistranscribes a telegram from Freud's publisher so that it seems to be about the body (rather than about books)—the message falls prey to "the telegraphist's hunger-complex" (p. 129)—the unconscious explanation manages to ignore economic and class difference. Such readings of Freud's errors lead, then, to revelations of the sort we have uncovered in Barthes or Heidegger. But do they show his hand? What difference does it make that he writes "O" instead of "S," that in withdrawing money he cuts off "o" when he meant to cut off "4," that in explaining the writing of *Buckrhard* (p. 117) he cites in a footnote the scene in *Julius Caesar* where Cinna the poet is murdered because of his name? What is the place of the letter, or the literary, in these scenes of self-writing?

An analysis of Freud that goes beyond what he offers is, of course, possible. Autobiography may extend beyond the examples offered as his own; mistakes made by other physicians may also be Freud's. The remark, "The doctor's relation to his mother must have been of decisive importance" (p. 124), written about an anecdote offered by Hitschmann (whose name is elsewhere mangled as "Hintschmann"), surely reflects upon Freud himself; and the belladonna story is told at great length, communicating perhaps with the bungled action in chapter 8, when Freud puts morphine in an old woman's eyes. The worries about ailing relatives, women who don't come when they are wanted: perhaps these are stories about Freud's mother. Perhaps, too, the interweaving of episodes from various hands are rewritten in Freud's hand, and the panoply of others, named or anonymous, are still retracing the Freudian text.

If we were to read these stories about Freud as Freud would read them, we would arrive at Oedipus. The chapter on slips of the pen arrives, however, at another literary text, a passage from a John Galsworthy novel (supplied by Dr. Hanns Sachs) in which the protagonist fails to sign a check as a way of extricating himself from a romance—and of getting his penurious male friend to arrive instead. No doubt the character's self-reflection, "you don't want to part with your money, that's all" (quoted p. 133), reflects on autobiographical revelations in the chapter, and goes beyond them. Money is never, we can be sure, all that such denials are about. But, again, it would seem that sexuality will explain everything. Will it explain the literary trajectory of the chapter, however, or the choice of a text in which the hero states, as he "forgets" to sign and refuses "a helping hand," that "The line must be drawn!" (quoted p. 133)? What would it mean not to read Freud himself in these instances, but to read Freud's repressed signature, or to trace the lines, written and rewritten, in the chapter?

We would still be reading along Freudian lines, but in the direction of the *nachträglich* rewriting that constitutes the originary and primal scene. One chapter in *The Psychopathology of Everyday Life* leads there too, chapter 4, "Childhood Memories and Screen Memories." Its topic might seem out of place in a book on parapraxes; yet it is in that chapter, not in the one on slips of the pen, that the question of a psychoanalytic graphology is raised, in a form, moreover, that might elucidate the question of why the only thing that the unconscious seems to have on its mind is sexuality. The episode recounted there intimates (this is, of course, no surprise) that writing may be equated with textually determinate forms of sexuality. Explaining why a chapter on screen memories is not out of place in the book, Freud elaborates theories of substitution, repression, and re-impression that are also textual theories. Both forgetting and misremembering, effacement and replacement, come about in the same way, Freud claims, "by means of displacement along a superficial association" (p. 45), a "tendentious factor" (p. 45). Here, that "alien effect" is a "verbal bridge" (p. 49) or, more exactly, a slip of the hand, a transposition of the letter. For, as Freud insists, the quality of screen memories is their combination of an intense visual component coupled to a seemingly indifferent content. They have, he remarks, a "plastic form, comparable only to representations on stage" (p. 47). If the drama is *Oedipus Rex*, it is the script of the play that is played as the screen memory. What it offers is "not the genuine memory-trace but a later revision of it" (pp. 47–48). Such second editions and replays are as close to primordiality as one ever comes.

Because screen memories are so deeply embedded in the revisionary rewritings that dictate the subject, they are, Freud says, difficult to extract from context. But he has one "good example" that can be lifted whole:

> A man of twenty-four has preserved the following picture from his fifth year. He is sitting in the garden of a summer villa, on a small chair beside his aunt, who is trying to teach him the letters of the alphabet. He is in difficulties over the difference between *m* and *n* and he asks his aunt to tell him how to know one from the other. His aunt points out to him that the *m* has a whole piece more than the *n*—the third stroke. (p. 48)

It is a lesson in sexual difference in which masculinity is equivalent to a supplementary stroke of the pen, a lesson that depends upon the instrument of writing. "For just at that time he wanted to know the difference between *m* and *n*, so later he was anxious to find out the difference between boys and girls" (p. 48). It might suggest that, even if Freud is not this little boy, he writes with a pen—and thus inscribes and reinscribes sexual difference as determinant. (The chapter ends with a long autobiographical moment, the screen memory of the child Freud screaming that his much older half-brother has locked his mother in a cabinet.)

The point about this exemplary scene, I would argue, is simply this: sexual difference arises from the instrument of writing. The unconscious is a historical phenomenon. If it is written, it is, in Freud, or Heidegger, or Barthes, written by hand. The instrument held in the hand is all too easily phallic. (Indeed penis and pencil are etymologically cognate.) The scene that is inscribed on the psyche—the primal scene—is the scene of writing by hand. No wonder, then, that Derrida concludes "Freud and the Scene of Writing" by producing the primal scene in Freud's textual metaphors of the machine as male genitalia, the paper as the body of the mother, and the pathbreaking, breaching, violence, and resistance, by which traces are produced, as coitus (p. 229).

Such, too, is the lesson Melanie Klein reads in her 1923 essay, "The Role of the School in the Libidinal Development of the Child," which Derrida cites with approval. With her patient Fritz, "i" and "e" play the role played by "m" and "n" in Freud's story. Fritz has different explanations of the production of the Latin alphabet and German Fraktur: in Latin miniscules, "'i' and 'e' are the same, only in the middle 'i' has a little stroke and the 'e' has a little hole"; in Fraktur, however, "e" has a "box" rather than a hole.[16] These letters are male and female genitalia. But might not Fritz's "box" communicate with the cabinet in which Freud fears his mother has been locked? Six-year-old Ernst with his "'I' box" (Klein, *Love, Guilt and Reparation*, p. 65)—an explicitly theatrical setting—may point in this direction too (male genitalia trapped in female genitalia), and may help explain Freud's slips with "O" and "o," just as Fritz's speculations on the letter "S" may explain why Freud wrote "O" instead of "S": "In general he regarded the small letters as the children of the capital letters. The capital S he looked upon as the emperor of the long German s's; it had two hooks at the end of it to distinguish it from the empress, the terminal s, which had only one hook" (*Love, Guilt and Reparation*, p. 100).

Klein reads in these childhood scenes anxiety about castration—an anxiety perhaps manifest when Freud has to clip the numbers, and starts at the end of the line ("The line must be drawn!"), rather than at the beginning. But, everywhere, Klein reads ordinary life—walking on roads, riding on scooters, sailing on lakes—as scenes that are sexually invested because they are graphically invested: "For in his phantasies the lines in his exercise book were roads, the book itself was the whole world and the letters rode into it on motor bicycles, *i.e.*, on the pen. Again, the pen was a boat and the exercise book a lake" (p. 100). The pen, for Fritz, is at once a writing *machine* and the phallus. Might his journeys by hand or on foot relate to Freud's preoccupations with travel? Or might Fritz's road be put next to Heidegger's text, not to reveal that sexuality is the truth of the road we are said to tread on the way to Being—a journey whose end will never come—but because the sexual way is also, and always already, graphic? We can perhaps only generalize the scriptive formation of Freud's text on slips of the hand because we do not know the encryptment of letters in his unconscious, but, at the least, Klein's text reveals that the unconscious (which she thinks is sexual) is rather graphic. For her, speech has a libidinal cathexis, and so too does all motor activity; in her young patients, these motor activities find their symbolic site in the hand, and even speech appears to be a derivative effect of this more generalized scripting of (human) being. For Fritz, as Klein reports in "Early Analysis," "we found that the spoken word was to him identical with the written. The word stood for the penis or the child, while the movement of the tongue and the pen stood for coitus" (*Love, Guilt and Reparation*, p. 100).

These investments in writing by hand have a history that may be as long as that of the West. Yet the terms of the Freudian unconscious perhaps first became available when writing by hand became a more general phenomenon, when it was not simply the privilege of monks and scribes. The historical moment I have in mind is the Renaissance, and even Lacan, in the closing pages of "The Agency of the Letter," summons up the name of Erasmus to indicate the beginning of a shift in the nature of the unconscious allied to changes in the practice of writing. It is a well-chosen name, and not merely because it is virtually synonymous with rhetoric.

In *De recta Graeci et Latini sermonis pronunciatione* (1528), Erasmus interprets a fable about the invention of the alphabet, about Cadmus, sower of the dragon's teeth and bearer of the letter to Greece: "The matter is symbolised in the fable which depicts him sowing the teeth of a dead snake in the ground; from this seed there suddenly leapt up two lines of men, armed with helmets and spears, who destroyed themselves by dealing each other mortal wounds." What are these teeth? "If you . . . look . . . and count the upper and lower teeth [of a snake], you will find that they are equal in their number to the letters introduced by Cadmus. . . . At first the letters are at peace, being set in the alphabethical order in which they were born; then they are scattered, sown, multiplied in number and, when marshalled in various ways, come alive, burst into activity, fight."[17] Erasmus's allegory is not simply about speaking and writing, explicating the "fact" "that the Latin word for speech (*sermo*) comes from the word for sowing (*serendo*)" (*Scribes*,

98

p. 35)—and it does not merely offer a view of writing in which the life of the text is also disseminative strife and destruction. For we must remember who was born in the line of these alphabetic teeth. Cadmus was the mythical founder of Thebes; he sowed that line with those alphabetic teeth. Oedipus was among his progeny.

We might close with another confession of Roland Barthes, one that (re)writes these primordial scenes of writing. It is a parenthesis in "Faute de frappes": "In what I write by hand, I always make only one mistake, though a frequent one: I write *n* for *m*, amputating one leg—I want letters with two legs, not three" (*Barthes*, p. 97). It is with "M" that Barthes concludes his essay on Erté; "M" is "the inhuman letter" (*Responsibility*, p. 128), connected with "love and death (at least in our Latin languages)"—and with man in Germanic tongues—connected, either way, with castration. Not anthropomorphized in Erté's alphabet, and therefore, not *feminized* (what else is the body for Barthes?), "M" is, Barthes concludes, "the loveliest object imaginable: a script." And when the hand writes "n" for "m"? We return to the mirror with "N, the specular letter par excellence" (*Responsibility*, p. 125), "N" the truth of "M." Ready-to-hand in the writing implement par excellence, the pen: "In the end," Barthes tells his interviewer in *Le Monde*, "I always return to fine fountain pens. The essential thing is that they can produce that soft, smooth writing [*cette écriture douce*] I absolutely require [à laquelle je tiens absolument]" (*Grain*, p. 178). Barthes holds—absolutely—his being in his hand; he rewrites the screen memory of sexual difference.

What it would mean to write otherwise, we hardly yet know. It is reported that Derrida has only now just begun to compose his texts on a word processor. What form will a psychoanalytic graphology take when texts are no longer produced by phallic instruments, when it is no longer the flow of liquid onto the page that produces traces? No longer "the letter 'i,' which, with its simple 'up and down'" serves as "the foundation of all writing" (Klein, *Love, Guilt and Reparation*, p. 66), of the subject—the I—by hand? It is—as the examples of Barthes and Heidegger, and Freud and Klein would seem to suggest—too soon to be able to answer such questions except in a speculative mode. "Now, a certain form of support is in the course of disappearing, and the unconscious will have to get used to this, and this is already in progress."[18] The end of rhetoric.

Lurid Figures

NEIL HERTZ

This essay is about a characteristic, and characteristically unsettling, aspect of Paul de Man's writing: his particular way of combining analysis and pathos, of blending technical arguments about operations of rhetoric (often presented in an abstract, seemingly affectless idiom) with language—his own and that of the texts he cites—whose recurrent figures are strongly marked and whose themes are emotively charged, not to say melodramatic.

Take, as an initial example, the concluding paragraphs of his discussion of Kleist.[1] De Man has been commenting on the description of the puppets in *Über das Marionettentheater*, treating it as a "model . . . of the text as a system of turns and deviations, as a system of tropes" (*RR*, p. 285), and stressing the "machinelike, mechanical predictability" of the puppets' (or tropes') motion. De Man had begun his essay by quoting Schiller's "image of a beautiful society [as] a well-executed English dance, composed of many complicated figures and turns" (*RR*, p. 263). Now he recalls that opening citation, contrasting its edifying talk of the harmonious integration of individuals, each respecting the freedom of the others, with what he finds in Kleist's text: a mechanical dance "which is also a dance of death and mutilation," puppets "suspended in dead passivity," "an English technician able to build such perfect mechanical legs that a mutilated man will be able to dance with them in Schiller-like perfection." This in turn reminds de Man of the "sheer monstrosity" of "the eyeless philosopher

A version of this essay appeared in *Reading de Man Reading*, edited by Lindsay Waters and Wlad Godzich, © 1989 by the University of Minnesota. Reprinted by permission of the University of Minnesota Press.

Saunderson in Diderot's *Lettre sur les aveugles*," who is himself, de Man notes, like Kleist's dancing invalid, "one more victim in a long series of mutilated bodies that attend on the progress of enlightened self-knowledge, a series that includes Wordsworth's mute country-dwellers and blind city-beggars." At this point, having culled and clustered this lurid bouquet, not willfully and not without textual justification, but certainly deliberately, de Man draws himself and his readers up short:

> But one should avoid the pathos of an imagery of bodily mutilation and not forget that we are dealing with textual models, not with the historical and political systems that are their correlate. The disarticulation produced by tropes is primarily a disarticulation of meaning; it attacks semantic units such as words and sentences. (*RR*, p. 289.)

We are warned, too late, to avoid a pathos that has been placed, unavoidable, in our paths. Moreover, should we vow to be more alert in the future, the task is made no easier by the remaining sentences of de Man's essay, in which the grim connotations of words like "dismemberment," "trap," and "deadly" are inextricable from de Man's own concluding formulations. When he writes of "the dismemberment of language by the power of the letter," one cannot say, "But of course he means 'dismemberment' only figuratively"; nor can one say, reassuringly, of the essay's last phrase, that the dance it speaks of as "the ultimate trap, as unavoidable as it is deadly" (*RR*, p. 290) isn't *really* "deadly." The prose has been working precisely to forestall any such assurance. It is that textual work—the forms it takes and its consequences—that I propose to explore in these pages.

This essay is organized around a reading of the ten pages in *The Rhetoric of Romanticism* entitled "Wordsworth and the Victorians," a text that seems to have been intended to serve as a preface to a reissue of F. W. H. Myers's 1881 volume in the English Men of Letters series.[2] A brief occasional piece, it stands in something of the same relation to the essays that surround it ("Autobiography as De-Facement" and "Shelley Disfigured") as the talk called "Kant's Materialism" does to the longer and more polished "Phenomenality and Materiality in Kant,"[3] that is, it reads like either an intense trial run or a rapid glance over hard-won ground, both sketchier and more abrupt than the other two essays in its deployment of similar arguments and figures. It is an intriguing text, and I intend to move through it slowly, glossing its language by juxtaposing it with other writings of de Man's. I chose it partly for its brevity and informality, partly because it focuses on two key "figural terms" (RR, p. 92) in Wordsworth's poetry—"hangs" and "face"— commonplace words, which, along with their more abstract synonyms—"suspends" and "figure"—are also persistent and central in de Man's work. "Wordsworth and the Victorians" thus offers an economical way of engaging the problem of the relation of technical and pathetic language in de Man, for the problem inheres in his recurrent use of concepts like "suspension" and "disfiguration" in puzzling (and sometimes disturbing) proximity to images of hanging or of physical defacement such as those in the Kleist essay. We shall want to look into the necessity behind this idiosyncratic punning.

"Wordsworth and the Victorians" falls conveniently into two halves. Its first five pages present, in highly condensed form, what de Man takes to be "the canonical reading which has dominated the interpretation of Wordsworth from Victorian to modern times" (RR, p. 85). De Man is prepared to acknowledge the differences between the ethically oriented commentaries of nineteenth-century critics and the phenomenologically informed close readings of contemporary Wordsworthians, but he would minimize the effect of these differences, stressing instead the ways in which accounts of Wordsworth continue to be dominated by moral and religious categories. De Man presents the contemporary version of the canonical reading sympathetically, but adds a decisive reservation: "And yet, the very alacrity with which Wordsworth's major texts respond to this approach should make one wary" (RR, p. 88). He then goes on in the essay's last five pages to offer an alternative reading, centered on the "Blessed Babe" lines in The Prelude.

Before looking at that alternative, however, it is worth pausing at certain points in de Man's characterization of the canonical reading and noticing his way of positioning his own work in relation to it. He grants the Victorians at least an oblique awareness of what he calls "a certain enigmatic aspect of Wordsworth" or "the truly puzzling element in Wordsworth," and he locates that awareness in their worrying the question of whether what Wordsworth wrote was to be thought of as poetry or philosophy, a concern he believes is prompted by their wish to keep the two modes of discourse clearly distinct. Why should they be kept apart? Because, de Man explains, "to couple such power of seduction with such authority is to tempt fate itself":

> Hence the urge to protect, as the most pressing of moral imperatives, this borderline between both modes of discourse. Many poets can easily be enlisted in the service of this cause but others are more recalcitrant, though not necessarily because they are formally involved with philosophical systems. Wordsworth, rather than Coleridge, is a case in point. It is as if his language came from a region in which the most carefully drawn distinctions between analytic rigor and poetic persuasion are no longer preserved, at no small risk to either. Trying to state why this is so is to suggest an alternative to the canonical reading which has dominated the interpretation of Wordsworth from Victorian to modern times. Some contemporary writing on Wordsworth begins to break with this tradition or, to be more precise, begins to reveal the break that has always been hidden in it. (*RR*, p. 85.)

Notice that these lines are about an epistemological threat figured in spatial terms, the possibility that the "borderline between [two] modes of discourse" will be blurred, a threat which is carried, like a virus, by language issuing from a "region" where those borderlines, certain "most carefully drawn distinctions," do not exist. But notice, too, that there is a whiff of the oedipal triangle in that image of the dangers readers face when confronting poetry's "power of seduction" coupled with the "authority" of philosophy: the danger that prompts the urge to reestablish clear demarcating lines would seem to be the threatened collapse of that triangle into a more archaic structure, at once cognitively unsettling and menacing to the integrity of the pre-oedipal subject. But is it the subject who is being threatened here? Not explicitly: what is at risk is the integrity of modes of discourse, the analytic rigor of the one, the persuasive power of the other. I have exaggerated the salience (and the immediate pertinence) of a psychoanalytic reading in order to point out the brief appearance of a drama of subjectivity within a discourse, de Man's, which is committed to questioning subjectivity's privilege as an interpretive category.

I call attention to these shifts in idiom and connotation because the question of finding appropriate language is precisely what de Man is discussing here, just as he is necessarily engaged in the business of finding appropriate language himself. His account of the tradition of Wordsworth criticism is a story of repeated

attempts to define that "enigmatic aspect" of his poetry, a dangerous "something" that philosophy, presumably, "is supposed to
shelter us from." This remained "unnamed and undefined" by the
Victorians, but the "effort of all subsequent Wordsworth interpreters has been, often with the poet's own assistance, to domesti-
cate it by giving it at least a recognizable content" (*RR*, p. 86). The
climax of de Man's summary of contemporary criticism—a climax
followed immediately by that deflating "And yet . . ."—is his tribute to a powerfully apt, if recuperative, act of identification: "The
threat from which we were to be sheltered and consoled is now
identified as a condition of consciousness. Maiming, death, the
wear and tear of mutability are the predicaments of 'the unimagin-
able touch of time' and time, in this version of Wordsworth, is the
very substance of the self-reflecting, recollecting mind." A lurid
thematics, to be sure, but once conceived as a subject's response to
the real, to the "touch of time" rather than to "a disarticulation of
meaning," it loses the added sting of incomprehensibility and becomes strangely consoling, a "triumph of consciousness over its
ever-threatening undoing" (*RR*, p. 87).

What would it mean to "break with this tradition"? First, it
would mean resisting the "urge" to name "the threat" at any cost.
More specifically, it would mean acknowledging the provenance of
Wordsworth's language as a region of *verbal* indistinction, but it
would also mean, de Man insists in an effort to "be more precise,"
revealing "the break that has always been hidden" within the canonical reading. That juxtaposition of figures is slightly puzzling:
on the one hand, de Man would confront "a region in which the
most carefully drawn distinctions between analytic rigor and poetic persuasion are no longer preserved," that is, he would risk a
dissolution of difference; on the other hand, his break with the canonical would "reveal the break that has always been hidden in it," a
residual, if minimal, difference in what had appeared to be a seamlessly coherent critical position. But where exactly does the threat
lie: in the loss of clear distinctions? or in the discovery of a hidden
and irreducible difference? The puzzle is not to be brushed aside by
insisting that, in context, these apparently contradictory figures
apply to quite different critical acts: that one is about reading
Wordsworth, the other about aligning oneself with previous readings. De Man's prose works to conflate those activities into one

thing called "reading," and to characterize reading as invariably entangling the reader in alternating apprehensions of difference and indifference.

We would do better by looking at some other places in de Man's writing where the image of a hidden break or flaw appears, in "Shelley Disfigured," for example, where de Man claims that a reading of *The Triumph of Life* "exposes the wound of a fracture that lies hidden in all texts" (*RR*, p. 120), or in the essay on Walter Benjamin's "The Task of the Translator," where de Man writes:

> All these activities—critical philosophy, literary theory, history—resemble each other in the fact that they do not resemble that from which they derive. But they are all intralinguistic: they relate to what in the original belongs to language, and not to meaning as an extralinguistic correlate susceptible of paraphrase and imitation. They disarticulate, they undo the original, they reveal that the original was always already disarticulated. They reveal that their failure, which seems to be due to the fact that they are secondary in relation to the original, reveals an essential failure, an essential disarticulation which was already there in the original. They kill the original by discovering that the original was already dead. They read the original from the perspective of a pure language (*reine Sprache*), a language that would be entirely freed of the illusion of meaning—pure form if you want; and in doing so they bring to light a dismembrance, a decanonization which was already there in the original from the beginning. (*RT*, p. 84.)

Here the force of "dismembrance" (like the disarticulation of Kleist's puppets or his amputees) or of "de-canonization" (like the effort to break with a tradition of criticism) is given a familiar deconstructive turn: its activity discovers a disarticulation always already there. What these lines add to that (by now) reassuring notion—for anything heard often enough is a comfort—is the discomfiting, because seemingly gratuitous, violence of construing "disarticulation" as murder and murder as, paradoxically, "discovering that the original was already dead." That is, what they add is, fleetingly, the pathos of uncertain agency. A subject is conjured up—perhaps a killer, perhaps only the discoverer of the corpse—who can serve as a locus of vacillation: did I do it? or had it already been done? This particular version of undecidability—between the activity or passivity, the guilt or innocence of a subject—must be added to those already adduced, between the original and the secondary, between the totalized and the fragmented, between difference and indistinctness, if the "threat" associated with Wordsworth's poetry, or the necessity of breaking with its canonical reading, is to be understood.

When de Man refers to Wordsworth as "a poet of sheer language" (*RR*, p. 92), the phrase combines one of his preferred honorific adjectives[4] with an echo of Benjamin's "reine Sprache." And de Man's further remarks on that expression are helpful in characterizing the "region" he associates with Wordsworth's poetry. After noting how, in "The Task of the Translator," Benjamin "put[s] the original in motion, to de-canonize [it]," de Man adds:

> This movement of the original is a wandering, an *errance*, a kind of permanent exile if you wish, but it is not really an exile, for there is no homeland, nothing from which one has been exiled. Least of all is there something like a *reine Sprache*, a pure language, which does not exist except as a permanent disjunction which inhabits all languages as such, including and especially the language one calls one's own. (*RT*, p. 92.)

In Kenneth Burke's terms, this is the Scene that serves as background, or container, for the Agent we have just observed, a subject ambivalently guilty and innocent, alternately present in and absent from de Man's discourse. Because of a "permanent disjunction which inhabits all languages as such"—the "enigmatic aspect" or "puzzling element" that interpreters of Wordsworth seek to come to terms with—we are led to figures like "homeland" or "pure language" or to a notion like that of a language to "call one's own," a mother tongue, in an effort to delineate the contour and sketch in the contents of that "region." But container and thing contained are unstable figures here: language would seem to "come from" a region at one moment (*RR*, p. 85), yet at another moment language serves as the space "inhabited" by a disjunction (*RT*, p. 92). What is clear is that the "region" is sometimes registered as a "shelter," sometimes as a "threat"; and, as de Man points out, it is common to confuse the two: "The strategy of denegation which calls a threat a shelter in the hope of thus laying it to rest is all too familiar" (*RR*, p. 86). Given this "predicament" we can perhaps best approach the nature of the "threat" by dwelling for a while on the word "shelter."

106

"We think we are at ease in our own language," de Man remarks, still glossing Benjamin on translation; "we feel a coziness, a
familiarity, a shelter in the language we call our own, in which we
think we are not alienated" (*RT*, p. 84). "Shelter" may have entered
de Man's lexicon by way of Heidegger, or Wordsworth, or both;[5] it
remained there as a constant resource, recurring throughout *Allegories of Reading* and *The Rhetoric of Romanticism*. Often, for obvious reasons, it is paired with "threat." More interesting, for our
purposes, are two other linkages, implicit in the sentence I've just
quoted, one bringing "shelter" into relation with language, particularly figural language, the other drawing its connotations of
"coziness" and "familiarity" off in the direction of the erotic or
seductive. "All remains implicit, inward, sheltered in the unsuspected nuances of common speech" (*RR*, p. 87): de Man is here
characterizing "the miracle of Wordsworth's figural diction." A
more surprising, because unidiomatic, usage occurs in a discussion
of Rousseau: "The threat remains sheltered behind its metaphoricity" (*AR*, p. 297). One would have expected a threat to be "hidden," and its potential victim to be the one who was or wasn't
"sheltered" from it. But the possibility of a reversal of the menacing and the menaced is precisely de Man's point: we may wish now
to look back at those "unsuspected nuances of common speech"
with a more apprehensive glance: why that suspicious word "unsuspected"? have we been led to mistake a threat for a shelter
there, too? If we have, it was because we have been lured or
"tempted" or "seduced" by Wordsworth's figural use of common
speech into a scene of familiarity, a family scene. "Shelter," for de
Man, always blends the architectonic with the "familial."[6] Reading
Nietzsche's *The Birth of Tragedy*, for example, he can call attention to the combined attractiveness of "the seductive power of a
genetic narrative," with its promise of rendering things intelligible
by means of a model of natural descent, and the "rhetorical complicity" generated by the narrator's manner: "We are guaranteed intellectual safety as long as we remain within the sheltering reach
of his voice. The same seductive tone safeguards the genetic continuity throughout the text" (*AR*, p. 94). Nor is it fortuitous that a
mode of explanation (a genetic narrative) and a mode of address (a
seductive tone) should be found working in tandem here: both
draw their force from the pathos of the familial.

But it is not your average family that de Man is concerned with, either in the texts he chooses to discuss or in his own figurative language. Or rather, it is not an oedipally triangulated family, with child, mother, and father occupying relatively stable positions. Instead, the configurations that interest him, and that he associates with all acts of reading and understanding, are variations of the specular.[7] In privileged texts like the "Blessed Babe" lines in *The Prelude,* or in phrases like that describing the merging of poetry and philosophy into a daunting combination of seduction and authority, he would seem to be attending to narcissistic or "borderline" structures of the sort Julia Kristeva has recently explored, structures that play out the earliest exchanges between infant and mother.[8] Hence the pathos of the familial, when it appears in de Man's writing, is often concerned with the maternal. The central argument of "Wordsworth and the Victorians" takes as its text lines celebrating "the Babe, / Nurs'd in his Mother's arms," a passage that provides de Man with an occasion for some of his own boldest statements. But before engaging that "alternative reading," I want to look at a much earlier reference to the maternal, a bizarre footnote de Man appended to a discussion of Yeats in his dissertation.

In a reading of Yeats's career that was startling in 1960 and has, if anything, gained in persuasive power in the years since, de Man sees the poet's development as generated by the tension between two kinds of figurative language, mimetic images of natural things and what Yeats came to call emblems, that is, images that had their meaning, in Yeats's phrase, "by a traditional and not by a natural right" (quoted in *RR,* p. 165). Yeats's mature manner, in this account, "is a tenuous equilibrium, in itself an extraordinary feat of style and rhetoric, but no reconciliation [of image with emblem], not even a dialectic." But such an equilibrium was bound to be short-lived, and the poet's "fundamental bewilderment," according to de Man, prompted a thematic crisis in his late work, a crisis played out primarily around the theme of erotic love (*RR,* pp. 204–6). De Man's understanding of this crisis requires him to dispute the canonical reading of Yeats as a celebrator of Eros and to document instead the poet's "most negative conception of the pleasures of sex" (*RR,* p. 217), an attitude that extends to the "natural seduction" of images as well: the devaluation of sexual love is the thematic sign of the drive to realize an unequivocally emblematic poetry. In the course of establishing this reading, de Man cites a number of poems that render desire not as a natural craving for satisfaction, but as a desire for the destruction of desire, for postcoital stillness or death. He then comments:

> One begins to understand, perhaps all too well (though one should beware not to confuse ontology and psychoanalysis), Yeats's interest in the castration myth of Attis. The rejection of all feminine and maternal elements of sex,[115] brings to mind Mallarmé's *Hérodiade*. (*RR*, p. 231.)[9]

Note 115, in its entirety, reads as follows:

> 115. To the point of a kind of matricidal indifference:
>
> > What matter if the knave
> > That most could pleasure you,
> > The children that he gave,
> > Are somewhere sleeping like a top
> > Under a marble flag?
> > > ("Those Dancing Days Are Gone,"
> > > *Var.*, p. 525)

The initial problem is that it's hard to read those lines—or the rest of the ballad—as "matricidal." The singer is certainly indifferent to the old woman's displeasure: this stanza begins "Curse as you may I sing it through; / What matter if the knave . . ." And the woman is old, and her lover and her children are dead. But is it obvious that being forced to listen to these bitter truths will be the death of her as well? Still more puzzling is the expression itself, "matricidal indifference": it sounds at once crabbed and hyperbolical, and it arrives in this text with the same air of gratuitous violence (and some of the same thematic resonance) as the sentence in de Man's Benjamin essay I remarked on earlier: "They kill the original by discovering that the original was already dead." I took that sentence to be expressive of a pathos of agency, signaling the appearance in de Man's text (for however brief a stay) of a fantasmatic subject, ambivalently active and passive, guilty and innocent, murderous or bereft or both. Something similar seems at work here: a passage to the limit, a rejection of the maternal carried "to the point of a kind of" matricide, produces a lurid figure— the dead mother—who functions as the disfigured specular double of the subject of a pathos, the poet as Attis, "castrated before he can return to Cybele, the mother of the gods" (*RR*, p. 201). How might this have come about? By what necessity would a subject, lurid or not, appear in this text?

De Man's mention of Attis here alludes to a moment in his argument some thirty pages earlier where he is considering Yeats's attempts to resolve the tension between image and emblem in his poetry. One recurrent figure, the tree, would seem to emblematize the tension itself; de Man quotes a stanza from the aptly named "Vacillation":

> A tree there is that from its topmost bough
> Is half all glittering flame and half all green
> Abounding foliage moistened with the dew;
> And half is half and yet is all the scene;
> And half and half consume what they renew,
> And he that Attis' image hangs between
> That staring fury and the blind lush leaf
> May not know what he knows, but knows not grief.

Aligning "foliage" with the natural image, "flame" with the emblem, de Man notes that "a synthesis is suggested by Attis' image or, more precisely, by the poetic act of hanging Attis' image between the two halves," then goes on to show how the synthesis is only apparent: what we have instead is "one more veiled statement of the absolute superiority of the emblem over the image" (*RR*, p. 201). The slight fine-tuning of his observation, his noting that it is not Attis's image but ("more precisely") the poetic act of hanging it on the tree that makes the difference, prefigures de Man's later explicit (and explicitly theorized) interest in the distinction between the meaning and the performance of a text. But it also exhibits how slippery the category of performance is, how easily "the poetic act" can be displaced, by an anthropomorphizing gesture, into the poet's act. De Man might even have pointed out an ambiguity in Yeats's stanza that goes along with the general drift of his argument: the phrasing of "he that Attis' image hangs between" rearranges the normal sequence of subject, transitive verb, and direct object so that the line allows a glimpse of the poet hanging on the tree: "he that, Attis' image, hangs between . . ." Is the stanza about an image or an action or a poet, a figure or a performance or a "figure"?

Moreover, de Man's most general statement about what it is like to read Yeats locates "the reader," that figure, in a similarly dangling position. Faced with the "tenuous equilibrium" of Yeats's style, "the reader vacillates between two extremes . . . the tendency to give in to the natural seduction of the images . . . or, on the other hand, the tendency to read them as if they were esoteric puzzles" (*RR*, p. 204). But the natural seduction of images is, as de Man will argue years later, a seduction into identification, into the positing of a specular subject as the reader's double, a "poet" behind the "poetic action."[10] Once Attis's image, the poetic act, and the vacillating reader are thus aligned, it is possible for the "threat" of Attis's castration to be communicated down the line to the poet and on to the reader, in this case de Man. The pathos of matricide would then mark the excess of force with which one reader is swung away from "the natural seduction" of Yeats's figurative language and released from suspended vacillation. In the vocabulary de Man would later adopt, it is a gesture of dis-figuration, at once an insight into the transferential dynamics of reading and a conjuring up of what is, in one sense, an unmotivated pathos.

De Man would have us register this pathos but not be quite taken in by it: hence the parenthetical warning not to confuse ontology and psychoanalysis.[11] But, like the admonition to "avoid the pathos of an imagery of bodily mutilation" that we began by noticing in the Kleist essay, this warning is hard to heed; at best—and this is, if not de Man's point in issuing such warnings, at least one consequence of our reading them—we can acknowledge the "predicament" they place us in. That is, we can acknowledge that a tug-of-war between "analytic rigor" and "poetic persuasion" is unavoidable in each act of reading/writing—in Yeats's, in de Man's, in our own—and acknowledge it all the more readily when the felt pressure of some other reader's pathos, here the imposition of the words "matricidal indifference," seems at once so palpable and so gratuitous. Whatever else "matricidal indifference" represents, it is certainly, and to begin with, a forced reading of "Those Dancing Days Are Gone," and it is by no means the only moment of interpretive violence a reader of de Man will encounter.[12] It is this question of forcing that I would like to engage now, in returning to "Wordsworth and the Victorians."

De Man bases his "alternative reading" (*RR*, pp. 88–92) on the results of two exceptional earlier investigations of Wordsworthian "key words," William Empson's account of "sense," which showed that "it is impossible . . . to make sense out of" the ways "sense"

functions in *The Prelude*, and Wordsworth's own "technical rhetorical analysis" of "hangs," which displayed "a remarkably consistent pattern" of meaning in uses of that term. De Man notes the
difference between the two analyses, one ending, to its credit, in
"near-total chaos," the other in a "perfectly coherent" account of a
semantic field. Noting too that "'hangs' is, by Wordsworth's own
avowal, *the* exemplary metaphor for metaphor, for figuration in
general," de Man is led to conclude that "the figural scheme that a
philosophy of consciousness allows one to reach" is insufficient to
account for all operations of Wordsworth's language.

The linking of hanging to figuration and of figuration to intelligibility,[13] as well as a drive to exhaust and move beyond that cluster of concepts, is characteristic of de Man's work in and after *Allegories of Reading*. It is nowhere more explicit than in the essay
that reads as a more developed companion piece to "Wordsworth
and the Victorians," "Shelley Disfigured," most particularly in
de Man's analysis of the sequence in *The Triumph of Life* that nar-
rates Rousseau's encounter with the feminine "shape all light." In
this poem, de Man observes, it is the shape that serves as "the
model of figuration in general," epitomizing the ways in which
"the seduction of the figure . . . creates an illusion of meaning."
Hence the shape allows itself to be read, finally, as figuring "the
figurality of all signification" (*RR*, pp. 115–16). It is represented
as "hovering" or "glimmering" with "seductive grace" in "near-
miraculous suspension" (*RR*, pp. 108–9) throughout a scene that,
as it unfolds, "makes this knot, by which knowledge, oblivion and
desire hang suspended, into an articulated sequence of events that
demands interpretation" (*RR*, pp. 106–7).

De Man's response is twofold: he will read the sequence rhetorically, as an allegory of figuration, and offer conceptual formulations of the sort I have just cited; but he is bound to respond in
another idiom as well, as he blends citation and interpretive paraphrase into a narration of the action and pathos of Shelley's lines.
So he will gloss the "disfiguration" of the shape as the active forgetting, within the language of the poem, of "the events this language in fact performs" (*RR*, p. 118). But he will also find "disfiguration" exemplified within the poem's narrative as a "drowning" of
the shape when it "traverses the mirror [of the stream's surface]
and goes under" (*RR*, p. 114), "to finally sink away 'below the watery floor'" (*RR*, p. 119). De Man is unaccustomedly emphatic in
his insistence on this version of the shape's disappearance or death:

"There is no doubt that, when we again meet the shape (ll. 425 ff.) it is no longer gliding along the river but drowned, Ophelia-like, below the surface of the water" (*RR*, p. 111). Yet just such a doubt may persist; de Man has imposed his interpretation on lines that contain no demonstrable images of drowning; rather they offer Rousseau's account of the gradual fading of the "shape all light," overwhelmed by the blaze of a "new Vision":

> "so on my sight
> Burst a new Vision never seen before.—
>
> "And the fair shape waned in the coming light
> As veil by veil the silent splendour drops
> From Lucifer, amid the chrysolite
>
> "Of sunrise. . . .
>
> "So knew I in that light's severe excess
> The presence of that shape which on the stream
> Moved, as I moved along the wilderness,
>
> "More dimly than a day appearing dream,
> The ghost of a forgotten form of sleep,
> A light from Heaven whose half extinguished beam
>
> "Through the sick day in which we wake to weep
> Glimmers, forever sought, forever lost.—
> So did that shape its obscure tenour keep
>
> "Beside my path, as silent as a ghost;
> But the new Vision, and its cold bright car,
> With savage music, stunning music, crost
>
> "The forest . . ."[14]

If we ask how de Man could have read a drowning into these lines, and ask it not rhetorically, as if to deplore a blatant error ("How could he?!"), but seriously, we are led to the drowned body of the poet himself, which if it cannot be located within Shelley's lines nevertheless "is present in the margin of the last manuscript page and has become an inseparable part of the poem" (*RR*, p. 120). "Shelley Disfigured" concludes by insisting that our knowledge of the poet's death is not knowledge of an irrelevant anecdote, whose poignancy can be surreptitiously counted on while ostensibly ignored in our dealings with the poem. Rather, de Man would include the death in the series of disfigurations he finds both in the poem and, necessarily, in any subsequent writing about it. The argument is strong and unsentimental, and depends on a subtly articulated meditation that has been developing throughout the essay, a progressive raising of the stakes of interpretation that turns on the question of how we are to understand the disappearance of the "shape all light." I can't hope to reproduce either the analytic care or the persuasive force of that argument, but I need to roughly indicate its path and some of its turns, for it is backward along that path that what de Man would call the disfiguring figure of drowning is communicated from Shelley to the shape.

The moment when de Man declares that "there is no doubt" that the shape is drowned is, as it happens, precisely the moment when he is about to stop taking Shelley's images at face value: the "chain of metaphorical transformations can be understood, up to this point," he writes, "without transposition into a vocabulary that would not be that of their own referents." But if we are to understand why the shape is "allowed to wane," he argues, we are obliged to "read in a non-phenomenal way," that is, to resist the seductions of the "representational code of the text" (*RR*, p. 115) and instead to construe Shelley's language as offering, allegorically, an account of its own workings (*RR*, pp. 111–13). That account, as de Man reconstructs it in the last dozen pages of his essay, has about it the intellectual excitement of a compressed survey of the path his own research had taken him: from a concern with the ways figurative language can unite "perception and cognition undisturbed by the possibly disruptive mediation of its own figuration" (*RR*, p. 112) to a deepened understanding of two other disruptive instances—that of the "play of the signifier" (the "literal and material aspects of language") with its power to "undo the representational and iconic function of figuration"(*RR*, pp. 113–14), and that of the performative aspect of language, which he refers to as "the positional power of language considered by and in itself," or again as "the senseless power of positional language" (*RR*, pp. 115–17). It is this latter power, the power of the performative, that de Man finds alone capable of accounting for the disappearance of the shape. He notes the abruptness with which one visionary scene replaces another in *The Triumph of Life*, as though the "previous occupants of the narrative space [were] expelled by decree, by the sheer power of utterance, and consequently at once forgotten." Thus he reads the poem as a fragment of a potentially endless story of disfiguration, "since the knowledge of the language's performative power is itself a figure in its own right and, as such, bound to repeat the disfiguration of metaphor as Shelley is bound to repeat the aberration of Rousseau in what appears to be a more violent mode" (*RR*, p. 120).

That last sentence offers a clue to de Man's conversion of the shape's waning into a drowning: it is his repetition of the poem's disfigurations "in what appears to be a more violent mode." But how would that play itself out? The language with which de Man works Shelley's "actual death" into his reading is instructive:

> At this point, figuration and cognition are actually interrupted by an event which shapes the text but which is not present in its represented or articulated meaning. It may seem a freak of chance to have a text thus molded by an actual occurrence, yet the reading of *The Triumph of Life* establishes that this mutilated textual model exposes the wound of a fracture that lies hidden in all texts. If anything, this text is more rather than less typical than texts that have not been thus truncated. The rhythmical interruptions that mark off the successive episodes of the narrative are not new moments of cognition but literal events textually reinscribed by a delusive act of figuration or forgetting.
>
> In Shelley's absence, the task of thus reinscribing the disfiguration now devolves entirely on the reader. The final test of reading, in *The Triumph of Life*, depends on how one reads the textuality of this event, how one disposes of Shelley's body. (*RR*, p. 121.)

How has de Man, as reader, performed "the task of . . . reinscribing the disfiguration," that is, what has he done with Shelley's body? He has indeed, as he says all readers are bound to do, "monumentalized" it by burying it in its own text, but with a difference. His discussion of the performative power of language has allowed him to name as "events" interruptions within the poem as well as the "actual" event that interrupted the writing of the poem. He can then not merely analogize these events in general, but insist on the particular analogy of the extratextual drowning with another interruption, the disappearance of the shape, by delusively figuring the latter *as a drowning*. This act has the effect of repositioning Shelley's body at the point in the poem where the shape "goes under," where meaning yields to "sheer" performance, at the site of "the wound of a fracture that lies hidden in all texts." Shelley's death thus can serve as a means of "exposing" a death that has been there all along: it is like saying that one kills the original by discovering that the original is already dead. The difficult but powerful argument of the essay, which allows de Man to read the shape's disappearance as an allegorical gesture unmasking the "figurality of all signification," is accomplished in language that reinscribes the drowned shape and the drowned Shelley in a specular structure, paired with each other like the imagined victim of Yeats's matricidal indifference and the figure of the castrated Attis. Another way of putting this would be to say that de Man has shown how and why readers cannot help forcing their texts, but (or rather: *and*) this awareness in no way prevents him from forcing his text.

"Wordsworth and the Victorians" follows the same trajectory, and exhibits the same bifurcation, once de Man moves beyond the word "hangs" and turns his attention to another key Wordsworthian term, "face." By dwelling on the meaning of "face," in Wordsworth's text and in his own, he will produce, in brief, the alternative reading he had promised, as well as a compelling sketch of the alternative poetics he lays out more fully in "Shelley Disfigured." But he will do so by means of a series of interpretations that culminate in another strange, delusive act of figuration, a surfacing of the specular figures buried in the longer essay.

The difficulty of de Man's discussion of "face," and of the analysis of the "Blessed Babe" lines that it draws on, lies partly in the way the word itself shifts, in de Man's usage, between its ordinary meaning and an idiosyncratic, nonphenomenal sense, partly in the puzzles about priority and dependency that any speculation on beginnings is bound to raise. De Man takes the lines as "Wordsworth's essay on the origins of language as poetic language" (*RR*, p. 90); that is, he takes them as seeking to map that "region" where poetry originates by offering a genetic narrative of its birth, a narrative that de Man must then read allegorically. Wordsworth presents a sequence of causes and effects, claiming that they are merely his "best conjectures," acknowledging that what he would describe has, properly speaking, "no beginning"; and de Man retells Wordsworth's story within the frame of his own poetics, his own understanding of what comes before what, what depends on what. The two stories both sustain and interfere with one another.

"Face," for de Man, can only be thought in relation to "language": for "face" is not just "the locus of speech, the necessary condition for the existence of articulated language" (*RR*, p. 89); it is also the product of language, ineluctably figurative: "Man can address and face other men, within life or beyond the grave, because he has a face, but he has a face only because he partakes of a mode of discourse that is neither entirely natural nor entirely human." When Wordsworth writes in *The Prelude* "my mind hath look'd / Upon the speaking face of earth and heaven," de Man glosses that as designating a "prior encounter," a visual exchange that underwrites later verbal exchanges: "One can speak only because one can look upon a mode of speech which is not quite our own" (*RR*, p. 90). It is important to notice that the encounter is with a speaking face that is not, however, that of another human: it is with a face that figures "language."[15] The difficulty of the interpretation arises from the fact that the lines de Man goes on to consider, which must bear on this encounter if they don't exactly illustrate it, are about what we may take to be the commonplace, if highly charged, face-to-face encounter of mother and infant. I cite them in full, before turning back to de Man's reading:

> Bless'd the infant Babe,
> (For with my best conjecture I would trace
> The progress of our being) blest the Babe,
> Nurs'd in his Mother's arms, the Babe who sleeps
> Upon his Mother's breast, who, when his soul
> Claims manifest kindred with an earthly soul,
> Doth gather passion from his Mother's eye!
> Such feelings pass into his torpid life
> Like an awakening breeze, and hence his mind
> Even in the first trial of its powers
> Is prompt and watchful, eager to combine
> In one appearance, all the elements
> And parts of the same object, else detach'd
> And loth to coalesce.
>
> (1805 *Prelude* 2.237–50)

Is the child looking at "language" or at his mother? At both, de Man would say; or rather he would point out that the question was badly put: "language" is not an object; "language" is already there in the looking. Hence he stresses the child's "claim of manifest kindred" as a moment of abrupt performance, an "active verbal deed . . . not given in the nature of things," which initiates the subsequent process of exchange, an exchange that allows the child to construct a widening and increasingly meaningful perceptual field through successive acts of figuration. The first of these acts is the imposition of a figure, the producing of a "face," the coordination of visual details into "a larger, total entity," which serves as the model for all further processes of totalization. I shall quote de Man's analysis of this sequence at length, because it has its own abruptnesses, which are worth attending to:

The power and the structure of this act are described in sufficient detail to give meaning to the by itself enigmatic phrase: to "gather passion." The "gathering" is a process of exchange by which the eye is "combin[d] / In one appearance . . ." with "all the elements / And parts of the same object, else detach'd / And loth to coalesce. . . ." Without having to evoke the technical vocabulary of associationist psychology which is used here, *it is clear* that what is being described is the possibility of inscribing the eye, which is nothing by itself, into a larger, total entity, the "same object" which, *in the internal logic of the text, can only be the face*, the face as the combination of parts which the mind, working like a synecdochical trope, can lay claim to—thus opening the way to a process of totalization which, in the span of a few lines, can grow to encompass everything, "*All* objects through *all* intercourse of sense." Language originates with the ability of the eye to establish the contour, the borderline, the surface which allows things to exist in the identity of the kinship of their distinction from other things. (*RR*, p. 91; first two emphases mine.)

The phrases I've italicized indicate the urgency with which de Man would insist on this reading, even though its central claim is an intuitively plausible one: that the "object" constructed by the child "in the first trial of its powers" should be the mother's face, and that its own having a face will be an effect of that construction, would suit contemporary gestalt theorists, or partisans of the mirror stage, as well as eighteenth-century associationists. Nevertheless there is a tension between the canonical reading and de Man's nonphenomenal alternative; the signs of strain can be located in his gloss on "gathering." The image of an eye "gathering passion" need not be as enigmatic as he would have it. Earlier in *The Prelude* one can find a similar figure, one that resonates with these lines on the babe at the breast, for it links seeing and sucking:

> yet I have stood,
> Even while my eye has mov'd o'er three long leagues
> Of shining water, gathering, as it seem'd,
> Through every hair-breadth of that field of light,
> New pleasure, like a bee among the flowers.
> (1805 *Prelude* 1.604–8)

De Man had remarked on how, in the "Blessed Babe" passage, the word "'eye' . . . is prominent enough to displace 'breast' where one would most naturally expect it" (*RR*, p. 90), and it is precisely the reader's natural expectation that he would thwart, by insisting on the displacement and suppressing the possibility that the eye's "gathering passion," like its "gathering pleasure," is a scopic analogue of nursing. Hence he comments on "gather" but not on "passion," and, by eliding the next lines ("Such feelings pass into his torpid life / Like an awakening breeze, and hence his mind . . ."), he can telescope Wordsworth's account of the progress of consciousness. The totalizing activity, as Wordsworth describes it, is a *result* of the passage of feelings into the child's torpid life: de Man omits the "hence" and relocates synecdochical totalization back at the onset of the process, almost contemporaneous with the initiating "claim." That interpretation is what allows him to conclude in this fashion:

> "Face" then, in this passage, not unlike the earlier "hangs," designates the dependence of any perception or "eye" on the totalizing power of language. It heralds this dependency as "the first / Poetic spirit of our human life." The possibility of any contact between mind and nature depends on this spirit manifested by and in language. (*RR*, p. 91.)

The child hangs at the mother's breast, the child depends on her, its sense of having a face depends on her having a face; but it is not that "dependency" that is being repeatedly evoked in these sentences. It is rather the logical dependence of perception and cognition on figurative language—on the figure of an outlined surface, a field or a face—that is stressed, and stressed at the expense of a more conventional intersubjective reading of the passage: the words "Mother" and "Babe" (which until now have only appeared within quotation marks in de Man's text) now disappear altogether. The characters in de Man's story of origins are named "eye" and "face" and "language."

By insisting so forcibly on the difference between the two readings, by endorsing whatever it was that led Wordsworth to substitute "eye" for "breast," for example, de Man is pointing to a differentiating force already at work, a "wound of a fracture" in the text of *The Prelude*. He is also, we should note, performing the work of that force in suppressing the figure of the maternal as he does. The displacement from "breast" to "eye" is a gentle one, however, barely indicting the naturalness of the nurturing activity it describes. But the same force is responsible for more violent declensions in *The Prelude*: de Man goes on to relate how, later in the poem, "this same face-making, totalizing power is shown at work in a process of endless differentiation correctly called perpetual 'logic,' of which it is said that it [i.e., the poet's eye] 'Could find no surface where its power might sleep.'" And here, as he is glossing that line, dwelling on the words "surface" and "power," something peculiar happens to de Man's text. He writes:

> The face, which is the power to surface from the sea of infinite distinctions in which we risk to drown, can find no surface. How are we to reconcile the *meaning* of face, with its promise of sense and of filial preservation, with its *function* as the relentless undoer of its own claims? (*RR*, p. 92.)

The noun "surface"—which had, in the previous paragraph, indicated the bounded area of an intelligible "face," enclosed within a "contour" or "borderline"—has here turned into a verb for coming-up-for-air, and the reader is back in the thematics of drowning, made more plangent by the pathos of the first person plural: "the sea of infinite distinctions in which we risk to drown." Moreover the phrase "in which we risk to drown"—not so much its words as the tune they make up—sounds suddenly familiar:

> Like this harsh world in which I wake to weep . . .
>
> Through the sick day in which we wake to weep . . .

Those are lines from *The Triumph of Life*, spoken by "Rousseau" and cited by de Man in his discussion of the "shape all light"; both cited and, in the case of the latter line, re-cited as "the *sad* day in which we wake to weep" (*RR*, pp. 104, 106). It is as if "Rousseau" (defaced) and the "shape" (drowned) were linked in that phrase, both surfacing together at this moment in an essay about an altogether different poem. And behind that mediating Shelleyan couple we can glimpse the most heavily invested pair in de Man's own writing, de Man's Rousseau and Rousseau's Julie.[16]

What can be made of this strange irruption? why should these figures surface just here? Consider the second of the sentences just cited: "How are we to reconcile the *meaning* of face, with its promise of sense and of filial preservation, with its *function* as the relentless undoer of its own claims?" It draws together the conceptual threads of the essay into an aporetic formulation familiar to de Man's readers, the impossibility of reconciling language as signification with language as performance. But it does so in a syntax that is familiar in another way: for it is the syntax of "How can we know the dancer from the dance?"—the line de Man has taught us to read not only as a (celebratory) rhetorical question but also as a genuine and genuinely "anguished question" (*AR*, p. 11; *RR*, pp. 201–2). And in fact a note of anxiety clings to the question as it is formulated here—a tone created by words like "filial" and "relentless." The effect is of still another surfacing, in this case of the pathos that had been suppressed in de Man's reading of the "Blessed Babe" passage. It returns here as another specular pairing, mother and child, but equivocally charged. It can be read as an attempt to align "meaning" with the mother's preserving (read: sheltering) tenderness, "function" with the child's aggressive (read: both positing and undoing) "claims." But the ambiguity of "filial preservation"—the child could be taken as either the beneficiary or the agent of that saving act of sense-making—keeps the sentence from stabilizing itself in any clear-cut fashion. It remains open to the unsettling shifts of position characteristic of specular structures, and haunted by the pathos of intimacy and loss (that is, of seduction and threat) such structures generate, here indeterminately that of Wordsworth's Babe and its Mother; of the Drowned Man in *The Prelude*, whom de Man had earlier coupled with the poet's own dead mother (*RR*, p. 73); of the drowned Shelley and the shape that "goes under" (*RR*, p. 114);[17] of "Rousseau" and the shape; and so on.

This is a moment of madness, that "madness of words" that de Man names as such in "Shelley Disfigured" (*RR*, p. 122): figuration turns hallucinatory in an attempt to render intelligible what, according to de Man, cannot be rendered intelligible, the "radical estrangement between the meaning and the performance of any text" (*AR*, p. 298). Or, again in the language of *Allegories of Reading*, it is the moment in which "the writer severs himself from the intelligibility of his own text," one that "has to be thematized as a sacrifice" (*AR*, p. 205–7)[18] or that, "from the point of view of the subject . . . can only be experienced as a dismemberment, a beheading or a castration" (*AR*, p. 296). Or as a drowning, we could add, if we would include the particular obsessive figure encountered here. For the form this madness adopts is that of obsession, of the repeated filling-in of unavoidable structures with images drawn from a limited set of anxieties. The attempt to dwell, speculatively, on the difference between language as meaning and language as performance cannot issue in a coolly univocal discourse. Instead the effort will trigger what I earlier called a pathos of uncertain agency, in which questions of intelligibility will be reinscribed as questions of activity or passivity, guilt or innocence, and play themselves out in obsessively repeated figures.[19] De Man has to warn himself and his readers against this pathos, for it will always appear as a distraction: it will never be quite what he is talking about. But he cannot avoid falling into it, nor—and this is a stronger claim—can he or any other reader make do without it.

A final word about gender, since that has been one of the concerns of this paper from the start. Unlike Jacques Derrida, de Man has little to say, explicitly, about gender; it has been left to his readers to begin the work of articulating his implicit positions with those of other discourses, Derrida's, for example, or Lacan's or Kristeva's.[20] But we have seen how de Man has been drawn to analyze—and sometimes led to construct—scenarios in which characters face off against each other, and in which sexual difference is strongly marked. We need to ask in what ways, and at what point, the rhetorical operations he is concerned to track engage questions of gender. Of the various pairings I have been considering, the most illuminating for this issue is the confrontation of Rousseau and Marion in the last chapter of *Allegories of Reading*.

The tale of the "Purloined Ribbon," as de Man reconstructs it from the *Confessions* and the *Fourth Rêverie*, condenses the violent themes we have been examining—the "abjection" of a woman, the "castration" of a man. Rousseau imagines ("with some relish," de Man notes at *AR*, p. 279) that his slander has almost certainly driven Marion to prostitution and an early grave; in (partial and belated) compensation, he associates her story with stories of his own near-mutilation and near-beheading (*AR*, p. 297). De Man presents this narrative of "desire, shame, guilt, exposure and repression" (*AR*, p. 289) in all its pathos, but, in a characteristic move, questions its primacy. He cites Rousseau's explanation of how he was led to accuse Marion in the first place: "It is bizarre but it is true that my friendship for her was the cause of the accusation. She was present to my mind, I excused myself on the first thing that offered itself." And he acknowledges the possibility of a psychoanalytically informed reading: "Her name is pronounced almost unconsciously, as if it were a slip, a segment of the discourse of the other." In this account Marion is the "object of a desire" whose presence within the discursive chain is "motivated as the target of the entire action" (*AR*, pp. 288–89). Here her gender makes a difference; it is no accident that what can be considered the "hidden center" of the story is "Marion" and not, say, "Jules" or "Jim." But de Man doesn't stop there. After sketching this reading he goes on to offer an alternative, by first stressing the element of contingency in Rousseau's use of the odd phrase "le premier objet qui s'offrit" and then, by a passage to the limit, absolutizing that contingency: "Marion just happened to be the first thing that came to mind; any other name, any other word, any other sound or noise could have done just as well and Marion's entry into the discourse is a mere effect of chance" (*AR*, p. 288). At this point de Man adds a variant of the warning we have encountered at other points in his work:

> In the spirit of the text, one should resist all temptation to give any significance whatever to the sound "Marion." For it is only if the act that initiated the entire chain, the utterance of the sound "Marion," is truly without any conceivable motive that the total arbitrariness of the action becomes the most effective, the most efficaciously performative excuse of all. The estrangement between subject and utterance is then so radical that it escapes any mode of comprehension. When everything else fails, one can always plead insanity. (*AR*, p. 289.)

This is a warning with a difference, for the temptation we are being asked to resist is not that of being seduced by the pathos of Marion's plight, but rather that of giving "any significance whatever to the sound 'Marion,'" and thus putting oneself in a position to either enjoy or condemn Rousseau's misogynistically tinged speculations on what must have become of his victim. That is, we are being asked to resist, in Cynthia Chase's phrase, "giving a face to a name" (*Decomposing Figures*, p. 82), or, still more puzzlingly, we are being asked to resist conferring the status of "name" at all on the cluster of phonemes that makes up the utterance "Marion." Is this a case of de Man's adding the insult of depersonalization to the injuries Marion had already received, in reality and in lingering fantasy, at Rousseau's hands? Is a deconstructive reading here in complicity with the misogyny of its text? I think not, although the reading serves to reveal the forces at work behind that misogyny. Most explicitly, de Man's insistence on the in-significance of "Marion" asks to be taken, rather, as a counterirritant to Rousseau's lurid narrative, draining it of its misogynistic pathos by attributing the utterance "Marion" to chance, to "the absolute randomness of language, prior to any figuration or meaning" (*AR*, p. 299). At that radically "prior" moment (or, we could say, drawing on another of de Man's figures, in that puzzling "region") "Marion" is neither gendered nor otherwise determined.

De Man grants that to take the enunciation of the sound "Marion" in this fashion, as an assertion of the "radical irresponsibility of fiction," no doubt "appears paradoxical and far-fetched to the point of absurdity":

> It seems impossible to isolate the moment in which the fiction stands free of any signification; in the very moment at which it is posited, as well as in the context it generates, it gets at once misinterpreted into a determination which is, *ipso facto*, overdetermined. Yet without this moment, never allowed to exist as such, no such thing as a text is conceivable. (*AR*, p. 293.)

What is this moment whose half-life is zero, which never exists "as such" but only as necessarily misinterpreted in (more or less) lurid figuration? It is not, as some of de Man's critics have imagined, his mystified conjuring up of a moment of "pure language." De Man is quite explicit on that point, as the passage quoted earlier from his essay on Walter Benjamin makes clear: "Least of all is there something like a *reine Sprache*, a pure language, which does not exist except as a permanent disjunction which inhabits all languages as such" (*RT*, p. 92). That "permanent disjunction," we have seen, is neither a moment nor a region but a construction of the theorist's, arrived at in the process of coming to terms with the "radical estrangement between the meaning and the performance of any text,"[21] and imaged variously as a "dismembrance," or as a "hidden break," or as "the wound of a flaw," or, in the discussion of the *Fourth Rêverie*, as "the almost imperceptible crack of the purely gratuitous" (*AR*, p. 291). This means not just that the "radical estrangement" that is the object of the theorist's attention can only be addressed in further figures, but also that it can only be experienced by the theorist as an "estrangement between subject and utterance" (*AR*, p. 289)—that is, as a sense of uncertain agency. But we have seen that the elective embodiment of the pathos of uncertain agency is the specular structure, one that locates the subject in a vacillating relation to the flawed or dismembered or disfigured (but invariably gendered) object of its attention. Here questions of sexual difference, desire, and misogyny come back into play. They are, in de Man's writing, both recurrent and judged nevertheless to be derivative. What he liked to call "rigor" meant, among other things, adopting the (necessarily unstable) position from which that judgment could be made.[22]

PART IV

The Analytic of Rhetoric

Analytic Speech: From Restricted to General Rhetoric

MIKKEL BORCH-JACOBSEN

Has rhetoric ended? Or can we today still make it serve some end? Is it still the productive, influential *techné* of which the Ancients spoke? Is it dead, "dried up" (as Martin Heidegger says of the flowers of rhetoric),[1] or is it "living" (as Paul Ricoeur says of metaphor)?[2]

All depends on what is meant by "rhetoric." Defined as the theory of tropes or of figures of speech, rhetoric undoubtedly died in the mid-nineteenth century. Roland Barthes, Gérard Genette, Ricoeur, and Tzvetan Todorov have all variously written out its death certificate by imputing what they see as rhetoric's two-thousand-year decline to a progressive restriction of its range and objectives: "natural eloquence" was reduced to a codification of probable argumentation; the great edifice of oratorical eloquence then shrank to the study of literary and poetic *elocutio; elocutio* subsequently diminished to a theory of tropes; tropes were limited to metaphor and metonymy; and, to end it all, the whole of rhetoric was defined as metaphor alone.[3] Thus, in their accounts, the history of rhetoric is a lethal "generalized restriction" (Genette, "La rhétorique," p. 158).

To say that rhetoric is dead by restriction, however, is also to say that only restricted rhetoric is dead. Nothing prevents one part or another of ancient rhetoric-in-general from surviving, reviving, or simply prospering under another name. How could it be otherwise? The *techné rhétoriké* dealt with language that allows effective action on another; thus its vast "empire" (Barthes, "L'ancienne

Translated from the French by Douglas Brick.

rhétorique," p. 174) comprised almost all aspects of language taken as an act of communication: *inventio, dispositio, elocutio, actio, memoria.* It would be very surprising if we had not kept or recaptured something of this domain, albeit unknowingly. To discover present-day relatives of ancient rhetoric, we need not invoke specialized research on "speech acts" or on the "pragmatics of communication," both attentive to the active and operant value of language. It suffices to think of the modern techniques of mass communication, whether advertising or political propaganda. Our "mediatized" societies, however different from Sicilian or Athenian democracies, are nonetheless similarly regulated by a rhetorical politics centered on the persuasive power of the probable and of popular opinion, of *eikos* and *endoxa.* Given the phenomenon of the mass media, how can we doubt that rhetoric is alive and well in the heart of our societies? Our very lives, both public and private, tend to turn (or to return) to rhetoric, to pure "commonplace."

Therefore it may be retrospective illusion to speak of the "end" or "death" of rhetoric. The history of rhetoric is not the continuous and closed story of its progressive restriction, but the discontinuous and indefinite one of a permanent tension between two uses of the term: one of extreme generality (and therefore also extreme vagueness), which makes it an art of persuasion (this is its oratorical, pragmatic, or "impressive" pole, corresponding roughly to what G. A. Kennedy calls "primary rhetoric");[4] the other of more restricted scope, which makes it an art of speaking well (this is its literary, poetic, ornamental, or "expressive" pole, corresponding roughly to what Kennedy calls "secondary rhetoric" and V. Florescu *letteraturizzazione*).[5] Between these two poles there is a constant oscillation punctuated by "deaths" and "renaissances" of rhetoric. That "secondary rhetoric" has regularly tended to replace "primary rhetoric" does not exclude (but, on the contrary, explains) the latter's having no less regularly reasserted its rights each time that historic conditions made the need of return to a persuasive or "impressive" use of language felt. No doubt today we are witnessing a resurgence of "primary rhetoric": the very fact that we ask ourselves about the "ends" of rhetoric testifies that we are living the nth chapter of that tension between a taxonomy of the figures of speaking well and a pragmatics (or politics) of effective speaking.

Conforming to the old probationary technique of the exemplum, in the interest of persuasive effectiveness, I propose to illustrate this "chapter" with a limited case, psychoanalytic rhetoric, or rather—for it is necessary to qualify immediately—what is conventionally called psychoanalytic "rhetoric."

The assimilation of dream work, slips of the tongue, and symptoms to the figures of rhetoric has become one of the most insistent topoi of our linguistico-psychoanalytic culture since Emile Benveniste, Roman Jakobson, and Jacques Lacan first advanced it in a series of famous articles that appeared in 1956–57.[6] Benveniste, in a rather vague and prudent manner, outlined a comparison between the oneiric processes described by Freud and the stylistic figures of speech: metaphor, metonymy, synecdoche, but also euphemism, allusion, antiphrasis, litotes, ellipsis, and so on. Jakobson, more precisely (or more audaciously), proposed assimilating displacement and condensation to metonymy, identification and symbolism to metaphor—these two rhetorical figures being themselves reduced, by a perilous leap, to the two properly linguistic operations of syntagmatic combination and paradigmatic selection. Lacan, extending the hypotheses of Jakobson, with no less temerity suggested identifying condensation and symptom with metaphor, displacement and desire with metonymy, thus promoting a linguistic interpretation of the unconscious. These formulations, however different, agree that there is a "figurality" of desire, a "rhetoric of Freud," a "rhetoric of denial," and even a catachretical "anasemy" of psychoanalytic conceptuality.[7]

Is this "rhetorical" interpretation of the unconscious legitimate—beyond the objections that can be made to details touching such and such a more or less improper (more or less metaphoric) displacement of concepts? The principal reproach I would make is not that such an interpretation reduces the unconscious and its manifestations to rhetorical processes. Many passages in Freud's work can support such a reading, and I will return to them in a moment. Rather I would point out that this interpretation restricts the operations of the unconscous to a rhetoric that is itself restricted, whether the restriction takes the extreme form of an integral reabsorption of rhetoric into linguistics (as in the works of Jakobson and Lacan) or the inverse form of a boundless generalization to simple figural displacement (as in the Lyotard of *Discours, figure*). Psychoanalytic "rhetoric," as it has been understood and practiced for nearly thirty years, is in reality *restricted* rhetoric, rhetoric restricted to the figures of speaking well (or, in this case, the impossibility of speaking well), and also, therefore, to a language amputated from its effective, pragmatic, or persuasive dimension. We should recall that the inverse of such amputation—an examination of the persuasive power of language—was Freud's initial point of departure. Moreover, this point of departure is also, I will show, Freud's point of arrival: a pure question mark. To examine this is to explore the understanding that we today can have of psychoanalysis, of rhetoric, and of their common power.

The psychoanalytic "talking cure" is historically rooted in the practice of hypnosis, more precisely in what Hippolyte Bernheim, in his 1886 *De la suggestion et de ses applications à la thérapeutique*, called "suggestive psychotherapy." But what is "suggestive psychotherapy" or "psychical treatment," as Freud, who translated the work in 1888, preferred to call it? In the article "Psychical Treatment," a "defense and illustration" of psychotherapy published by Freud in 1890, we find the following definition: "'Psychical treatment' [*Seelenbehandlung*] denotes treatment taking its start in the mind [*Behandlung von der Seele aus*], treatment (whether of mental or psychical disorders) by measures which operate in the first instance and immediately upon the human mind. Foremost among such measures is the use of words; and words are the essential tool of mental treatment."[8] Contrary to modern medicine, which treats body and soul by means of the body, psychical treatment treats soul and body by means of the soul, by utilizing the word. Freud concedes, however, anticipating certain developments in *Totem and Taboo*, that this attributes a quasimagical power to words: "A layman . . . will feel that he is being asked to believe in magic. And he will not be so very wrong, for the words which we use in our everyday speech are nothing other than watered-down magic" ("Psychical Treatment," p. 283). This will necessitate, he adds, "a roundabout path in order to explain how science sets about restoring to words a part at least of their former magical power" (ibid.).

The goal of this roundabout path—which is the detour by hypnosis—is clear. Science (here medical science) must recuperate, to its profit, the power of language abandoned to magicians, preachers, and healers. That power—of which Freud remarks in passing that it is all the more effective in that it is employed in isolation from the discourse of science, in the domain of religious faith and popular prejudice—that properly miraculous power of the word, is persuasion, *Einreden*. In brief, it is the rhetorical *dunamis*, the power of enchantment stigmatized by Plato under the name of *goétèia* (*Menexenus* 234c–235a) of which Nietzsche said, anticipating Freud, that it "does not intend to instruct, but to transmit to others a subjective emotion and apprehension."[9] How, in fact, does the soul act on the body? Essentially by the intermediary of affects that "are characterized," says Freud, "by a quite special connection with somatic processes": grief, terror, anguish, joy, enthusiasm, or *gläubige Erwartung*, "confident expectation" vis-à-vis the therapist. It is by language that a person can communicate an affect to another person, can influence him, convince him, move him, and so forth. (One will have recognized in passing the two objectives of rhetorical *inventio*: *fidem facere et animos impellere*.) Freud's provisional conclusion is: "Words are the most important media by which one man seeks to bring his influence to bear on another; words are a good method of producing mental changes in the person to whom they are addressed. So that there is no longer anything puzzling in the assertion that the magic of words can remove the symptoms of illness" ("Psychical Treatment," p. 292).

But this is not all. The affective power of the word would remain abandoned to chance and empiricism (that is, would remain "magic") if science did not have at its disposal a *techné* capable not only of provoking such and such an affect, but also of inducing *patheia* as such, a "mental compliance," or what Freud calls, after Bernheim, "suggestibility" ("Psychical Treatment," p. 293). That technique (that "specific therapeutic method"; "Psychical Treatment," p. 294) is hypnotism, with which, Freud tells us, "modern mental treatment has taken its start" ("Psychical Treatment," p. 293). In effect, he explains, playing on the word *Ein-reden*, one can "talk" the patient "into" a special state of "mental compliance," in which he becomes "obedient and credulous" vis-à-vis the hypnotist, submits himself to the hypnotist's injunctions, models his "mental life" on the hypnotist's, and so on ("Psychical Treatment," pp. 293–95). In brief, by a fabulous process (which would have been the dream of the ancient rhetoricians) one can persuade the listener to be "persuadable," "affectable." Suggestion (which is, says Freud, the technical name of the "words spoken by the hypnotist which have [these] magical results"; "Psychical Treatment," p. 296) possesses the remarkable property of annulling (at least for the hypnotized person) the distance between locutor and listener, emitter and receiver. It does not communicate a message (information, or even an order), it communicates a state of faith (*Gläubigkeit*)—that is to say, both a receptivity to the message and an identification with the emitter. Freud wrote in his preface to the German edition of Bernheim's book: "What distinguishes a suggestion from other kinds of psychical influence, such as a command or the giving of a piece of information or instruction, is that in the case of a suggestion an idea is aroused in another person's brain which is not examined in regard to its origin but is accepted just as though it had arisen spontaneously in that brain."[10] Hence its affective (pathogenic or, contrarily, cathartic) power, since the listener completely appropriates for himself this discourse of the other; hence also its contaminating, contagious power, since the listener identifies with and mimics it. As Freud says, "Words have once more regained their magic" ("Psychical Treatment," p. 296)— that is, their mimetic magic, their mimologic omnipotence, described (and condemned) by Plato in Books 3 and 10 of the *Republic*.

This reading of "Psychical Treatment" could take us far toward what Freud later called the "magical omnipotence of thoughts" and the absence of doubt and negation proper to unconscious "primary processes":[11] the singular "logic" of the unconscious is, undoubtedly, the mimo-patho-logic of hypnotic suggestion. That is to say, it is the rhetorical mimo-patho-logic understood as the "art of conducting souls by words" (which is Socrates' definition in *Phaedrus*).[12] If the effectiveness of the psychoanalytic cure rests entirely on the power of speech, as Lacan has repeated many times, this power was originally, in Freud's work, that of "suggestive," affective, and impressive—in brief, persuasive—speech. What Freud rediscovered, around 1890, in Bernheim's, Joseph Delboeuf's, or Pierre Janet's researches on verbal suggestion, was at base a new version (with scientific and experimental pretensions) of the "pathic" part of ancient rhetoric, as we know it in its codification by Aristotle in Book 2 of the *Rhetoric* (1377b–1391b). How can we not see that the project outlined in "Psychical Treatment" is a sort of medical rhetoric, fallen away from its relation with scientific medicine and yet, nevertheless, sufficiently "technical" (thanks to hypnotism) to escape from empiricism and from the magic of healers? It is the project—halfway between *épistémé* and *empeiria*—of a *patho-logy*, in the double sense of an affecting discourse (capable of provoking certain *pathé*) and of a discourse *on* affects (of an *Affektivitätslehre*, as Freud would later say).

One might object that this patho-logical *techné* has exactly nothing to do with psychoanalysis and that Freud quickly abandoned it in favor of the technique of "free association" (by the patient), and an "art of interpreting"[13] (by the therapist). The hypno-suggestive technique was expressly rejected by Freud (even in its "cathartic" form), for a very simple reason, which is, at bottom, reason itself. The patho-logy, understood as discourse *on* affects (thus as theoretical discourse), can only compete with, and finally eliminate, the patho-logy, understood as affective, persuasive discourse. For how is one to say the truth about this false power, this *pseudologos* that makes one believe in no-matter-what and causes, according to Socrates, "that which is small to appear large, and that which is large, small"? As Plato says in *Phaedrus*, the rhetoricians do not know what they are saying (that is to say, what they are doing): they speak *to* the soul of their listeners, but not *of* the soul in its relation with speech, and therefore they cannot produce the truth of their own psychagogic discourse (266e–267c; 270b–272d).

Beginning in 1895, Freud directed just such a reproach against suggestion, and that reproach is a sign of a forceful return in his discourse to the values of truth and scientificity, in the very place where the hypno-suggestive *techné* was only interested in therapeutic effectiveness. Freud does not object to the effectiveness of suggestion (on the contrary, here and there Freud even regrets its loss),[14] but rather to its irrational, "mysterious,"[15] and thus unmanageable and "uncheckable" character.[16] This critique is made explicit in chapter 4 of *Group Psychology and the Analysis of the Ego*: Suggestion—which is supposed to explain everything—cannot even explain itself; a word for the "magic of words," it would itself be a "magic word," a *Zauberwort*, incapable of resolving the enigma (*Rätsel*) of an "influence without adequate logical foundation" (pp. 88–90); in brief, it designates a power not that of the truth, not a knowledge. Hence, of course, its condemnation as "violence" and as a hold exercised on another, a condemnation that is itself very violent (indeed "magic") and that evokes Plato's expulsion of rhetoric from the philosophical *logos*. Psychoanalytic dialogue has often been compared to Platonic dialectic,[17] and here this comparison is more pertinent than ever: the passage from suggestive technique to analytic "talking cure" corresponds almost point for point with the Platonic passage from rhetorical argumentation, in which the stakes are persuasive "probability," to the "true rhetoric" or *dialèktikè*, in which the stakes are "the truth about the subject that you speak . . . about" (*Phaedrus* 277b).

The "thing of which one speaks" in the analytical *dialegesthai* and about which one is to arrive at a consensus or *homologia* is here the speaking subject himself, however. (In this the psychoanalytic cure is already much closer, as Lacan has noted, to dialectic in its modern Hegelian form.)[18] The post-Cartesian Freud conceives of truth as certitude, as the self-knowledge of consciousness. This attitude explains, beyond historical vicissitude, why "psychical treatment" passes from the persuasive setup of hypnosis, where it is the other who *ein-redet* the subject (in a state of unconsciousness), to the auto-enunciative setup of psychoanalysis, where the subject speaks of himself to another who is now only the mediator of his certainty (of the *Erinnerung*, the "realization" of the repressed). The treatment continues to be a treatment by words and by affects, though now in the sense that the words of the subject must adequately express (and thus "abreact," as Freud says)[19] an affect that has been detached from its proper representation because of repression. As for the therapist, he no longer speaks (or he speaks very little); moreover, he becomes himself one of the "transferential" forms in which the subject fallaciously expresses his affect. In a word, he becomes a *figure* of the subject and of his auto-enunciative discourse.

It is here that Benveniste, Jakobson, and Lacan have, more or less legitimately, grafted on the rhetorico-linguistic interpretation. Once one admits that the subject's discourse (which includes his dreams and symptoms) is the indirect expression of an affect that cannot be directly expressed because of repression and censorship, then the different operations of symbolization located by Freud can all be described as the distance between a proper sense and a transposed or tropic sense (one need only think of *Übertragung*, which exactly translates Aristotle's *metaphora*). By radicalizing certain Freudian themes (for example, the necessary inaccessibility of the unconscious apart from its "translation" to consciousness,[20] or the figural character of the analytic *Bildersprache*),[21] one easily arrives at Lacan's thesis: the subject can only signify himself by metaphorizing himself in the signifier by which he expresses himself, and therefore, he cannot signify himself except by losing himself as subject of the enunciation, in accordance with a metaphoricity without proper sense (or a *signifiance* without signified), which makes the whole structure of the unconscious like language and the "discourse of the Other."

This interpretation, however, continues to make the analytic setup into a setup of auto-expression (even if this is declared impossible), and the "rhetoric" of the unconscious into a rhetoric restricted to the figures of discourse (even if these are defined in terms of signifying substitution, and no longer as figures of sense). The Lacanian subject cannot properly express himself, since his discourse is always already that of the Other—but that is exactly his most proper truth (which says, "I, truth, speak" and which, as we know, must be taken "literally"; *Ecrits*, p. 411), and the "discourse of the Other" has nothing to do with some "persuasive" or "suggestive" discourse of the analyst. Lacan's whole enterprise is expressly directed against an interpretation of the analytic cure as persuasion or suggestion, which he always denounces in the name of "Freudian truth" as "imaginary identification with the analyst" and "alienation" into the specular "petit autre." Freudian rhetoric is perhaps that of the "metaphor of the subject,"[22] but it should definitely not be that of the persuasion of the subject, according to Lacan.

Such an interpretation would be unproblematic if Freud had kept to his initial rejection of verbal suggestion and of the persuasive dimension of words. But that is not the case, and on this point the "truth" or "the letter of Freud" is much less univocal (in any case, much less appropriable) than Lacan says. Suggestion—more precisely, the *question* of suggestion—returned in many ways to the center of Freud's preoccupations, above all in the practice of the cure itself, under the form of the transference. Freud realized very early on that the analyst's abandonment of all forms of suggestion or verbal persuasion did not prevent the "spontaneous" reappearance in the patient of the suggestibility that is characteristic of hypnosis. On the contrary—this is the phenomenon of transference called "positive"—the more silent and reserved the analyst remains, the greater the patient's passion for him: the subject "loves" his analyst, thinks only of him, submits to his "influence," has faith in his interpretations, and so on. All of these traits being those of the hypnotic "relation," Freud could not miss making the connection. To quote the *Selbstdarstellung*, one among many analogous passages: "In every analytic treatment there arises, without the physician's agency, an intense emotional relationship between the patient and the analyst which is not to be accounted for by the actual situation. . . . We can easily recognize it as the same dynamic factor which the hypnotists have named 'suggestibility,' which is the agent of hypnotic *rapport*."[23]

This affirmation has many implications (for instance, for the henceforth problematic "objectivity" of analytic interpretations, or for the no less problematic possibility of a final "dissolution" of the transference). Here I will simply note that the connection between transference and suggestibility causes an inevitable resurgence in reverse, so to speak, of the whole problem of the pathologic, understood as affective power, and of the "magic" of language. At bottom, what is transference as described by Freud if not hypnosis without a hypnotist, if not persuasion without a rhetorician, since it is produced in the absence of any direct suggestion? Paradoxically, the phenomenon of the transference reveals that the influence of the hypnotist and/or analyst is based not on a particular technique or power, but rather on an a priori affectability (a "spontaneous receptivity") in the patient—that is to say, on the "rhetoricity" of the affect *as such*, a rhetoricity anterior to any verbal persuasion and also to any metaphoric expression of passions. The analytic pathology in its ensemble, now understood as *Affektivitätslehre* and the theory of drives, thus finds itself concerned with the problem of rhetoric and its power. Why does another affect me? Why am I affectable, suggestible, persuadable by the discourse of the other—even, and especially, when he says nothing? Is it because I feel an affect in his regard (because I love him, or the unconscious personage that he represents "transferentially")? Or does he affect me with "my" affect, because I have no affect of my own?

This is the question of the "affective tie" with another, alias the "enigma of suggestive influence." This last question appears (or reappears) in *Group Psychology and the Analysis of the Ego*, in a detour made in an inquiry on the nature of the social tie. Why there rather than elsewhere? Because Freud, in conformity with the analyses of Gustave Le Bon (and also Gabriel Tarde and William McDougall), understands the essence of social being on the model of the crowd (or *Masse*) dominated by a leader (or *Führer*). This

136

model is that of collective hypnosis, as the characteristics of "group psychology" enumerated by Freud, following Le Bon, can testify: disappearance of any individual will or personality, affective contagion, suggestibility, hypnotic submission to a "prestigious" leader, and finally, the "magic power of words." Freud writes: "The crowd is extremely credulous and open to influence . . . the improbable does not exist for it. It thinks in images . . . whose agreement with reality is never checked by any reasonable agency. . . . A group, further, is subject to the truly magical power of words; they can evoke the most formidable tempests in the group mind, and are also capable of stilling them. . . . And, finally, groups have never thirsted after truth" (*Group Psychology*, pp. 78, 80). This dramatic picture is not an aberrant or pathological phenomenon. It is the very image of our mediatized societies, which I invoked earlier. It is also the vision that the fascist ideologues, great readers of Le Bon (if not of Freud), made into a historical reality in the 1930's with the terrifying efficiency that we all know. And it is, finally, almost to the last detail, the picture accusingly painted by Plato of the listeners enchanted by poets and orators. Here we arrive at the common root of the patho-logic, of rhetoric, and of politics.

Significantly, Freud, while subscribing unreservedly to this description of "group psychology," refuses the hypno-suggestive theory that underlies it in the work of Le Bon. (It is in *Group Psychology* that Freud's virulent critique of suggestion as *Zauberwort* is to be found.) If the individuals assembled in a mass are so easily persuaded by another, it is not, he explains, by virtue of a mysterious "suggestibility," but because of *love* for the leader. More precisely, if the social tie is really a mimetico-affective tie—an identificatory *Gefühlsbindung*, according to Freud—it is because the members of the mass identify with each other in the mode of hysteria (here a collective one) as a function of their love for a common "object," the *Führer*. Far from being a mass affective contagion, the social tie indirectly expresses the affects of individuals: the identification is a sort of libidinal metaphor (a comparison on the base of an "analogy"),[24] and the *Führer* takes his power from being a transferential figure of desire just like the analyst or hypnotist. Exit, consequently, the phantom of suggestion and of the "magic of words."

In *Group Psychology*, however, this official doctrine of the social tie is paralleled by a different, much more problematic doctrine, which returns us to the "enigma of suggestive influence." For the affective tie with the *Führer*, Freud had to concede, is not a libidinal tie. It is a perfectly "desexualized" tie of submission, analogous if not identical, he says, to the "mysterious" hypnotic rapport; he proposes to assimilate it to the tie with the narcissistic ego ideal. Now, this tie, Freud had expressly established in chapter 7, is really just identification, understood as the "earliest and original form of emotional tie," anterior to any libidinal-erotic investment (p. 107). "Identification is known to psychoanalysis as the earliest expression of an emotional tie with another person. . . . A little boy will exhibit a special interest in his father; he would like to grow like him and be like him, and take his place everywhere. We may say simply that he takes his father as his ideal" (p. 105).

To summarize briefly, the affective social tie—that is, the whole domain of suggestion, of mimetico-affective contagion, of the magical power of words, and so on—reposes on the equally hypnotic tie with the *Führer*-Ego-Ideal, itself reduced to the affective tie of "primary identification."[25] This solution to the "enigma of suggestive influence"—and therefore to the *Einreden*, the power of rhetoric— is merely *that enigma itself*, brought back to the vanished ground of the "subject." For what is the identificatory *Gefühlsbindung* if not another word for stating (or restating) openness to influence, passiveness in regard to another, or depropriation of the affect? To affirm that "the earliest emotional tie with another person" is identification is, in effect, to assert that affect as such is identificatory, mimetic, and that there is no "proper" affect except on the condition of a prior "affection" of the ego by another. Another does not affect me because I feel such and such an affect in regard to him, nor even because he succeeds in communicating an affect to me by way of words. He affects me because "I" *am* that "other," following an identification that is my affection, the most strange alteration of my proper auto-affection. My identity is a passion. And reciprocally, my passions are always identificatory.

Here, therefore, is the enigma—the renewed enigma of rhetoric—and I do not believe that it can be resolved. This enigma hides nothing, dissimulates nothing—or only *the* nothing, the absence of any ground, of every *subjectum* and of every subject. It is the irrevealable enigma of a *mimesis* that is all the more effective and "technical" because it has nothing of its own, and because it creates from nothing. Thus there is absolutely nothing to say about it unless it be to repeat, following Freud and so many others, that this enigma is not that of truth. This does not render it any less powerful, as those who have tried to silence rhetoric have always recognized. For, as rhetoric herself says, through the mouth of Socrates in *Phaedrus*: "Why do you extraordinary people talk such nonsense? I never insist on ignorance of the truth on the part of one who would learn to speak; on the contrary, if my advice goes for anything, it is that he should only resort to me after he has come into possession of truth: what I do, however, pride myself on is that without my aid knowledge of what is true will get a man no nearer to mastering the art of persuasion." (Plato, *Phaedrus* 260d.)

Rhetoric and Relevance

DAN SPERBER AND DEIRDRE WILSON

The student of rhetoric is faced with a paradox and a dilemma. We will suggest a solution to the dilemma, but this will only make the paradox more blatant.

Let us begin with the paradox. Rhetoric took pride of place in formal education for two and a half millennia. Its very rich and complex history is worth detailed study, but it can be summarized in a few sentences. Essentially the same substance was passed on by eighty generations of teachers to eighty generations of pupils. If there was a general tendency, it consisted simply in a narrowing down of the subject matter of rhetoric: one of its five branches, *elocutio*, the study of figures of speech, gradually displaced the others, and in some schools became identified with rhetoric *tout court*. (We ourselves will be guilty of this and several other simplifications.) This narrowing was not even offset by a theoretical deepening. Pierre Fontanier's *Les figures du discours* does not substantially improve on Quintilian's *Institutio oratoria*, despite the work of sixty generations of scholars in between.

The combination of such institutional success with such intellectual barrenness is puzzling. Moreover, the history of rhetoric cuts across major social changes: the eighty generations of pupils had little in common, yet Greek politicians, Roman lawyers, medieval clerks, Renaissance aristocrats, and nineteenth-century bourgeois were taught the same thing. This extraordinary institutional resilience of an otherwise rigid rhetoric turns puzzle into paradox.

Then came the Romantics—and the end of rhetoric, or so it seemed. The Romantics were particularly scathing about the treatment in classical rhetoric of metaphor, irony, and other figures of speech. In classical rhetoric, figures were seen as ornaments added to a text, which made it more pleasant and hence more convincing, but without altering its content. It was said that tropes in particular achieved this ornamental effect by replacing a dull literal expression of the author's thought by a more attractive figurative expression: that is, an expression whose literal meaning is set aside and replaced by a figurative meaning.

A mother says to her child:

"You're a piglet!"

A rhetorician would analyze "piglet" in this context as a metaphor figuratively meaning "dirty child." Or the mother might say:

"You're such a clean child!"

A rhetorician would analyze "clean child" as an irony figuratively meaning, again, "dirty child." The figurative meaning of the metaphorical or ironical expression is claimed to be identical with the literal meaning of the ordinary expression it replaces.

Against the notion of a figure as a mere ornament, the Romantics maintained that a felicitous trope cannot be paraphrased. Thus Coleridge argues that the "infallible test of a blameless style" is "its *untranslateableness* in words of the same language without injury to the meaning. Be it observed, however, that I include in the *meaning* of a word not only its correspondent object but likewise all the associations which it recalls."[1] Though only a modest stylist, the mother who calls her child a piglet achieves some unparaphrasable effects: for instance, she appears more forgiving than if she had called him a dirty child. Or in saying "You're such a clean child!" the mother conveys not only that the child is dirty but also—with a light touch that explicit paraphrase would lose—that he ought to be clean.

The Romantic critics were unquestionably right to point out the richness and importance of those effects of figures of speech that are not maintained under paraphrase. These effects were merely mentioned by classical rhetoricians; they were not described, let alone explained. But for all their well-taken criticisms and subtle observations, the Romantics were content to talk about tropes in metaphorical terms and proposed no explicit theory of irony either; if anything, they cast doubt on the very possibility of developing a nonmetaphorical theory of tropes, by entirely rejecting the notion of a literal meaning—the "proper meaning superstition," as I. A. Richards calls it.[2]

The Romantics' criticisms have been generally accepted by the contemporary academic heirs of the rhetoricians. It has become almost a commonplace that, in Jonathan Culler's words, "one can never construct a position outside tropology from which to view it; one's own terms are always caught up in the processes they attempt to describe."[3]

This academization of Romanticism led—paradoxically—to a resurgence of classical rhetoric. For if "words are equal, free, of age," as Victor Hugo said,[4] scorning rhetorical typologies, then the words occurring in these typologies are themselves inferior to none and can be freely used. And so we find, in modern literary studies, a Romantic use of classical rhetorical terms: they no longer have "proper meanings," but they suggest subtle distinctions and evoke scholarly sophistication and historical depth.

Let us make our position clear: we see nothing wrong with a free use of all the resources of language—poetic use and rhetorical jargon included—to interpret particular experiences or particular texts. However, we do not believe that interpretations of particulars can be generalized into proper theories. Proper theories should be descriptive and explanatory rather than interpretive.[5] We are aware that post-Romantic, poststructuralist sophisticates have even less faith in proper theories than they do in proper meanings. But we are not sophisticated. It seems to us a worthwhile pursuit to develop a theory dealing with the kind of phenomena classical rhetoric tried to describe, but with even greater explicitness than it tried to achieve.

And so, the dilemma: it seems that we must either keep to the relative rigor of a rhetorical approach and miss an essential—maybe *the* essential—dimension of language use, or start from the Romantic intuition that linguistic creativity cannot be reduced to a mere set of combination rules, and abandon all ambition in the direction of a scientific theory forever. More specifically: On the one side, we have the view that an utterance or a text has a literal meaning, which, in the absence of indications to the contrary, it is presumed to convey; this view allows a neat definition of semantics as the study of literal meanings, and of tropology as the study of departures from literal meanings. On the other side, we have the view of meaning as mishmash in motion, analytically unappealing, but true to life.

Note that both classical rhetoricians and their Romantic critics take it for granted that if there is such a thing as literal meaning, then utterances come with a presumption of literalness. We disagree. It is possible to keep a notion of literal meaning, which is analytically useful, and drop the presumption of literalness, which is implausible, provided that a presumption of relevance is introduced. In this way, we will argue, theory and intuition can be reconciled.

The rhetorician's dilemma is a special case of an even more fundamental problem in the study of human communication. From ancient rhetoric to modern semiotics, communication has been seen as a process of encoding (by the communicator), followed by a process of decoding (by the audience). The existence of a common code has been taken as a necessary and essentially sufficient condition for communication. The code model of communication has an appealing simplicity. However, it has become more and more manifest that human communication cannot be fully explained in terms of this model.

Given a rich enough code—and human languages are certainly rich enough in the required sense—whatever can be encoded in one way can be encoded in another, that is, can be paraphrased. The fact that communication achieves some unparaphrasable effects—which particularly interested the Romantics—strongly suggests that more is communicated than is actually encoded. Moreover, as modern pragmatics has repeatedly shown, communicators somehow manage to convey implicitly, and without encoding it, information that *could* have been explicitly encoded.

How are unencodable poetic effects, and encodable but unencoded "implicatures," communicated? Modern pragmatics has an answer for implicatures: they are inferred by the audience on the basis of what can be decoded, together with contextual information and general expectations about the communicator's behavior. Inference, then, is viewed as a supplement to encoding and decoding, designed to economize on effort. However, the special flavor and uses of implicit communication, and of poetic effects, remain as mysterious in modern pragmatics as they were in classical rhetoric.

In *Relevance: Communication and Cognition,* we have developed a novel approach to human communication, based on a general view of cognition, an approach that, we will try to show, helps solve the rhetorician's dilemma and its modern pragmatic counterpart.

Instead of viewing the fully coded communication of a well-defined paraphrasable meaning as the norm, we treat it as a theoretical limit that is never encountered. Instead of treating a mix of explicitness and implicitness, of paraphrasable and unparaphrasable effects, as a departure from the norm, we regard it as normal, ordinary communication. We define communication not as a process by which a meaning in the communicator's head is duplicated in the addressee's, but as a more or less controlled modification by the communicator of the audience's mental landscape—or "cognitive environment" as we call it—achieved in an intentional and overt way.

A person's cognitive environment can be modified by the addition of a single piece of new information, but it can equally well be modified by a diffuse increase in the saliency, or in the plausibility, of a whole range of assumptions, yielding what will be subjectively experienced as an "impression." Between the communication of specific information and the communication of an impression, there is, in our approach, a continuum of cases. Thus, instead of contrasting "meaning" and "rhetorical effects," or "denotation" and "connotation," we include both under a single unitary notion of "cognitive effects." The communication of such cognitive effects is essentially inferential. Decoded meaning structures are not directly adopted by the audience as thoughts of their own; they serve rather as very rich evidence that can be exploited by largely unconscious inferential processes to arrive at comprehension proper. Exploited, but how? Under what guidance? This is where considerations of relevance come in.

Human information processing requires some mental effort and achieves some cognitive effect. The effort required is an effort of attention, memory, and reasoning. The effect achieved is the alteration of the individual's cognitive environment, by the addition of new beliefs, the cancellation of old ones, or merely the alteration of the saliency or strength of beliefs already held. We may characterize a comparative notion of *relevance* in terms of effect and effort as follows:

(a) Everything else being equal, the greater the cognitive effect achieved by the processing of a given piece of information, the greater its relevance for the individual who processes it.

(b) Everything else being equal, the greater the effort involved in the processing of a given piece of information, the smaller its relevance for the individual who processes it.

We claim that humans automatically aim at maximal relevance, that is, maximal cognitive effect for minimal processing effort. This is the most general factor that determines the course of human information processing. It determines which information is attended to, which background assumptions are retrieved from memory and used as context, which inferences are drawn.

To communicate is, in the first place, to claim someone's attention. People will not pay attention to a phenomenon unless they expect it to be relevant enough to them. Hence, to communicate is to imply that the phenomenon displayed, the linguistic utterance for instance, is relevant enough to be worth the audience's attention. Any utterance addressed to someone automatically conveys a presumption of its own relevance. This fact we call the *principle of relevance*.

A communicator puts a conceptual structure into her audience's head—by means, say, of an act of mimicry that calls to mind a description of the act or object it resembles, or by means of an utterance that is automatically decoded into a semantic representation. If the presumption of relevance conveyed by such an act of communication is borne out, then the effort needed to construct this conceptual structure will not be wasted. That is, this structure will yield enough cognitive effects to justify the effort. A demand for effort amounts to a promise of effect (how well the promise is kept is another matter).

The task of the audience, then, is to identify the effects the communicator could have foreseen, and on the basis of which she could guarantee the relevance of her communication. Those effects that are (or might have seemed to the communicator to be) enough to make the signal adequately relevant to the audience are intended effects. Together, they make up an interpretation consistent with the fact that a presumption of relevance has been communicated: that is, in our terms, an interpretation *consistent with the principle of relevance*. Consistency with the principle of relevance is the guiding criterion in the comprehension process. (Note, incidentally, that the interpretation selected by this criterion is not the most relevant one, but one that is relevant enough to confirm the presumption of relevance.) In *Relevance*, we work out in detail how the principle of relevance guides inference and enables the explicit and implicit content of an utterance to be identified. Here we will merely indicate how it gives rise to metaphorical or ironical interpretations.[6]

If verbal communication were guided by a presumption of literalness, then every second utterance would be an exception. If it is guided by a presumption of relevance, or more precisely by a criterion of consistency with the principle of relevance, then there are no exceptions: the interpretation of every successful act of communication meets this criterion, figurative utterances included.

At a party in San Francisco, Marie meets Peter. He asks her where she lives, and she answers:

"I live in Paris."

It so happens that Marie lives in Issy-les-Moulineaux, a block away from the city limits of Paris. Her answer is literally false, but not blatantly so. If Peter presumed it was literal, he would be misled.

In ordinary circumstances, however, Marie's answer is quite appropriate, and not misleading. How is that so? It is easily explained in terms of relevance theory. A speaker wants, by means of her utterance, to make her hearer see a certain set of propositions as true or probable. Suppose these propositions are all quite easily derivable as implications of a proposition Q. Q has other implications whose truth the speaker does not believe and does not want to guarantee. Nonetheless, the best way of achieving her aim may be for her to express the single proposition Q, as long as the hearer has some way of selecting those of its logical and contextual implications that the speaker intends to convey, and ignoring the others.

Our claim is that such a selection process is *always* at work, plays a role in the understanding of *every* utterance. Whenever a proposition is expressed, the hearer takes for granted that some subset of its implications are also implications of the thought being communicated, and aims to identify this subset. He assumes (or at least assumes that the speaker assumed) that this subset will yield enough cognitive effects to make the utterance worth his attention. He assumes further (or at least assumes that the speaker assumed) that there was no obvious way of achieving these effects for less effort. He aims at an interpretation consistent with these assumptions, that is, consistent with the principle of relevance. When this criterion yields a single interpretation (or closely similar interpretations with no important differences between them), communication succeeds.

In our example, Peter will be able to infer from Marie's answer quite a lot of true or plausible information: that Marie spends most of her time in the Paris area, that she knows Paris, that she lives an urban life, that he might try to meet her on his next trip to Paris, and so on. It is such cognitive effects that make Marie's utterance relevant enough to be worth his processing effort, in a way Marie manifestly could have anticipated. Hence, Peter is entitled to assume that Marie intended him to interpret her utterance in this way. Peter would be misled by Marie's answer only if he were to conclude from it that she lives within the city limits of Paris. However, it is clear that Marie had no reason to assume that Peter would have to derive such a conclusion in order to establish the relevance of her utterance. Therefore her utterance does not warrant it.

Utterances such as Marie's answer are, typically, loosely understood. This loose understanding is not achieved by first considering a strictly literal interpretation, and then discarding it in favor of a looser one: in the example just given, Peter would have no ground for discarding the literal interpretation to begin with. In fact, at no point is literalness presumed.

An utterance may be literally understood, but this happens at the end of the comprehension process rather than the beginning, and only when relevance requires it. Suppose Marie is asked where she lives, not at a party in San Francisco, but at an electoral meeting for a Paris local election. If she answers that she lives in Paris, the proposition expressed will itself be crucially relevant, hence the utterance will be understood literally, and Marie will have lied.

The same procedure—deriving enough cognitive effects to make up an interpretation consistent with the principle of relevance—yields a literal interpretation in some cases, a loose one in others. In still other cases, it yields a figurative interpretation. For instance, an author writes:

"Clarissa's face was a perfect oval."
If there were a presumption of literalness, the reader would first have to consider the literal interpretation of this utterance, and then reject it, since it is common knowledge that no human face is a perfect oval. The reader would then look for a figurative interpretation, and in this case somehow recognize a hyperbole: what the author presumably means is that Clarissa's face was remarkably close to being oval. That it should be interpreted as a case of hyperbole rather than, say, irony, is obvious, but why this is so is not obvious at all in the classical approach.

In terms of relevance theory, the reader does not first consider and then reject the hypothesis that the writer meant to assert that Clarissa's face was a perfect oval. He simply uses the idea expressed as a source of cognitive effects: he builds a mental representation of Clarissa's face that contains enough of the implications of the idea of its being a perfect oval—the general shape, a striking degree of regularity and symmetry—to justify the presumption of relevance. The utterance so understood produces enough effects, for a minimum of effort. If the author had spelled out such an interpretation instead of relying on her readers' abilities, the effect would have been roughly similar, but the processing effort would have been much greater, hence the relevance would have been less.

Let us return to our example of a mundane metaphor:
Mother to child: "You are a piglet."
While calling somebody a pig is quite standard—the metaphor is "lexicalized"—calling a child a piglet puts the hearer to some extra processing effort, which justifies him in searching for added effect. For instance, young animals are endearing, even when the adults of the species are not; so, the child may feel encouraged to derive not only the obvious contextual implication that he is dirty, but also the further implication that he is, nevertheless, endearing.

The wider the range of cognitive effects, and the greater the degree of initiative left to the hearer (or reader) in constructing them, the more creative the metaphor: "piglet" is, if only marginally, more creative than "pig." In the richest and most successful cases, the hearer can go beyond just exploring the immediate context and the background knowledge directly invoked, accessing a wider area of knowledge, entertaining ad hoc assumptions that may themselves be metaphorical, and discovering more and more suggested effects. The result is a quite complex picture, for which the hearer has to take a large part of the responsibility, but the discovery of which has been triggered by the speaker (or writer).

Take Prospero's words to his daughter, Miranda:

> The fringèd curtains of thine eye advance
> And say what thou see'st yond.
>
> (Shakespeare, *The Tempest*,
> I.ii. 409–10)

Coleridge argues, against Pope and Arbuthnot, that these words should not be taken as equivalent in meaning to "Look what is coming yonder." They are uniquely appropriate to the characters and situation:

> Prospero sees Ferdinand and wishes to point him out to his daughter not only with great but with scenic solemnity. . . . Something was to appear to Miranda on the sudden, and as unexpectedly as if the hearer of a drama were to be on the stage at the instant when the curtain is elevated. . . . Turning from the sight of Ferdinand to his thoughtful daughter, his attention was first struck by the downcast appearance of her eyes and eyelids.[7]

Coleridge's comments are indeed illuminating, but they invite an objection and a question. The objection is that it is possible to appreciate Shakespeare's metaphor without understanding it exactly as Coleridge does. The question is how such an understanding is arrived at.

Our way of answering the question also takes account of the objection. To understand Prospero's metaphor, the hearer must take into account his knowledge of the appearance of eyelids and of curtains, theater curtains in particular. But this is not enough, for merely selecting the most obvious implication—that Prospero is telling Miranda to raise her eyelids—would result in an interpretation requiring too much effort for too little effect. A more attentive hearer will invest a little more effort and get much more effect. This extra effort may consist in creating a metaphor of his own— for instance Coleridge's metaphor of the hearer of a drama being brought on stage—and adopting some of the joint implications of Prospero's metaphor and his. In such a process, the hearer takes a large share of the responsibility for the conclusions he arrives at. As a result, different hearers, with different background knowledge and different imaginations, will follow somewhat different routes. However, they are all encouraged and guided by the text, and they all proceed by exploring its implications as relevantly as they can.

How does this approach to metaphor compare with the classical and Romantic accounts? In many ways we are on the Romantic side. If we are right, metaphors are based on fundamental and universal psychological mechanisms. They are in no sense departures from a norm, or, as modern pragmatists would have it, breaches of a rule or maxim of communication. We also reject the classical claim that tropes in general, and metaphor in particular, have a purely decorative function. For us, as for the Romantics, tropes have a genuine cognitive content, which, particularly with the more creative metaphors, is not paraphrasable without loss. This content we have proposed to analyze in terms of an wide array of weak cognitive effects whose recovery is triggered by the speaker, but whose content the hearer actively helps to determine.

Despite our general sympathy with the Romantic view of metaphor, we differ sharply from the Romantics on the nature of language and meaning. For us, the existence of loose uses does not mean that language is irremediably vague, and the pervasiveness of metaphor does not make it an aspect of word and sentence meaning. Similarly, the fact that hearers approach utterances without fixed expectations as to their literalness, looseness, or metaphorical nature does not mean that literalness, looseness, and metaphor cannot be distinguished. The distinction, however, is one of degree rather than of kind. Words and sentences have a literal meaning, but that meaning is an instrument of communication rather than its content. What hearers expect is that the literal meaning of an utterance will help them infer, with a minimum of effort, the thought that the speaker intends to convey. This expectation itself derives from, and is warranted by, a more basic expectation of relevance, which is automatically encouraged by any act of communication.

Just as we deny that the literal meaning of an utterance constitutes its preferred interpretation, we challenge the view that the mood of an utterance (declarative, imperative, interrogative, etc.) determines its speech act type (assertion, request, question, etc.). A sentence mood encodes not an illocutionary force, but a more abstract and by itself inconclusive piece of evidence concerning the speaker's intentions.[8] Thus, the same imperative sentence might be used in several ways:

—to express a request:

>   *Mother to son*: "Be a good boy!"

—to express the antecedent of a conditional assertion:

>   "Be a good boy and you will become a good man."

—to report another person's utterance:

>   *Girl*: "What did Mommy tell you?"
>   *Boy*: "Be a good boy!"

—to echo a preceding utterance:

>   *Mother to son*: "Be a good boy!"
>   *Son to mother*: "Be a good boy! Be a good boy!
>   I *am* being a good boy!"

—to echo (in an extended sense of the word) another person's utterance (or another's thought, or one's own past thoughts or utterances, or public opinion, etc.), however removed in time:

>   *She*: "What kind of an upbringing did you have?"
>   *He*: "Oh, you know, be a good boy! and all that
>   sort of thing."

Any utterance will be taken to have whatever illocutionary force is required in order to arrive at an interpretation that is relevant as expected.

What makes an *echoic* utterance relevant? An echoic utterance indicates to the hearer that the speaker is paying attention to a representation (rather than to a state of affairs); it indicates that one of the speaker's reasons for paying attention to this representation is the fact that it has been entertained (and possibly expressed) by someone; it also indicates the speaker's attitude to the representation echoed. An echoic utterance achieves relevance by making it possible for the hearer to recognize, and perhaps to emulate, the speaker's interest in, and attitude to, somebody else's thought.

The speaker may express any one of an indefinite variety of attitudes to the representation she echoes. The attitude expressed may be one of approval or even of reverence, as when popular wisdom or holy scriptures are echoed by a speaker who hopes thereby to command greater acquiescence than she would if she were merely to speak in her own voice. The attitude may be one of surprise or even disbelief, as when a speaker echoes some amazing statement. There is, too, an attitude, or rather a range of attitudes, that may properly be called ironical: the representations echoed with such an ironical attitude are worth paying attention to because of their very inappropriateness, falsity, or even absurdity, *and* because of the fact that, nevertheless, they have been or are being held by some as true beliefs or as realistic expectations.

Irony, then, rests on the perception of a discrepancy between a representation and the state of affairs that it purports to represent. Such a characterization encompasses all varieties of irony from Socratic irony (where the discrepancy lies between the self-confidence and sense of superiority that Socrates allows his interlocutor to indulge in and the true *rapport de force*), to Romantic irony (where all representations—and in particular the poet's own ambitions—are seen as illusory).

When verbal irony is seen as the use of a linguistic expression in order to convey the opposite of its literal meaning, the usefulness of that rhetorical device and its relationship to irony as an attitude are quite mysterious. The mystery dissolves when verbal irony is seen as the echoing of an utterance or a thought to which an ironical attitude is taken.

In verbal irony, the ironical attitude is implicitly rather than explicitly conveyed. As a result, the hearer who recognizes and shares that ironical attitude will feel that the speaker and he stand above the victims of the irony; those who accept the representation echoed at face value. In the special case where the representation echoed is a belief or an expectation of the hearer himself, or a norm that the hearer has failed to conform to, the hearer is not given the option of sharing with the speaker a sense of superiority: the hearer is himself the victim of the irony.

Thus the mother who says ironically:

"You're such a clean child!"

is evoking the discrepancy between the norm of cleanliness that the child is supposed to meet and his actual appearance. That, by the way, explains why there are many fewer situations where it would be appropriate for the mother to say ironically to a *clean* child:

"You're such a dirty child!"

Unless the child had been expected to be dirty, there would be no antecedent representation to evoke. Irony is moralistic, not because, as D. C. Muecke suggests, "all literature is moral,"[9] but because an easy way of achieving relevance by means of irony consists in echoing moral norms right when they are being violated.

Echoic utterances are a well-defined type. Ironical utterances, on the other hand, are a loosely defined subclass of utterances of the echoic type. Ironical attitudes are many; they shade off imperceptibly into other attitudes, anger or aloofness, for instance. Because of that, the same representation can be echoed several times in the same discourse, but with a changing attitude: the utterance type and content remain the same, but the disposition evolves and relevance is renewed.

Four times, Shakespeare's Mark Antony repeats "Brutus is an honorable man." The first time, all agree, his audience is not intended to take these words ironically. The fourth occurrence, on the other hand, is blatantly sarcastic. What happens in between? Wayne Booth, subtle interpreter though he may be, is hampered by the classical model of irony, however much enriched:

> For the populace, when Mark Antony says for the first time that "Brutus is an honorable man," the invitation is simply to agree or disagree. If any one of them takes the further step of judging that Mark Antony does not believe what he says, they will probably decide that he is a liar, not an ironist.[10]

Booth envisages only two alternatives: either Mark Antony is making a literal assertion, or else he is being ironical, and since irony is excluded at that stage, then a literal assertion it must be (and hence a lie). For lack of intermediate forms between literalness and irony, a total reversal of meaning must take place at the second or third occurrence of "Brutus is an honorable man." In order to give a richer account of the passage than classical rhetorical tools permit, Booth must resort to metaphor. Mark Antony's hearers, he writes,

> do not just translate into the opposite conclusion: "Brutus is really *dis*honorable." They are forced to make the ironical leap in order to stand with Mark Antony on his platform (a good deal higher, one might say, than the literal one on which he stands) and they must feel themselves drawn to his conclusions by the acrobatic skill which they themselves have shown. (*Rhetoric of Irony*, p. 42)

Relevance theory provides a more powerful analytical tool and thus permits a more fine-grained, explicit account of the rapidly evolving mood expressed by Mark Antony. When he first says that Brutus is an honorable man, we do not have to describe him as *asserting* his own opinion, and even less as asking his audience to agree. They are already on Brutus's side ("'Twere best he speak no harm of Brutus here," a citizen cautions). What Mark Antony does is *echo* their opinion with what they must take, at this stage, to be a conciliatory attitude. Considerations of relevance cause his audience to understand Mark Antony, not as telling them, but as granting them that Brutus is honorable (and granting what you do not believe is not lying and may even be the moral thing to do).

Then, as he gives his audience reasons to renounce the favorable opinion of Brutus that he repeatedly echoes, Mark Antony conveys a more and more scornful attitude to that opinion (and to Brutus himself, who would like to be thought of as honorable). The utterance type is the same throughout: it is echoic. Only the attitude changes. The echoic character of the utterance and the speaker's evolving attitude are not encoded and therefore cannot be decoded; the audience recognizes them by looking for a *relevant* interpretation.

Again, we side with the Romantics: irony is not an occasional device; it is a fundamental attitude. Unlike the Romantics, however, we believe that the expression of this attitude by linguistic means can be analyzed and indeed explained without recourse to further tropes and by means of an unambiguous and testable model.

If relevance theory is right, then it offers a solution to the rhetorician's dilemma, a way of being precise about vagueness, of making literal claims about metaphors and ironies, without abandoning any of the Romantics' intuitions. However, rhetoricians could not adopt this solution without jeopardizing the very foundations of rhetoric. For this solution implies that metaphor and irony are ordinary exploitations of basic processes of verbal communication, rather than devices based on codified departures from the ordinary use of language. Moreover metaphor and irony exploit quite different basic processes and are more closely related to other forms of speech—the former to loose talk, the latter to a variety of echoic uses—than to one another. The very notion of a trope is better dispensed with. If so, then rhetoric has no proprietary subject matter to study, or to teach.

Rhetoric has no proprietary subject matter to study because the phenomena and issues it claimed as its own make up a disparate collection rather than an autonomous category. The collection should be broken down and the parts studied within the larger framework of a cognitive approach to human communication. Rhetoric has no subject matter to teach because its effects and procedures are known by every human communicator. Teaching metaphor or irony, or, for that matter, the more esoteric sounding antapodosis or zeugma, has only one indisputable result: it makes people do self-consciously what they were already doing spontaneously. From an aesthetic point of view, no one nowadays would argue that self-conscious rhetoricality is an unmixed blessing. From a cognitive point of view, the teaching of rhetoric turns out to have been less a source of self-understanding than a source of self-misunderstanding.

Because rhetorical effects are achieved in the normal course of the ever-present pursuit of relevance, the institution of rhetoric as a separate subject for teaching and study defeats its avowed purpose. This, of course, makes the historical resilience of rhetoric all the more paradoxical. What covert role, what addictive power, what indirect relevance, should we attribute to rhetoric in order to solve the paradox?

The Emancipation of Rhetorical Elements in Art: From Postmodernity to the Technological Era

WALTHER CH. ZIMMERLI

If we agree with the view put forward by Hans-Georg Gadamer, we must regard rhetoric as the counterpart of hermeneutics. Both are concerned with the *eikos*, with the verisimilar, that is, with the probable. Whereas hermeneutics is the art of understanding the probable, rhetoric is the art of expressing it. This, of course, leads to consequences, as Gadamer observed when he spoke, for example, of the significance of rhetoric for communicating science:

> It is only through rhetoric that science becomes a social factor in life. What would we know about modern physics, which has so obviously changed our lives, from physics alone? All presentations of it which extend beyond the circle of experts (and we should perhaps add: as far as they are not limited to a very small circle of initiated specialists) owe their impact to the rhetorical elements they bear. . . . There is no question about the fundamental role they play within social life. All sciences, if they are to become practical sciences, depend on it.[1]

Gadamer leaves us in no doubt that rhetoric and hermeneutics are *theories* that as such endeavor retrospectively to conceptualize the human linguistic *practice* that precedes them. However, rhetoric and hermeneutics do not have the same origins. Rhetoric already existed as a practice *and* as a theory in the heyday of Greek philosophy; hermeneutics existed at this point also, but only as a practice. It has existed as a theory since the time when the relation of man to his linguistically transmitted history was no longer that of the unquestioned acknowledgment of authority. "In view of this," Gadamer states, "it was not until the modern era that hermeneutics really became aware of the distance between it and an-

To Hans-Georg Gadamer, who is my teacher without my being his student.

cient times. Something of this could already be found in the theological claim of reformational understanding of the Bible and its principle of *sola scriptura*; it was not actually unfolded, however, until its historical consciousness emerged from the Enlightenment and Romantic periods and established a broken relation to all tradition" ("Rhetorik," p. 62).

Rhetoric and hermeneutics are related by their intended purpose, that is, of making the *probable* valid. Consequently they are related to one another by their opposition to the ideal of truth and certainty in methodological and analytic proof operative in modern science:

> To convince and clarify without being able to prove is evidently just as much the aim and measure of understanding and interpretation as of the art of speaking and persuading, and this whole wide realm of convincing persuasion and views that exist generally is not being hampered gradually by the progress of science—as great as that progress may be—but extends to every new piece of knowledge produced by research in order to adapt itself to it and appropriate it. ("Rhetorik," p. 63)

Gadamer's theory serves to correct the biased scientistic orientation toward the ideal of method in the sciences. He attempts to exchange this ideal for the right to a "different," to a "new" culture.[2] In other words, he is concerned with replacing the truth of the sciences with the truth of the humanities. Gadamer's convincing strategy consists in not proceeding according to the pattern of demarcation, as was the general practice since neo-Kantianism and Dilthey, but rather in developing hermeneutics and rhetoric as the medium of transmitting knowledge relating to both the arts and the sciences. If, as Gadamer maintains, the hermeneutic dimension proves to be the dominant one in all sciences and all cultural contexts,[3] then the same must also hold for its counterpart: the rhetorical dimension is equally universal. My intention is to amplify and clarify this assumption.

Gadamer's position has been developed further by the various attempts of semiotics concerning the philosophy of language. But at the same time, that which Gadamer considered to be scientifico-scientistic truth has likewise considerably changed: it has become apparent that today it is in fact a matter of technology.

"Being that can be understood is language" ("Rhetorik," p. 71). It was this often-misunderstood formula that both led Gadamer to the ontology of language *and* expressed the unavoidable relation between semiotics and hermeneutics. We should therefore search for hermeneutics' counterpart in a rhetoric of that "being that can be understood." I shall explicate what is meant by this in the following three stages. First of all, I shall analyze the present relation of the two cultures, not according to the "old" topos of "humanities versus sciences," but following the leitmotivs "postmodernity" and "technological era." Next I will investigate the semiotic turn in aesthetics by analyzing the basic aesthetic-semiotic relation. This will set the scene for the third and last stage, in which I will examine the technological rhetorics of postmodernity in the most exemplary form I know of, namely, in architecture.

We are now in an age that we can label both "postmodern" and "technological." What we mean by this, as far as my diagnosis of the current situation in science and culture in our society is concerned, is a peculiar inversion of the relation between "singularity" and "plurality." Whereas according to general opinion the chaotic plurality of appearances can be structured by the singularity of the culture that ultimately determines our orientation (although this has not been the case for a long time), it now looks as if the search for orientation through culture is being replaced by a confusing lack of orientation, by plurality and variety of color. Even art and the arts no longer offer a reliable canon; it seems that anything goes. The fact that we can no longer rely even on the boring architecture of modernity has to be the object of further thought.

The singularity sought is found in quite different places. It is not found in a unified philosophical theory that comprehends everything, not in poetry or religion, and not in the second culture therefore, but in the first—in technology. Technology is the singularity of the pluralistic world, the oneness that pervades and governs it. It is not technics in the classical sense (although this certainly does still exist in some places), not knowledge in the form of "being able" ("know-how"), with its embodiments minute and large; instead, the type of technology we are concerned with is yet a new form of merger, a hybrid. In it, to give Martin Heidegger's formulation a new meaning, art, which was separated from technics in ancient times and which had lost the function of unifying, regains new powers. In other words, it is here a matter of the antiplatonic turn[4] of culture itself. Since Plato, all thinking had sought unity in an idealistic and cultural superstructure, whereas it had sought plurality in the diversity of appearances of its basis. We see, however, that the postmodern technological era turns this relation upside down. Johann Beckmann, a philosopher and economist from Göttingen, introduced the term "technology" in 1777 in order to describe and classify the various crafts and trades.[5] But only today, in our computer-dominated world, has the term been granted its actual meaning: "technology" means that technics today is conveyed logically, and that logic is conveyed technically.

The helpful illusion of the late modern period that science and technics can be rigidly separated according to a pattern of application can no longer stand in view of this almost inextricable interlacement. For who would dare to find criteria for "pure" as opposed to "applied" research? The history of the modern period has only one feature that persists and that now becomes clear: effective technization is being pursued more and more, both in the usage of instruments and in application, and is now laying hold of science itself. Even prizes for great contributions to basic research are being awarded for discoveries that are more and more concerned with technics; we need only think of the recent Nobel prizes for physics, awarded, e.g., for the development of microscopes and superconductive materials. Moreover, *one* of the new forms of technology has become omnipresent in our world today: the dissemination of data-processing equipment has led to the formation of a new cultural technique alongside reading, writing, and calculating. In short, we are now in a transition period heading toward full realization of the technological age.

This culture, unified by technology, now exhibits in its intellectual superstructure those elements of plurality and color that it is obliged to integrate. This results in the plurality of values, the abandonment of a unified instinct and desire for style in art, the complexity of external forms of appearance, and the loss of traditional identity. These, however, are the very characteristics of a lost superstructure that was once unified: it would be pure sentimentality to yearn for it, and it is up to technology to replace it. This plurality and loss of orientation—considered positively—are characteristics of postmodernity. For this reason, the most diverse intellectuals, among them aestheticians, use this phrase to describe the present.[6]

The most important meaning contained in the phrase "technological era" is that it takes a critical stance toward modernity.

Modernity was the epoch characterized by the project of a unified superstructure, that is, the project of emancipating mankind by rational planning of the world and by realizing all technical plans. In being carried out, this project not only determined our way of thinking, but also the entire change that has taken place on earth, and that is why it is called "modernization." Postmodernity and criticism of the characteristics of the lost superstructure therefore go hand in hand as the intellectualized development of modernity with other means and in a reversed situation; the two are not, as Jürgen Habermas has claimed, eternal enemies.[7]

In this rough analysis, the current situation represents the point at which we become aware of the shift: the identity of the technological era and postmodernity becomes in principle more and more noticeable, with the result that we talk, as far as our consciousness of the situation is concerned, of being on the way from postmodernity to the technological era. And this does not even stop at the so-called "hard" sciences. The times have swung drastically away from the classical notion, to which Gadamer was opposed, that the natural sciences are concerned with deductively and nomologically establishing conformity to natural laws and the arts have the function of considering the individual. By means of concepts like "self-organization," "hyper-cycles," and "dissipative structures," not only statistics or stochastics but even anomic, irregular, instable, creative states have entered the realm of "hard-nosed" scientific and technological thinking.[8]

In other words, the "historical turn" in the philosophy of science has had as a consequence a general historical way of thinking, even in the natural sciences. The connection of this to systematic trains of thought, as exemplarily expressed in the theory of self-organization and its reformulation of the theory of evolution, is itself already a compound paradigm of the patterns of the classical so-called "explanatory" sciences and the "understanding" humanities, and thus of the two cultures that are related to them.

It is against this background that the semiotic turn must be seen. It was actually introduced by Friedrich Nietzsche,[9] but it is only in the present technological context that we are able to understand its consequences. The fact that rhetorical elements have emancipated themselves from their traditional anchorage in language and have "migrated" to certain spheres of traditional aesthetics and its objects, for example art, can also be interpreted more clearly against this background.

Rather than give yet another introduction to semiotics (a large number have indeed already been given),[10] which would probably be rudimentary and false anyway, I have chosen to take a principally different path. I do not draw inferences from generalized suppositions about what is relevant for human beings. In other words, I comply with the recommendation of philosophical hermeneutics and infer—like Heidegger—from *"zunächst"* and *"zumeist."* This strategy corresponds best with the thematic: rhetoric, hermeneutics, and semiotics.

To be more exact, I proceed from the supposition that everything that can become the object of our comprehension, that is, everything with which human beings are concerned, be it theoretical, practical, or poetic, can be described as "meaning," indeed meaning that is either actual or potential. All things, conditions, and circumstances of this world have either already or not yet been recognized by human beings as far as meaning (or meaninglessness) is concerned. The way human beings deal with conditions of this world is like the way the Phrygian king, Midas, did it—in the same way that he turned everything he touched to gold,[11] we turn everything we even look at into something with meaning.

We can now express this as follows: human being-in-the-world determines itself as the process of constantly transforming world conditions into meaning conditions. Since, however, we normally talk of carriers of meaning units as signs, we should define being-in-the-world as the process of the constant transformation of world conditions into signs, that is, as a constant semiosis. Conversely, this process can be used to explain that human being-in-the-world represents a specific form of dealing with world conditions. Through the various forms of semiosis, we create what we believed in traditional philosophy before Nietzsche to be the regions of being; Nietzsche exposed this, however, as the universal illusion. (We must of course stress that a naive idealism, suggesting that not only the *regions* but also the *being* is established by the process of semiosis itself, is not the intended purpose of Nietzsche's critique.)

I think that this process of semiosis, which transforms all

world conditions into potential conveyors of meaning, can now be analyzed in its elements.[12] The smallest complex units that emerge are to be called "aesthetic-semiotic elementary relations." They are *aesthetic*-semiotic because the creating of meaning always occurs by the mediation of the senses. A human existence in vitro, as envisioned in the discussion of the mind-brain problem,[13] would always depend on the mediation of a sense apparatus whose signals and information it would have to process, even in the absence of a personal subject, in order to create meaning. That this is the only option open to it follows for analytic reasons, as the world cannot be reduced to the sphere of the self-experience of the empty ego. A basic apophantic occurrence takes place in the aesthetic-semiotic elementary relation transcendentally presupposed: something (s_1) is regarded *as* something (s_2), owing to the sensual mediation.

By a simple epistemological reflection, we can now show that the apophantic relation has to be extended by one element, namely, the subject, so that we must now say: something (s_1) is regarded as something (s_2) by a subject. If we consider this more closely, however, we realize that the subject thus introduced must for its part be apophantic in structure, as this subject is thematic for itself. The result is an infinite regress, if we introduce this subject according to a model of self-consciousness.[14] The approach constituted by self-consciousness theory thus leads us into the problem of infinite regress and must be avoided. Since the basic assumption, however, prevails that everything can only be considered insofar as it is considered *for* a subject because it is considered *by* a subject anyway, this assumption can be ignored with reference to the problem we are concerned with.

The aesthetic-semiotic elementary relation "s_1 is regarded as a symbol for s_2" is indeed not yet indifferent. It is still a matter of a one-way relation, which, when reversed, would read as follows: "s_1 is *posited* (produced) as a sign for s_2." Our language does not permit us to express the symmetry of the elementary relation in everyday terms. It must therefore be defined symbolically as "R_{as} (s_1, s_2)." This aesthetic-semiotic elementary relation contains potentially the conditions of both directions, which we could label the reception and production sides of the relation. If we call to mind what we said about the relation between hermeneutics and rhetoric at the beginning of this paper, we can then denote the two directions in the elementary relation as the "hermeneutic" and the "rhetorical" partial relations.

Every form of communication, every form of behavior, when it boils down to it, even our very presence before someone else, is composed of more or less coherent basic relations of this type. The ontological claim to the universality of hermeneutics made by Heidegger and even more sharply by Gadamer attempts to take this into consideration theoretically. This claim of universality has to be completed by its theoretical counterpart in rhetoric.

The following general semiological thesis is therefore valid:

> (1) Human relation to being is to be seen as the transformation of being into meaning. The smallest conceivable instance of this transformation relation is the aesthetic-semiotic elementary relation, which expresses the basic apophantic occurrence in which something can be both understood as a sign for something else (hermeneutics) and posited as a sign for something else (rhetoric): $R_{as}(s_1, s_2)$.

This shows with particular clarity that the description of the elementary relation as "aesthetic" is in fact correct, since, as Charles Morris observes, everything that is made the object of aesthetic perception could become a work of art.[15] However, in the case of objects of art, we must mention yet another characteristic. For although it is true that everything *can* become a work of art, it is not true that everything in fact *is* a work of art. The semiotic turn in aesthetics now makes do with a reference to a characteristic that has likewise been discussed for a long time: an aesthetic sign, or more precisely, a message with an aesthetic function, is structured *ambivalently* with regard to the system of expectation that the code represents and in which its sign character is actualized.[16] The constitutive ambivalence of messages functioning aesthetically prevents the message from being interpreted merely referentially and leads to the disappearance of its sign character. The message itself becomes more important *as a sign*. In other words, owing to the fact that the referential function of the sign cannot be clearly recognized in a context already identified as a message, the sign changes from being merely a means of transporting meaning to being itself meaning. The structure of the aesthetic-semiotic elementary relation depends on the context, insofar as each reception context is concerned, and determines the aesthetic function of a message. The far-reaching dimension of such messages therefore consists in the possibility of iterated inclusions (*Schachtelungen*) of expectations that have been disappointed, and this produces the specific artifact.

Bearing this in mind, we see that the aesthetic function of signs is tied up with the pragmatic context of their possible reception. This means that, as far as the determining of those regions in which messages can acquire an aesthetic function is concerned, the hermeneutic variable of the context of reception must be put in a constitutive place both historically and socially. Umberto Eco, however, has developed still another aspect in his aesthetics of the "open" work of art, namely, that in addition to this variable (Eco uses the term "openness"), we must take yet another stage into consideration. The break that took place in the nineteenth century, and that can be decidedly felt in the twentieth century, can be interpreted thus: Whereas if aesthetic functions were performed as messages by violating the system of expectation, that is, the code, something now takes place that we can call an "openness of the second degree," whereby violations of the code no longer constitute violations of individual rules of this code, but the availability of a basically different code. That this is due to the reflexive turn, which aims at the production of openness, and thus occurs consciously, Eco tries to prove by showing that this break introduced the completion of the general "aesthetics of openness" by the explicit "*poetics* of openness," the aim of which was to produce openness in its second meaning.[17] To put it another way, conscious rhetorical openness is now added to hermeneutical openness.

From this we derive the following (historical and systematic) definition:

(2) When we talk of art we refer to the class of constructs formed by the aesthetic-semiotic elementary relations that function aesthetically. These in turn are characterized constitutively by ambivalence, which can be seen as a variable in two ways: first, as a general hermeneutic variable of reception, and second, as the rhetorical variable of the conscious production of openness. This double variability is made possible owing to the fact that the aesthetic-semiotic elementary relation bridges subjective intention and objective being, and therefore

represents meaning. This becomes transparent when intentions are realized; however, it can be rendered opaque arbitrarily by denying fulfillment, through which it increasingly draws attention to itself.

Talk about ends for us finite postmodern beings is always restricted to intentions and does not extend to the actual telos (of the Greeks) that included both intentions *and* consequences. Although we are thus restricted in principle, we nevertheless have to presuppose an, as it were, eschatological notion of a last observer who actually knows whether the intended ends (of whatsoever) in the long run really did coincide with the consequences. Or, to put it in more fashionable terms: Who is able to compare input and output, and with respect to both "is" and "ought"?

The only possible way of doing this under the given conditions of finitude is hypothetically to identify the relative end of history, that is, our own present situation, with the presupposed absolute end of history and to assume that this is the real telos. If this is correct in every respect, then it must also be true for each single instance. Applied to the case in question, that is, the case of rhetoric, a *strong universalization thesis* results from what has been said so far:

> (3) By means of the semiotic turn of aesthetics in particular (and of epistemology and ontology in general) the universalization of hermeneutics put forward by Heidegger and Gadamer can be extended to rhetoric as well. Any single event, any set of data, can be considered as an element or a set of elements of a purposeful message.

That this is in my opinion generally valid does not of course preclude specific cultural and historical differences. And in order to bring my considerations to a point where what I have said about the ends-end dialectic becomes relevant not only with respect to theoretical paradigms but also to contents, I should like to apply what has been developed so far to the analysis of postmodernity and the technological era.

The best way to do that is, in my view, to do it exemplarily, and I choose architecture as the exemplary case because it seems to me a good incarnation of art and technology, that is, of telos.

The postmodern Aristotle, Umberto Eco, has, with respect to architecture, distinguished between the denotated first function and the connotated second function, and of course the code and the ideology. In developing further what he has said and applying it to our question of the transition from modernity to postmodernity, I would like to remind the reader of my antiplatonic postmodernity thesis, which claims that in the technological era a fundamental change is taking place as far as unity and plurality are concerned. Whereas in all previous periods the unifying force was located in the realm of ideas—that is, in the ideology, represented by the code—and the plurality was located in the realm of appearances or functions, represented by different signs—that is, materializations —the technological era is characterized by an almost incredible diversity and plurality of coexisting ideologies and a unifying monotony of materials, that is, of appearances. What we call "postmodernity," then, is an abstraction, brought about by focusing exclusively on the surface of the ideological code-level. Charles Jencks and others who have tried to conceptualize postmodern architecture semiotically necessarily *had* to fail because they were still searching for some kind of a meta-meta-level superideology represented by an equally high-level supercode, and the only thing they could find was the notion of a "radical eclecticism," which in itself indicates that it is not representing any kind of unifying ideology.[18]

To put it in a more genetic way: modern architecture (and modern art in general) *made use* of traditionally well-known denotations (roofs for weather protection, windows for light supply, etc.) and *refrained* from the use of almost all connotations, thus by its very sensual existence transmitting the message that the second functions actually *are* reducible to the first functions. The ideology codified hereby was what Habermas has called "the project of modernity";[19] in Adorno's terms, the aesthetic form *is* the function,[20] function is a representation of rationality, therefore the aesthetic form represents rationality.

Postmodern architecture in its turn (and postmodern art in general) also makes use of traditionally well-known denotations but packs them with connotations (mostly by means of quotations and allusions). And the effect is an almost complete nullification of any message. Therefore it is rather difficult to identify a code because the only ideology codified is that there is no such thing as a unifying rationality. (It follows from all we have seen that high-tech architecture is only *one* type of the present plurality of postmodern architecture).

We are talking about rhetoric. Rhetoric traditionally makes purposeful use of linguistic elements in order to convince or persuade somebody of something that is not capable of being *stricto sensu* demonstrated (i.e., to sell something).[21] We could now say that in postmodern architecture (and maybe in postmodern art in general) this has changed: postmodern art doesn't sell anything any more—except itself. And therefore the rhetorical elements in postmodern art are emancipated from external ideological purposes. We witness some kind of a *l'art pour l'art* renaissance, a *conscious* production of second openness, which, following Eco's numeration, would in actual fact be a *third* openness.

PART V

Rhetoric and Interaction in America

The Ends of American Puritan Rhetoric

SACVAN BERCOVITCH

My discovery of New England Puritan rhetoric was a journey from typology to ideology. It led from an attempt to recover the figural richness of Puritan language to an analysis of the function of Puritan figuralism in American culture. The analysis was basically "extrinsic," adversarial—I am neither a Puritan nor the son of Puritans, and not even an American, except in that chimerical commonsense view in which a marginal Canadian Jew may be termed American—but my ends were appreciative. I wanted not to debunk but to display. It seemed to me that a good deal of adversarial criticism was wrongheaded or superficial, or both—wrongheaded, because it assumed that to expose the hard facts was to dispel the claims of rhetoric; and superficial, because it failed to account for the very premises of the rhetoric it had set out to expose. Hence my concern with appreciation. There had never been a scarcity of debunkers. What was needed, I thought, was a realistic assessment of the culture's strategies of mystification. In part, these strategies were centripetal, turning exposé into a do-it-yourself form of assent (as in the case of debunkers, over three centuries of them, who had denounced American life in the name of some patently fictional American mission). In part, the strategies worked centrifugally, by pragmatic diffusion. They served to transmute antagonism into pluralism, as though this society had no dominant power structure—as though America were a synonym for diversity, a mythic unity represented here and now only in fragments, and comprehensible only under the ephemeral, shifting category of "experience."

Prophecy and pluralism: on the one hand, Martin Luther King proclaiming "his" dream without seeming to recognize that the very forms of his proclamation had been ingrained in the culture since the 1660's; on the other hand, a multitude of pragmatic historians searching for traces of dissent, without seeming to recognize that from its Protestant-capitalist origins this culture had been enlisting the energies of dissent in the service of society. These, briefly stated, are the ends of the rhetoric of America. Prophetic denunciation and pragmatic analysis would seem to contradict each other, as fusion contradicts fragmentation, and eternity the calculations of time; but in America, as "America," they are all made to correspond. My own ends (to repeat) were to explore the powers of mystification inherent in that long-nourished theory of correspondence. Looking back now over my writings, I see in them a fourfold process of appreciation as a cognitive act: first, a recognition of the sophistication and daring of the early New England imagination; then, a recognition of Puritan symbology as a mode of socialization; then, a recognition of socialization as a complex, resilient, and highly flexible system of interpretation; and finally, a recognition that interpretation, so systemized, can be an extraordinarily effective vehicle of cultural coherence, social revitalization, and co-optation by consent.

My purpose in this essay is to describe that process in its own terms, by recapitulating the stages not of my discovery of the Puritans, but of their discovery of America. And to bring these within the scope of a chapter, I focus on a particular moment: spring 1692, the bicentennial of Columbus's transatlantic passage. Looking back on April 16 of that year to the "antiquities" of colonial New England, Cotton Mather recognized that those "twin migrations," to San Salvador and Massachusetts Bay, were the key to a great design. To begin with, the voyage of 1492 was one of three shaping events of the modern age, all of which occurred in rapid succession at the turn of the sixteenth century: (1) "*the Resurrection of Literature,*" which had been made possible by the invention of the printing press (1456) and which in turn made the Bible accessible for the first time to the entire community of believers; (2) the discovery of America, which opened a New World, hitherto shrouded in "heathen darkness," to the light of the Gospel; and (3) the Protestant Reformation, which signaled the dawn of a new era "after the long night of Catholic persecution." And in turn all three beginnings—

textual, geographical, and spiritual—pointed forward to something grander still: the imminent renovation of all things in "a new heavens and a new earth." A new beginning, then, and a newly urgent sense of an ending; and intermediate between these, at once linking them in time and confirming the overall design, like an apocalyptic play-within-a-play, was the story of New England. That, too, had its providential beginnings, culminating in 1630 when the fleet under the *Arbella* set sail for British North America. Mather describes the journey in language appropriate to its momentous spiritual-geographical-textual significance:

> The *Church* of our Lord Jesus Christ, well compared unto a *Ship*, is now *victoriously* sailing round the Globe . . . [carrying] some thousands of *Reformers* into the Retirements of an *American Desart*, on purpose that . . . He might there, *To* them first, and then *By* them, give a *Specimen* of many Good Things, which He would have His Churches elsewhere aspire and arise unto . . . the HISTORY OF A NEW-ENGLISH ISRAEL . . . to anticipate the state of the *New Jerusalem*.[1]

By the 1690's all this was commonplace. Mather's recognition was a summing up of local tradition, the re-cognition of a long-nurtured view of the colony's origin and mission. One reason for its persistence was the power of the vision itself. Another reason was that on some basic level it told the truth. I mean not only the truth as rhetoric, the growth of New England as the Puritans perceived it, but historical truth, as the facts bore out their perception. For of course what we call history is rhetoric and fact entwined, inseparably the event interpreted and the interpretation become event. History is the dialectic between the two primary meanings of vision, the dynamic interaction between what is seen out there and how we see it, between what forces itself into our view and the view by which we force it to conform to our habits of perception. So understood, Mather's formulaic recognition is interchangeably the past seen under the aspect of prophecy and prophecy redefined through what historians now consider to be three central factors in the making of the modern world: the invention of the printing press, the discovery of America, and the growth of Protestantism.

Of the three, the invention of the printing press, along with "the resurrection of literature," is most obviously an example of the dialectics of rhetoric and fact. Gutenberg's galaxy, as Marshall McLuhan termed it, marks a turning point as decisive in cultural history as the Copernican revolution in the history of science. It has particular relevance to the New England colonists because of their extraordinary reliance on texts. Like all Puritans, they were a self-declared people of the Book. In these latter days, wrote the English martyrologist John Foxe, "the Lord began to work for His church not with sword . . . but with printing. . . . How many printing presses there be in the world, so many block-houses there be against the high castle of St. Angelo, so that the pope must either abolish . . . printing or printing at length will root him out."[2] That faith the colonists shared with their Calvinist brethren everywhere, but it held a special, heightened meaning for them. In leaving Europe, they had turned to the Book to discover their "true" identity—had invented the meaning of their community, that is, *ex verbo*, by the word; and increasingly through the seventeenth century, they kept asserting that identity to a bemused or indifferent world, expanding, modifying, and revising it in a procession of sermons, exhortations, and declarations, histories and hagiographies, covenants and controversies, statements and restatements of purpose, a sustained process of rhetorical self-definition unequaled by any other community of its kind (and proportionately, perhaps of any kind). That mode of identity, with its attendant anxieties, the Puritans bequeathed to the nation that was to usurp the symbol of America for itself. Not accidentally, it was the New England theocrats who first used the name "American" to refer to European immigrants, rather than (like other emigrants) to the continent's native inhabitants. The legacy of the Puritan vision, as the first-begotten corporate offspring of the printing press, was a rationale, a technique, and (in the material sense of the word) a *process* whereby a community could constitute itself by publication, declare itself a nation by verbal fiat, define its past, present, and future by proclamation, and justify its definition in histories, like Mather's *Magnalia Christi Americana* (1692–1702), which in one form or another translated geography into Christianography.

I mean Christianography in a broader metaphoric sense than Mather intended. The publications through which the republic established itself were political rather than theological, they appealed to reason, they celebrated civic virtues, and they addressed "a large, new class of readers, Franklin's middling class," which they "came increasingly to treat . . . as the very definition of the American."[3] But the same conditions applied *in kind* to Puritan New England. The transition from colony to province was not a process of secularization. It was an expanding sacred-secular process of textual self-identification from the *Arbella* covenant through Timothy Dwight's epic of the Revolution, *The Conquest of Canaan*. A distinguishing feature of this development was the confluence in the eighteenth century of three moral-political traditions that were to become the basis of American "civil religion" and that all depended upon the dissemination of the printed word: colonial Puritanism (especially in its revivalist transformation), civic humanism, and libertarian ideology. Significantly, the two best-sellers of 1776 were Samuel Sherwood's sermon *The Church's Flight into the Wilderness*, which politicizes the metaphor of sacred history, and Tom Paine's *The Rights of Man*, which heralds the American republic as New Israel.

In this sense, Mather's concept of Christianography may be said to apply after all. And the application extends as well to the two other germinal events to which he refers: the Puritan vision was also the offspring of the discovery of America and the growth of Protestantism. It was an unlikely mixed marriage at the start. The discovery of America was preeminently a secular venture, a process of exploration and appropriation empowered by what scholars have come to call the forces of modernization: capitalist enterprise, state nationalism, the expansion of Western forms of culture throughout the world. So considered, "America" meant the triumph of European imperialism. It was an act of naming that doubly certified the invaders' control of the continent: it meant control by symbol and trope. "America" denoted far more than the Italian entrepreneur whose falsified sightings, once published, claimed the terra incognita for the Spanish throne. "America" entitled a carnival of European fantasies. It meant the fabled land of gold, the enchanted Isles of the West, springs of eternal youth, and "lubberlands" of ease and plenty. It verified theories of "natural man" and "the state of nature." It promised opportunities for realizing utopia, for unlimited riches and mass conversions, for the return to pastoral arcadia, for implementing schemes for moral and social perfection. Columbus thought that it had been the actual site of Eden. Later explorers and settlers, translating the myths of biblical geography into the landmarks of Renaissance geo-mythology— spoke of America as a second Eden, inhabited by pagan primitives (or perhaps the ten lost Hebrew tribes) awaiting the advent of Civilization and the Gospel Truth.

History and rhetoric: conquest by arms and conquest by the word—the discovery or invention of America is the modern instance par excellence of how these two kinds of violence are entwined; how metaphor becomes fact, and fact, metaphor; how the realms of power and myth can be reciprocally sustaining; and how that reciprocity can encompass widely disparate outlooks. The same thing may be said about the rise of Protestantism, though from a wholly different perspective. Protestantism was in its inception a spiritual movement. It began as a protest against the worldliness of the Roman Catholic Church—against the Catholic emphasis on temporal authority (as in the papacy), geographic locale (the Holy Roman Empire), and mercenary practices, from the selling of indulgences to political alliances. According to the early Reformers, Catholicism had set itself as mediator between God and His people, whereas Christianity demanded a direct relation between the believer and Christ, the one true Mediator, as He manifested Himself in the believer's soul, and as He was manifest for all to see in the Bible (both the Old Testament, prophetically, and the New). *Sola fides* and *sola scriptura*, the primacy of personal faith and the supreme authority of Scripture: upon these twin principles Protestantism was established. But once established, it, too, like every other venture in transcending human limitations, found itself entangled in the web of history and rhetoric.

Scholars have described that tangle from various angles, including virtually every concept associated with the discovery of America: capitalist enterprise, nationalism, and the expansion of Western forms of culture. Indeed, in this case as in others, the very impulse toward transcendence may be traced to the needs of a certain historic moment and the logic of certain rhetorical modes. For my present purpose, I limit myself to one aspect of the process: the Protestant view of history. For in spite of their emphasis on the individual (*sola fides*) the Protestants identified themselves collectively, as a church or association of churches, in opposition to Roman Catholicism. And through their emphasis on the Bible (*sola scriptura*), they identified themselves temporally, as part of the gradual progress of God's people, from the chosen Israelites to the New Christian Israel to the "latter-day" Israel that would usher in the millennium. The main text for that divine plan, the book of Revelation, spoke in figures or types of an "elect nation," which in the "last days" would defeat "Antichrist, the Beast of Rome," and so prepare the way for the Second Coming. That became the frame-work of Martin Luther's view of the Protestant mission. For a time he identified Germany as the elect nation, and although he later abandoned that particular dream, he and the other founding Reformers retained the basic tenets of his historiography. Protestantism, they declared, was the true church; Catholicism, the Antichrist; and the conflict between these, the central action of this final period of time, attended by all the long-awaited "signs and wonders" (political and natural as well as ecclesiastical) of the apocalypse.

After its initial spiritual protest, then, Protestantism returned to history with a vengeance. But it was a special kind of history, sacred as distinct from secular. It was the story not of mankind but of God's "peculiar people," the covenanted saints who constituted the real subject of the unfolding drama of redemption. Basically, that is, Protestant rhetoric retained its traditional Christian roots—remained grounded in the belief that Christ's kingdom was not of this world—and so could break free, if necessary, of any national specificity. Thus Luther could reject the concept of national calling without qualifying his vision of universal progress. Thus, too, English Protestants of the late sixteenth century could abandon their revision of Luther's concept—their chauvinist rhetoric of *England* as elect nation—without in any way modifying their allegiance to the Reformation. It should be added that the rhetoric itself remained a force in the development of modern nationalisms. It would surface again in England under the Puritan Commonwealth and later in the imperial claims of Victoria's "British Israel." In Germany it informs Hegel's encomia to the Prussian State, and (in our century) the millennialist *Sturm und Drang* of the Third Reich. But in all cases the concept of national mission retains the imprint of its universalist origins. Prussia's decline did no basic damage to Hegelians' faith in the progress of the World-Spirit (just as, a century later, the failed communist revolution in any single nation would not basically contravene Marx's inverted Hegelian dialectics of the classless society). Milton could abandon the dreams of Cromwell's Revolution—as the English Romantics later turned from *their* political millenarianism—without forgoing his faith that New Jerusalem would one day renovate England's green and pleasant land.

The immigrant Puritans of 1630 shared this ambiguous nationalist-universalist outlook. Broadly speaking, they represented one of three Puritan groups of the time. The largest, most eclectic of these were the Presbyterians, who sought to purify the country at large to a state worthy of its special calling. The smallest of the three groups, the Separatists, took the opposite course. They purified their faith to the point where they refused allegiance to any institutional authority, including that of the English Protestant church, whether Anglican or Presbyterian. Instead, they hoped to join the progress of the "universal invisible church" in small congregations, modeled after the first Christian communities. Some remained in England, others fled persecution to Amsterdam, and then, in the case of the Plymouth Pilgrims, to the New World. The Massachusetts Bay immigrants sought a "middle way" between these extremes. In doing so, they meant not to compromise but to perfect. They set out to combine what seemed to them in each case a partial gesture at reformation, in church and in state. Accordingly, they proclaimed their "purified church-state" a model for all Christendom. They were congregationalists in a "federal" or "national" covenant; a community of "visible saints" gathered for a venture in history; de facto Separatists who insisted not only on their vital connection to English Protestantism, but (through this) on their central role in the worldwide struggle against Antichrist.

The European connection thus opened to the far broader connection, through New England's mission, between the Old World and the New. And that connection in turn opened up the meaning (again, mediated by the concept of New England's mission) of the New World as America. It seems a logical sequence in retrospect, but it was neither natural nor inevitable. The Puritan vision was not brought to New England aboard the *Arbella*, nor was it a flower of the New World wilderness. Rather, it was the product of certain unforeseen historical exigencies and certain possibilities for interpretation inherent in Puritan rhetoric.

The immigrants of the 1630's do not seem to have had a distinct vision of the continent at large. Their focus was on the Reformation already under way: New England was to be a "model of Christian charity" for Protestants abroad, "a city set upon a hill" as a beacon to Europe. These phrases come from John Winthrop's justly famous lay sermon aboard the *Arbella*, and when he added that "the eyes of all people are upon us" he was thinking mainly of the peoples of England, Germany, Holland, and other Protestant countries. His vision was transatlantic, rather than American; it tended toward the universalist aspect of the emigrants' ambiguously nationalist-universalist outlook. By placing New England at the apex of history, Winthrop was admitting its dependency on the Old World. It was not enough to set up "a specimen of New Jerusalem"; *their* eyes had to be on it, and their hearts and minds ready to follow. So it was that Cromwell's Revolution lured back a considerable number of immigrants. So it was, too, that after the failure of the English Puritan Commonwealth—and with it the waning of apocalyptic fervor throughout Protestant Europe—New Englanders found themselves trapped in an embarrassing paradox. They had declared themselves the advance guard of the Reformation, committed themselves to a worldwide mission, and invested their credentials of authority in scriptural prophecy. In 1660, the vision was intact, the community prospering, and their authority still dominant; but to all appearances history had betrayed them. They were a beacon unheeded by the world, a city on a hill that no one noticed, or noticed only to scorn. In Perry Miller's words, they "were left alone with America."[4]

Not entirely alone, however; for the rhetoric they carried with them offered a ready means of compensation. It allowed them by scriptural precedent to *consecrate* their "outcast," "exiled," "wilderness condition." If they could not compel the Old World to yield to their vision, they could interpret the New in their own image. That interpretation was implicit from the start. I said before that Winthrop emphasized the universalist aspect of the Protestant outlook, but the "national" or "federal" aspect—the sense of the importance of *this* people in *this* locale—was there as well. New England was to be an example for others by providing a model in its own right. From the opening reference to the immigrants as "Christian Tribes" to his concluding comparison of himself with Moses, exhorting Israel into Canaan, Winthrop was subtly redefining the emigrants' identity. Genealogically, of course, they were *English* Puritans, but as a *New* English community, he implied, they were a new chosen people, all "knit together as One Man in Christ" and together "commissioned by the God of Israel" to secure a new promised land, there to progress toward a better state "in wisdom, power, goodness, and truth than formerly" existed (Winthrop, "Model," p. 16).

Progress and *New Canaan*: these terms, though relatively

muted in Winthrop's address, were nonetheless organic to his vision. They became increasingly prominent as the first generation leaders consolidated the enterprise and defended its claims against an increasingly indifferent or hostile world. Gradually, in promotional tracts, apologias for the church-state, and evangelical treatises, in sermons on Indian conversion and the saint's preparation for salvation, in exegeses on Bible prophecy proof-texts of the millennium, histories of the Good Old Way, and polemics against sectarians at home and opponents abroad, from Antinomians to Anglicans, the colonists drew out the implications of their New England Way.

In doing so, they laid the ground for the great rhetorical shift that once and for all resolved the paradox of vanguard isolation. Having been left alone with America, the second- and third-generation Puritans felt free to incorporate Renaissance geo-mythology, as it suited their purposes, into their own vision. Explicitly and implicitly, they adapted the European images of America (land of gold, second paradise, utopia, primitivism as moral regeneration) to fit the Protestant view of progress. And having thus taken possession of the rhetoric of America, they proceeded one crucial step further. Reorienting their vision from a transatlantic to a transcontinental direction, they situated the Protestant apocalypse—or what amounted to the same thing, the Protestant road to the apocalypse—in the New World.

We can hardly overestimate the importance of that astonishing Westward leap of the imagination. It was an achievement comparable in its way to the two great rhetorical shifts on which it built: the Hebrews' redefinition (by verbal fiat) of Canaan—territory, name, "antiquities" and all—as *their* country; and the imperialism of the *figura*, or type, whereby the Church Fathers declared that the Old Testament, the story of Israel in its entirety, from Adam through Abraham and David to the Messiah, heir of David, really belonged to Christ.

The Hebrews' triumph was nationalist, the self-assertion of a scattered community in exile. The triumph of early Christianity was universalist, the self-assertion of marginal, multinational groups of believers. The nationalist-universalist vision of New England arose out of similar circumstances. Having been left behind by Europe, the Puritans proceeded to recapture Europe for themselves, rhetorically, as part of all that was not-America—the benighted "Old World," awaiting its redemption by the mighty works of Christ in America. Confronted with the uncertain meaning of their locale, the Puritans discovered the New World in Scripture—not literally (in the way Columbus discovered it), as the lost Eden, but figurally (in the way the Church Fathers discovered Noah in Moses and both in Jesus), as the second paradise foreseen by all the prophets. New Canaan was not a metaphor for them, as it was for other colonists. It was the New World reserved from eternity for God's latter-day elect nation, which He would gather as choice grain from the chaff of Europe/Babylon/Egypt, so that (to recall Cotton Mather's phrase) "He might there, *To* them first, and then *By* them, give a *Specimen* of many Good Things" to come. In short, driven back by history upon the resources of language, the second- and third-generation New Englanders united geography, textuality, and the spirit into something genuinely new and (as it turned out) enormously compelling, a cultural symbology centered on the vision of America.

The decisive decades in this development were the 1660's and 1670's, when a series of crises threatened to put an end to the enterprise altogether. First, the Restoration of King Charles endangered not only the colonial charter but the Puritan rule. Next, the apparent decline of religion among the immigrants' children—what the clergy bewailed as the "degeneracy of the rising generation"—forced important modifications in the New England Way. In the course of this turmoil, the last of the immigrant leaders died, and anxieties of succession became a main theme of pulpit and press. Then, in the mid-1670's, the several Indian nations in the region allied to reclaim their land, in a sudden attack that threatened to decimate New England from Stockbridge to Boston.

The literary result of these "Wars of the Lord" (as the ministry termed all the various events) was the first native flowering of New England mythology, through the first English-language genre developed in the New World, the American Puritan jeremiad. The immigrants had imported the jeremiad as an immemorial mode of lament over the corrupt ways of the world. Their heirs transformed it into a vehicle of social continuity. The lament continued, but here it served to celebrate the trials of a people in covenant. Here as nowhere else, the clergy explained, God's afflictions were like a "refining fire," intended to purify and strengthen, or like the punishment meted out by a loving father, the token of His special care. "God's

181

Controversy with New England," wrote the poet Michael Wigglesworth in 1662, *ensured* the colony's success. In the words of the
Reverend Dimmesdale in *The Scarlet Letter*, it signaled "a high
and glorious destiny for this newly chosen people of the Lord."[5]

Dimmesdale is an immigrant minister, of course, here deliver-
ing the election day sermon of 1649. This was not inaccurate on
Hawthorne's part: there were ample first-generation foreshadow-
ings of the American Puritan jeremiad, from John Cotton's *God's
Promise to His Plantations* (1630) through Edward Johnson's *Won-
der-Working Providence of Sion's Savior in New England* (1649–
54). But as a distinctive New World genre the jeremiad was essentially a ritual of continuity through generational rededication.
It required a set of *local* precedents, a pride of tribal heroes to whom
the community could look back in reverence, and from whom,
therefore, it could inherit its mission. The immigrants had imported the rhetoric; their children and grandchildren supplied the
antiquities needed to make the rhetoric American. They enshrined
their forebears in scriptural types, re-cognized them as giants of a
golden age, like Virgil's legendary Trojans entering upon the future
site of Rome. Winthrop could compare himself to Moses only by
implication; Cotton had only the story of the pre-American Israel
to illustrate the terms of "God's promise to His New World plantations." The next generations felt neither of these restrictions, personal or historical. They could sanctify Winthrop as the New England Moses—or the American Nehemiah (after the prophet who
rebuilt the walls of Jerusalem)—and Cotton as the American Abraham, Joshua, and John the Divine combined. These and other immigrant leaders they canonized as founding fathers, translated
their Atlantic crossing as the Great Migration, antitype of the Hebrew exodus, and consecrated their church-state as a venture that,
because it fulfilled Old World prophecy, was wholly an event of
this New World. It led by promise from New England *then* to New
England as it *would be*, when the "American desert" would reveal
itself to all people as the "Theopolis Americana, the Holy City, the
streets whereof are pure gold."[6] It was a mission into America, by
the American Israel, for America first and then the world.

So it was that the second- and third-generation colonists completed the founders' errand into rhetoric: they gave the Puritan vision a local habitation and a name. What they achieved has become
something so familiar by now, so much a matter of cultural reflex,
that it is difficult to convey its sheer audacity and sweep. Only

once afterward was there anything at all comparable to it in the culture. That was the consecration of the "nation's founding fathers" by the generation following the Revolution—a myth that relegated the colonial immigrants, by figural rite, to the role of *ur*-fathers, as Noah was to Moses and both were to Jesus—and undoubtedly the rhetoric of this second founding was much indebted to that of the first.

The Puritans made three lasting contributions to the American Way. First, they justified the New World in its own right. Other colonists and explorers brought utopian dreams to the New World, but in doing so they claimed the land (New Spain, New France, Nova Scotia) as European Christians, by virtue of the superiority of Christian European culture. In short, they justified their invasion of America through European concepts of progress. The Puritans denied the very fact of invasion by investing *America* with the meaning of progress and then identifying themselves as the people peculiarly destined to bring that meaning to life. "Other peoples," John Cotton pointed out in 1630, "have their land by providence; we have it by promise."[7] The next generation of New Englanders drew out the full import of his distinction. They were not claiming America by conquest, they explained; they were reclaiming what by promise belonged to them, as the Israelites had once reclaimed Canaan, or (in spiritual terms) as the church had reclaimed the name of Israel.

By that literal-prophetic act of reclamation the Puritans raised the New World into the realm of *figura*. America for them was neither an outpost nor a backwater of Europe. Nor was it simply an open stage for Europeans to experiment on with models of church-state, or quick ways to get rich, or schemes for social and moral perfection. All of these things might well happen in the New World, but only because the continent itself had a unique meaning, involving a special kind of teleology—an identity *in progress*, not so much defined by the past as directed toward the future; or rather, defined through its direction from past to future. Beginning with New England, continuing into the wilderness, and culminating as the New World Jerusalem, America, they announced, was nothing less than "the ends of the earth" prophesied in Scripture—"the ends of the earth" meaning literally, geographically, the end of exploration; historically, the "end-time" in the grand design of providence; and hermeneutically, the *summum et ultimum* of prophecy itself. From all three perspectives, America was "*pulcherrima inter mu-*

lieres, the youngest and loveliest of Christ's brides" (Mather, *Theopolis Americana*, p. 16), the last, best hope of mankind, whether mankind knew it or not.

That vision of the New World was the harvest of the Renaissance rhetoric of discovery. It marked the Puritans' first contribution to American identity; and the second was inextricably bound up with it. I refer to the corporate ideal through which they resolved the ambiguities of their nationalist-universalist venture. For as their opponents were quick to point out, this self-proclaimed latter-day Israel was unlike any other community, sacred or secular. It was not limited by genealogy, as was Israel of old. Nor was it circumscribed by territory, tradition, and custom, as was modern England or Germany. Nor was it a wandering congregation of Christians seeking a haven in the world's wilderness, as were the Plymouth Pilgrims or the Pennsylvania Quakers. And yet the Puritans insisted on incorporating all of these aspects, tribal, territorial, personal, and spiritual. Their key to incorporation, I have suggested, was the Protestant concept of national election. But the concept itself was by definition uncharted. It signified an entity that had never before existed: a "latter-day" community designed for (and confined to) the "end-time." That lack of specificity, that absence of precedent or principle of delimitation—of *frontiers*, in the European sense of the term—left the colonists open to attack from all quarters. But the same conceptual vagueness that made them vulnerable to historical analysis also freed them, rhetorically, to bring together what tradition and common sense had declared fundamentally separate: to open the *frontiers* (in the American sense of the term) between saint and state; sacred and secular; a community gathered by voluntarist, spiritual commitment and a community defined by locale, local origins, and territorial errand.

In retrospect, we can see how these ambiguities were latent in the idea of national election, inherent in the Reformers' historical re-cognition of their spiritual protest. But the ambiguities presented themselves as a problem to European Protestant nationalists. Elect nationhood was an interpretation, after all. As a textual abstraction it stood apart from whatever historically formed nationality it was meant to identify; and as a national designation it was preempted by more deeply rooted, pre-Reformation, even pre-Christian bonds of community. The Reformers tried to solve the problem by a rhetorical ambiguity. They spoke of the covenant of national election as being interchangeably national or *federal*. I stress the federal alternative to convey its distinctively Protestant character. National identity antedated Protestantism, but federal identity was a sort of wild seed of the Reformation, a by-blow of regional pride and apocalyptic hope that never found a stable home in the Old World. Despite its reappearance in various guises of chauvinism, it remained a suspect and disputed foster child in the ancient European family of nations and city-states, wandering uneasily from Luther's Germany to Calvin's Geneva to John Foxe's England—an identity in search of a community—until, in the westward course of empire, it found its proper home in Puritan New England.

For as Cotton Mather might have put it, the dream of national election was heaven-sent for the Massachusetts Bay colonists. As nonseparating congregationalists they had effectually dehistoricized their venture. Their effort at intellectual synthesis ("visible saints," "church-state") deprived them of their concrete connections with the past—all their English antiquities, except those inscribed in Protestant historiography—just as the past they invented for America deprived the continent's native inhabitants of *their* antiquities. They were a community in search of an identity commensurate with their New World mission. When they adopted the rhetoric of federalism as their "peculiar" social bond, the covenant of national election flowered, and the elect nation of Jeremiah, Isaiah, and John the Divine became incarnate in the first wholly Protestant contribution to modern nationalism, the American Israel.

"Nationalist" is not the accurate term for the colonial Puritans, of course, except as a figure of speech, a metaphor for the federal model of community. But then, the same may be said about the designation "American." The federal metaphor was designed to replace the communal past with a visionary history of the future. It signified a community in process, and therefore released from the usual restrictions of genealogy, territory, and tradition—a "nation born in a day," as the Bible put it, for the express purpose of making "the desert blossom as the rose." Thus New England came to signify a "Way," an "errand *into* the [indefinite American] wilderness." It denoted a people that was neither purely religious nor merely national, but that nonetheless combined both these concepts in a voluntary sacred-secular contract that merged the principles of *sola fides* and *sola scriptura*, the inward spiritual road to salvation and the communal road in time and space to the millen-

nium. Thus, too, the ritual I mentioned of generational rededication focused on the past in order to elicit the anxieties of progress.
To recognize the meaning of New England, as John Danforth explained in his great election day address of 1670, was to understand
the colony *now* in terms of its cause and end, in relation to its New
World antiquities and to the New World Jerusalem, of which those
antiquities were a specimen. Inevitably, this was to realize (through
an inward sight of sin) "how far we have fallen" and at the same
time to realize (through prophetic insight) "how far we must rise to
make ourselves worthy of our errand."[8] And that double sense of
shortcoming implied its own remedy: an *act* both personal and
public, through which the inward turning to the spirit issued in a
social commitment to progress.

It has been argued that the rhetorical assertions of the immigrants betray feelings of nostalgia and guilt. If so, it may be said of
their successors that they managed to redirect such feelings into a
positive anxiety about the future. Turning nostalgia into a com-
memoration of the fathers' "pristine wilderness," and guilt into an
incentive toward what still remained to be done, their rituals celebrate a federal identity expanding, in a movable symbolic-territorial
feast, from regional myth to continental prophecy.

Danforth's *Brief Recognition of New England's Errand into the
Wilderness* is characteristic in this regard. It echoes and is echoed in
turn by a long procession of exhortations, which together constitute
a triumph of the colonial Puritan imagination. To some extent the
addresses persisted in their own right, as a literary genre, through in-
tertextual connections from one ritual occasion to the next—on
fast and thanksgiving days, days of humiliation, election days, and
days of covenant renewal. But above all they persisted for functional reasons, as an organic expression of the community. They
were the *cultural* issue of a venture dedicated to the proposition
that prophecy is history antedated, and history, postdated prophecy. They represented a community in crisis and therefore using
crisis as a strategy of social revitalization; a settlement in peril and
therefore drawing strength from adversity, transition, and flux; a
company-in-covenant deprived by history of their identity and
therefore using their self-declared newness to create a vision of
America that reconceived history at large (including that of the Old
World) as hinging on *their* failure or success.

The legacy of this ritual mode may be traced through virtually every major event in the culture, from the Great Awakening

through the Revolution and the Westward Movement to the Civil War, and from that "Armageddon of the Republic" to the Cold War and the Star Wars of *our* latter days. At every point, the rituals of generational rededication build on the distance in terms of "errand" or its various equivalents ("manifest destiny," "continuing revolution," "new frontiers"). And at every point, the errand is defined as the special obligation of the "Israel of our time," federally covenanted as "the nation of futurity" to be "the heir of the ages" and "the haven for God's outcasts and exiles"—"a new breed of humans called an American," destined "to begin the world over again" and "to build a land here that will be for all mankind a shining city on a hill."[9]

These phrases come from a variety of Americans, as distant in time from each other as John Adams and Ronald Reagan, and as different in mind and imagination as Herman Melville and the manifest destinarian John O'Sullivan. My purpose in running their words together is not to blur the differences. On the contrary, it is to highlight the disparate uses to which the Puritan vision lent and continues to lend itself. In particular, I want to call attention to its legacy to our literary tradition: the internalized, ideal America that inspired Emerson and his heirs; "the only true America," as Thoreau called it, which the country's major authors have recurrently drawn upon (or withdrawn into) as an alternative to the dominant American Way. "Not America," was the way W. E. B. Du Bois put it, "but what America might be—the Real America." In the words of Langston Hughes:

> America never was America
> to me
> And yet I swear this oath—America
> will be.

It is a paradox explicable only in "America" that Hughes should have titled his poem, nostalgically, "Let America Be America Again."[10]

That alternative America, if I may call it so, is the third aspect I referred to of the Puritan legacy, and it has its roots in the last phase of the development of the New England Puritan vision. By the spring of 1692, when Cotton Mather started on his *Magnalia Christi Americana*, the church-state was defunct, and in his view New England had tragically abandoned its calling. The *Magnalia* self-consciously affirms the vision *in spite of* social continuities; it reconstitutes the entire errand, from its antiquities in the Great Migration to its fulfillment in the millennium, *as rhetoric*: "I write the *Wonders* of the CHRISTIAN RELIGION, flying from the deprivations of *Europe* to the *American Strand*" (p. 89). With this double allusion to what he considered the chief epics of classical and Reformation history—Virgil's *Aeneid*, the myth of Rome's founding, and Foxe's *Book of Martyrs*, the founding myth of England's national election—Mather began his would-be greater New World epic. Then he added, a little later in the general introduction, "But whether *New England* may *Live* anywhere else or no, it must *Live* in our *History*" (p. 94).

This poignant and defiant transvaluation of fact into trope may be seen as the logical end of the Puritan vision. The second-generation colonists had turned to rhetoric to compensate for the betrayal of the Old World. Mather took their strategy one step further: he transformed the rhetoric into compensation for history's betrayal of the New World. For him, too, "New England" was a conjunction of geography, Scripture, and the spirit; he also created his symbology out of the rhetoric of discovery, the authority of the word, and the primacy of personal faith. But his ends were not to clothe local history in myth. They were to preserve the myth from history. These were the ends, too, of many of his later works, through *Theopolis Americana* (1710) and *Terra Beata* (1726), as well as the works of other Old Guard visionaries—all of which might have been titled, like Samuel Sewall's tract of 1697, *Phaenomena Quedam Apocalyptica, or A Description of the New Heavens as It Makes to Those Who Stand Upon the New Earth*.

This procession of anachronistic visionary tracts would seem to be an apt *finale* to what I termed the apocalyptic play-within-a-play of "the history of New-English Israel." "Elect nation," "New World," "wilderness," "New Canaan," "latter-day Israel"—all the foundations of the New England Way were figures of speech. Conceived in rhetoric, they sprang to life for a season—a nation born *ex verbo* in a day—and then returned in due time to the realm of rhetoric.

There is a satisfying sense of closure in this view, and a certain poetic justice as well. But it happens to be historically inaccurate. The fact is that the Puritan vision survived the demise of the church-state. Like Hawthorne's anachronistic Grey Champion, it returned as an agent of social cohesion at every stage of cultural transition—including, ironically, the transition from Puritan colony to Yankee province. The fact is, too, that New England retained its mythic status as the origin of American identity (long after the region had lost its national importance), just as the telos it claimed to prefigure remained in one form or another (and quintessentially in scriptural form) inherent in the cloud-capped American dream. And the fact is, finally, that the strategy of Mather's *Magnalia*, his determination to make "history" of *his* Theopolis Americana—to bring interpretation to "life," whether it lived historically anywhere else or not—became a ritual mode of our literary tradition. What distinguishes our classic writers in this respect is what distinguished the latter-day New England Puritans from *their* European contemporaries and predecessors: they did not abandon the vision even when they were persuaded that the country had. Of course, they re-cognized the vision in their own terms (as the "open territories," or the Great Desert / Garden of the West); they made the spirit consonant with Romantic consciousness; and they reconceived the text as a vaguer expression, at once more general and more subjective, of the principle of *sola scriptura*.

But here as elsewhere re-cognition suggests the way a vision persists; it attests to the process of imaginative continuity *through* change. Intrinsic to that process, from the Romantic period onward, was the spiritual use of geography as *American* nature, the geographic specificity of consciousness as *American* self-realization, and the sustained use of Scripture as pre-text of *America*'s promise. That symbology our classic writers never disavowed. However universalist their outlook, however fixed they were on transcendence and the self, they invested the meaning of those concepts in the same federal vision. In their optative moods, they spoke as unacknowledged representatives of America. In their despairing moods they interpreted the betrayal of the vision as the betrayal of all human aspirations—inverted millennium into doomsday, and mankind's best hope into its last. From either perspective (or both), it made for a literary tradition distinguished by its active engagement in a volatile, contradictory, and often violent history, a procession of self-declared "isolatoes" sustained by the American vision even as they shaped the vision to accommodate the changing needs of the culture.

Looking back now at the antiquities of "New England"—reevaluating these through the interpretive modes of our own time (our suspicion of language, our dissensus about the meaning of the dream, and our tendency to replace Puritan providence with a metaphysics of material causation)—it seems clear that in part the vision persisted because it facilitated the development of a new way of life: the nascent capitalist modes that Christopher Hill has shown to have been dominant in seventeenth-century English Puritanism, and that applied equally to the society established by the Massachusetts Bay Company, Incorporated. The literary legacy is more problematic. The New World vision that the Puritans bequeathed became in our major writers variously a symbolic battleground, an ideal to which they could aspire *because* it could never be realized in fact, and an alternative *cultural* authority through which they could denounce (or even renounce) the United States. From either perspective, cultural or aesthetic, the inquiry into the ends of rhetoric returns us perforce to the problematics of history. The vision of New England was the child of Protestantism, Renaissance exploration, and the printing press. But America, as the single most potent cultural symbol of the modern world, and also (in its various re-cognizable forms) as the symbolic center of the nation's literary tradition—America as prophecy, telos and process entwined—was the discovery of Puritan New England.

The Rhetoric of Ethnic Identity

RICHARD SENNETT

Cities are places which draw together different groups of human beings; the lives of those who migrate to cities are further fragmented by the very pressure of numbers and population density. Imagine, therefore, someone taking the following hour's walk in New York. He starts in the drug-dealing-and-shooting galleries of the lower lower East Side, which give directly north to the rich-young-artist chic of the upper lower East Side; passing from these opposite but equal scenes of youthful squalor, he enters the staid, patrician precincts of Gramercy Park, then walks further up again through the sleek professional blocks of Turtle Bay, east past the welfare-hotel district, with its scenes of aimless children and harassed mothers fighting for turf in the lobbies with the elderly who are also condemned to these hotels; he comes finally to the forest of office skyscrapers, Grand Central Station, and his waiting train which he boards with a feeling of relief. Daily experience of difference on this scale does not breed belief in "the family of man." What common appeal to humanity could be made, what humanistic culture bred in such a city?

The answer may be, "none." This answer implies that people generate images of humanity only under conditions of social uniformity—a process the anthropologist Clyde Kluckhohn once called "pseudo-speciation," by which he meant that images of mankind are generalizations of immediate cultural beliefs and practices. If this were so, the degree of social complexity should vary inversely

This essay is an early version of a chapter that will appear in *Conscience of the Eye*, by Richard Sennett, forthcoming from Alfred A. Knopf, Inc. It is included here by permission of the publisher.

with a society's beliefs in "humanity"; the more textured, contradictory, or cosmopolitan its daily life, the less each man or woman should see on the street something of himself or herself in the faces of all the others.

How might cities, on the contrary, generate a humanistic culture out of the very facts of social diversity? How might an image of "the human being," and so of that adjective of virtue, "humane," be created precisely out of experiences of difference? The social phenomenon which seems to be most resistant to this urban humanism is the phenomenon of ethnicity, and its rhetoric seems a logical place to begin to look for necessarily difficult answers.

In 1962 James Baldwin published an essay in the *New Yorker* called "The Fire Next Time." This essay—part autobiography, part reportage on the Black Muslim movement, part homily—revealed to the liberal and affluent reader of that magazine something of the rage of black Americans that would break out during the next decade. Baldwin's text embodies the rage it explains. The tone moves rapidly from that of distant observation to ringing denunciation, then back again to detached description, the prose lapping forward on these waves as if Baldwin were drained by the outrage he feels within himself at what he tells. There's nothing lurid, particularly, in the scenes of Harlem in "The Fire Next Time." The shock of it at the time was that it challenged the liberal belief that blacks would become another ethnic group in America, one which, once granted civil rights, would enter and climb the American jungle gym. Moreover, in the early 1960's, liberal circles imagined blacks were gratified at the civil liberties at last coming to them. "Gratified" and "grateful" share a common root; what Baldwin's essay brought home to his readers was a kind of moral disgust blacks felt for their benefactors.

The liberal hopes of racial integration were perhaps the strongest practical expression of civic humanism in the liberal era. "The human being"—a creature eventually, ultimately, to be seen without color. Baldwin's essay could be read as a document of disillusion, even as an attack on the complacency lurking behind this liberal humanism: sheer goodwill so feeble in the face of the appalling facts of race. But the importance of this essay, its strength, is that it suggests ways of thinking about difference that are not quite those first evoked by Baldwin's angry "rhetoric," in the ordinary sense of that word. His subtlety is not that of an aesthete. His sentences lack traction. His imagery is often vague or faint, despite his tone of passionate assertiveness; the clauses in his sentences often trip over one another. Yet the reader stays with him because Baldwin is struggling within himself, despite what he knows of the world, struggling against the limitations of his artistic gift, to find some meaning for "humane." He does find that meaning, and he finds it as a writer; he finds it in what I shall call narrative violation.

This discovery happens as something totally unexpected during the course of the essay. The opening aims instead at calling the idea of "integration" to account. Baldwin prefaces "The Fire Next Time" with a letter to his nephew, ostensibly to let this young man know how to deal with whites, in fact to slip some bitter pills to those reading over his nephew's shoulder. Baldwin is perfectly aware of our snooping:

> . . . I hear the chorus of the innocents screaming, "No! This is not true! How *bitter* you are!"—but I am writing this letter to you to try to tell you how to handle *them*, for most of them do not yet really know that you exist.[1]

Baldwin puts the familiar device of the reader-over-the-shoulder to a peculiar rhetorical use: inversion of racial stereotypes. The racists of his youth considered blacks to be innocent, sweet-tempered if subjected to kind discipline, irrationally vicious if left to their own devices. This attitude toward blacks Baldwin inverts as the attitude his nephew ought to adopt toward whites: they are innocent and vicious unless properly guided. This inversion allows him to make a surprise attack on the sort of readers who might be attending him in the pages of the *New Yorker*; instead of enlightened benefactors they are children in need of help. He counsels his nephew:

> . . . these men are your brothers—your lost, younger brothers. And if the word *integration* means anything, this is what it means: that we, with love, shall force our brothers to see themselves as they are, to cease fleeing from reality and begin to change it. (*Collected Nonfiction*, p. 336.)

We seem headed for an accusatory orgy, but immediately Baldwin changes the subject. Now into the essay, he describes his own loss of faith in himself as a child preacher. He became a particularly inspiring orator during his early adolescence in Harlem but

193

gradually realized that "being in the pulpit was like being in the theater; I was behind the scenes and knew how the illusion was worked" (p. 347). Baldwin tells us how he gradually became more and more disgusted with his own powers of rhetoric, his own capacity to make a church audience "rock" until . . . until what? The narrative of his loss of religion suddenly breaks off, to be replaced by reflections on the relations of Christianity and race, cogent reflections on how the Christian doctrines of love are so easily perverted to love only of one's own kind, whereas the young Baldwin in his naivety thought Christian love was the love of anyone for anyone else. Baldwin accuses black ministers and devout South African whites equally on this score.

What is at work here is the following: a striking personal story, whose denouement is abruptly hidden from us. Our narrative expectations thwarted, we attend instead to a disquisition on Christianity and race, the waves of Baldwin's rage rising. But now we do not lose contact with the text; it does not seem the rhetorical excess of a black venting his contempt on whites through the inversion of the preface. Baldwin's anger is rising against race, against the loss of a common humanity to be seen when we stare at Christ's face. "The transfiguring power of the Holy Ghost," he says,

> ended when the service ended, and salvation stopped at the church door. When we were told to love everybody, I had thought that meant *everybody*. But no. It applied only to those who believed as we did, and it did not apply to white people at all. (*Collected Nonfiction*, p. 348.)

Then Baldwin turns to the separate but equal appropriation of Christianity by white missionaries for white purposes, and to the mantle of Christianity in which modern racist regimes clothe themselves. We attend to this homily on the racism of Christianity because Baldwin has aroused our curiosity about his own fate—perhaps these words will give us a clue to it.

Narrative violation makes passages work that would otherwise seem like rhetorical excursions. In the hands of a lesser writer, Amiri Baraka (LeRoy Jones), anger at whites becomes a judicial process; the story of the injuries is given as clearly as possible, and the black protagonists are charged by their author with drawing the right moral. It is a literature of witness. The stories Baldwin tells do not bear witness in this usual sense. The disappearing author engages us in his politics for an answer to the questions of where is he and what happened to him. In doing honor to this complexity in the writing, we must therefore honor the passion of the writer. Narrative violation has made us feel the loss of the human subject: Baldwin no longer a child preacher, the god to whom he prayed no longer a god for humanity. Nietzsche once spoke of metaphor's joining unlikes together to create the "miracle" of truth. Here narrative does that miraculous work, a story that ends in absence joined to the absence of a humane god.

Baldwin makes more of this miracle in the second half of "The Fire Next Time." We move ahead twenty years suddenly; the scene changes from New York to Chicago, where Elijah Muhammed's Black Muslims have their headquarters. The Muslims proclaim explicitly what Baldwin had heard implied in the churches of Harlem: "God is black." From this theological vision comes a social vision of total separation; the Muslims believe integration to be a slave's dream, fostered by those who want to continue to be masters, masters without guilt. Baldwin sees in these claims a version of power and self-respect—and something more. He might lose himself for good in this movement, which regulates everyday life down to the minutest details according to Black Muslim principles. In this severe, chaste, aloof house of daily life the Black Muslims define what it is to be human; for blacks, any other dwelling is a way of delusion or weakness, while there can be no entrance here for anyone who is white. The white man is a devil. After appearing on a television program with Malcolm X, Elijah Muhammed's lieutenant, Baldwin says:

> In the hall, as I was waiting for the elevator, someone shook my hand and said, "Goodbye, Mr. James Baldwin. We'll soon be addressing you as Mr. James X." And I thought, for an awful moment, My God, if this goes on much longer, you probably will. (*Collected Nonfiction*, p. 358.)

Finally he might disappear for good.

Baldwin is invited to dine with Elijah Muhammed and accepts. He is impressed with the discipline and good humor of Elijah Muhammed's followers, the monastic purity of their life. The leader himself impresses Baldwin by his softness. But Baldwin is also appalled: "I began to see that Elijah's power came from his single-mindedness" (p. 361). They begin to talk about Christianity, of Allah's allowing this infidel religion only as a testing and tempering

195

of black men; they speak of religious commitment, which leads Elijah Muhammed to ask Baldwin about his own. Here is Baldwin's reply:

> "I? Now? Nothing." This was not enough. "I'm a writer. I like doing things alone." I heard myself saying this. Elijah smiled at me. "I don't, anyway," I said, finally, "think about it a great deal." (*Collected Nonfiction*, p. 363.)

Carefully, stroke upon stroke, Baldwin has told us a story of what he might do to escape the enslaving, the fearful, and the blind Other, the white. Only a word and he can surrender his identity, become Mr. James X, and in these radical terms, solve the problem of race as his problem. Now, even more than in Harlem twenty years before, we have arrived at a denouement. With the single-mindedness Baldwin first remarked, Elijah challenges him—you should think about this all the time. Now what happens?

Well, nothing. The personal story almost stops. Baldwin begins to explain the Muslims a little more, indicating how they might see his weakness, but this en passant; as a first-person narrative, what now happens is that dinner politely ends, and a Black Muslim driver conducts Baldwin to another part of Chicago, where he has an appointment with some white friends. But by now this narrative violation has made us all the more attentive to the general reflections on race rolling into the text in ever larger waves: now the outcome of this dramatic confrontation is contained in them. Indeed, at this point in the text of "The Fire Next Time," something crucial does happen to the language. Baldwin addresses the reader less and less as "you"; more and more he employs "we." His readers know nothing about the outcome of the turning point in his life, the man's story more elusive than ever before, save that he has changed pronouns. This is his answer to Elijah Muhammed. The anger still reverberates in the prose but now it is anger outside the bond of that "we," that bond between an unknowable writer and his readers, readers who he is no longer defining rhetorically, as in the preface addressed to his nephew. Rhetoric—in his case the preacher's voice—no longer needs to be strategically managed. These are the last two sentences of "The Fire Next Time":

> If we and now I mean the relatively conscious whites and the relatively conscious blacks, who must, like lovers, insist on, or create, the consciousness of the others do not falter in our duty now, we may be

able, handful that we are, to end the racial nightmare, and achieve our country, and change the history of the world. If we do not now dare everything, the fulfillment of that prophecy, recreated from the Bible in song by a slave, is upon us: "God gave Noah the rainbow sign, No more water, the fire next time!" (*Collected Nonfiction*, p. 379.)

What does this story suggest, however obliquely, of the humanistic dimensions of ethnicity in a city? What role can rhetoric, narrative subvention, the disappearing subject play in the formation of a humane culture? A practical objection might instantly be lodged in so moving from art to society. Baldwin is writing about race, not ethnicity. Being black is a major fact of life in cities, but it is not the same fact as being Jewish or Italian.

In New York, it used to be American blacks who made this argument, and for a practical reason. The system of entitlements which grew up during the first fifty years of the twentieth century for ethnics failed to provide for the blacks who moved north to New York after the Second World War. New York City schools, for instance, created social order for the children of Italians and Jews in being orientated to local neighborhoods. The school counselors and teachers were often members of those neighborhoods; the curricula within the schools adjusted locally and informally to bilingual needs. Italian was spoken without bureaucratic sanction in the schools of Little Italy. Most important, the social order of ethnic schools was based on the fact that those mothers who did not work outside the community could supplement the presence of the school during the day in their children's lives. Black families entered New York at a point when all these factors—neighborhood homogeneity, locally employed white-collar staff, and locally laboring mothers—began to change radically in New York. The ethnic model could not serve because the city was not the same in the age of race. A different sense of "local" began to be required.

More recently, the assertion that blacks have little common ground with Italians, Jews, or Greeks has been made by these ethnic groups themselves, and in terms of culture. In New York, as in other large cities, those who have lost ethnic community are beginning to mourn the loss of the places they left, the disappearance of the gemütlichkeit of the lower East Side; the family life of the immigrant poor growing more and more rosy and warm through the binoculars of time. And this fog of nostalgia is saturated often by a kind of acid rain. It is "them," the blacks, who are somehow responsible. In a recent racially motivated murder in Howard Beach, members of the community, horrified at the death of a young black man as they were, invoked, in the midst of their empathy for the slain blacks, their own feelings of threat and loss about their predominantly Italian community, as though this loss explained the black young man who lay dead.

It's precisely this kind of cultural assertion, separating race from ethnicity with a hidden agenda, which suggests that the experience of a black writer in coming to terms with his race might have something to say to those ethnics who have turned within themselves. What would it take on their part to use "we"?

First of all, ethnicity denotes something more than a social group with distinct characteristics. For instance, few of the Italian or Polish laborers who came to America knew they were Italian or Polish before they embarked; they knew themselves as members of a family in a local landscape. When Florian Znaniecki interviewed Polish immigrants in Chicago in the 1920's, one woman remarked to him, "I didn't think of the language I spoke as Polish until I came to Chicago." Ethnicity is a sense of identity established by awareness of difference, and this awareness of difference comes in turn through a history of displacement: the peasant moves, and in the alien land becomes Polish.

If ethnicity is put in these words, this social condition begins to speak in a seemingly remote language, the language of modern literary theory. Ethnicity has indeed a live, tense relationship to art-making because ethnicity requires interpretive, imaginative work. Displacement from a familiar landscape provokes one to imagine who one is, when one is no longer there; one constructs oneself as having a character. Moreover, one's history becomes a story.

Feelings of loss organize this narrative work. In the course of the latter decades of the nineteenth century, Irish migrants to London gradually altered the origins of their migration. Laborers in the 1860's, the Great Famine fresh in their memories, spoke of escape from Ireland; by the late 1890's, London's Irish had created a more benign "old country," and spoke to interviewers like Edward Mayhew of their migration as something which happened to them or to their parents. No one would want to leave the old country. Imagination gradually endowed the memory of place, and correspondingly transformed a personal act into a passive event. The "I decided," the "I want to get out," disappears in the language of

American and Canadian immigration equally, from the French settlers in Quebec in the eighteenth century to the new wave of Koreans in New York. An identity found, oneself as an active historical subject effaced: this is the ethnic story.

Philosophic discussions like Heidegger's or Derrida's of the decentered subject assert that imaginative freedom comes through authorial displacement. The text is no longer chained to representing the interests of its author—this critical attitude is rather like that of an exuberant stockbroker who has decided he won't return the telephone calls of his worried clients. In the social construction of reality, however, these pleasures of the text are not to be found.

The creation of an ethnic identity entails a considerable amount of guilt. Guilt, in the exact psychoanalytic sense of the word, means awareness of transgression; one is aware of crossing a boundary which others lack the determination, skill, or sheer luck to cross. This boundary need not be moral, the emotional wall around the forbidden. Experience of transgression is more universal than that. Freud himself imagined the sole survivor of an accident as the perfectly guilty man. And as we know from the literature of the Holocaust, people who performed heroic and courageous feats were assailed afterward by profound sentiments of guilt simply for surviving.

Ethnicity is built on geographic transgression. Migrants leave others behind. And in the receiving culture, over time, the sons and daughters practice a new form of abandonment through assimilation into that alien world. Guilt we know to be a paralyzing emotion: How could you leave us? What right have you to be different? Why should you survive?—an inner, endless tape of self-accusation. This inner voice, which only the author hears, is one point of unity between racial and ethnic experience. It is a voice that spoke in the ears of Ralph Ellison's characters who moved north to avoid the horrors of the south, and now in those of Toni Morrison's; it is the steadiest voice to which Philip Roth listened, the parents in Maxine Hong Kingston's books. The "we" which speaks to itself of leaving . . .

In everyday social life, ethnic language is, as a consequence, spoken between people according to certain rules—they can be thought of as a triangle of assumptions people make when they speak out loud of "we Italians" or "we Jews": on one side of this triangle, hostility between the "willing subject," the man or woman who announces "I'm leaving," and the community; on another, time organized so that the time of community is the time of regret, time past; on the third, the willing subject who eliminates pleasure or desire in giving an account of his movement. History becomes passive experience.

Triangles are rigid structures, when all the sides are equal. If these three ethnic rules become of equal dimension, the language of ethnicity becomes rigid, paralyzing its speakers in two ways. One is a matter of silence: the side of "I'm leaving" is neutralized, and conflict between the mobile individual and the community is replaced by a more passive account of the individual's life in the face of historical necessity. Thus a group identity of the ethnic sort can accustom the individuals in its grasp to losing a sense of being responsible for their lives: the active acceptance of social participation which Hannah Arendt called the "vita activa" is warded off by the ethnic shield. Secondly, strangers and outsiders become necessary figures of blame. The guilt, repression of actual history, and sense of real community as a lost community are transferred to the outsiders, who are held responsible for people's eschewing responsibility for themselves.

Ethnic formulas of "us" and "them," insiders and outsiders, aren't mere pretexts for racism, nor do they necessarily lead to racism. Rather, ethnicity is a real language; in technical terms, if you like, its triangle of rules forms a trope of ethnicity, so that employing pronouns like "us" or "them" and using the present or the past tense and the active or the passive voice all become highly charged linguistic activities. Viewing ethnicity as a language implies, moreover, a certain optimism.

For if ethnicity has real textual properties, it might be revised. In the act of writing, Baldwin came to revise his own racial rage, which speaks well for him as a man. What speaks well for him socially is how he proceeded as a writer, the means he employed to break apart his own construction of "us" and "them." He did so through narrative subversion. An act of this sort has a textual consequence: it creates irony.

On the West Side, below 23rd Street, along 9th Avenue, many of the expensive boutiques feature street-chic clothes, shirts stained with beer or artistically torn jeans; these clothes evoke, at outrageous prices, the look of the undesirables who are being moved by high rents from this part of town. The restaurants lining the street offer ethnic food in two versions. In one sort of place it is served on elegant plates in rooms faced with mirrors, trimmed in chrome, and in these rooms the carefully scruffy young people dine; in the other sort of restaurant, where the decor is grubbier but the diners are older and appear friendlier, ethnic food is still served to ethnics.

Gentrification is an operation in which those who destroy the past often then reconstruct a nostalgic, fake version of it. The nautical cutesy-poo of the restored seaports in Boston and in Baltimore is cousin to the ersatz tough-guy style of this part of New York. And now, in the places in Harlem in which James Baldwin grew up, that same process of destruction and faking has begun. Replicas of the old jazz clubs are being launched with bartenders and bouncers dressed in "period style"—but again with enough mirrors and chrome to reassure people it's safe, it's clean, it's fake. A big church in the center of Harlem now has a film crew in it on Sundays, to record the old people—cleaning ladies, nurses aides, and porters downtown during the week—praying fervently, nothing fake at all in their prayers, a fervor which the film crew voyeurs call "authentic," that tribute which is the first step in placing prayer within the downtown circle of style.

The culture built on suffering and withdrawal and faith has proved no more durable here than elsewhere, only the visible marks of race insuring that prejudices against those blacks who remain will persist. As long as a communal identity seems to be a prison house in which one might serve a life sentence, breaking its barriers has a strong meaning; it is an act of freedom. But if that community is frail? To look to the outside might instead simply mean not caring about one's own, they who could not hold you in any case, who lack the power to bind. One perverse definition of belonging: they need you, and you are suffocating.

A humane language of belonging implies a sense of responsibility to others. What the destruction of Baldwin's Harlem might seem to suggest is that, when all is said and done, a man has to identify himself with those he cares about, simply because they need him, whether he wants to or not. If he does not become Mr. James X, then he will become something like that; he won't be long held, in any case, for soon "soul-food" recipes will appear in the pages of fashionable magazines, and the culture which covered him tight, perhaps too tight, will become as comfortably loose as designer clothes.

The fear of oppressed groups is always that they will lose the inquisitive and intelligent among them to the outside world, lose those who could best hold the group together; indeed, Baldwin himself was reproached by some blacks, for all that his writing turns on the issue of race in America, because he chose to live in the south of France. Further, it would seem that the particular forces in the city which will consign Baldwin's Harlem to nostalgic memory, as they have consigned the Irish and Greek communities to that fate, offer little possibility of a humane future for those who are left. They offer instead a postmodern city whose widened public realm consists of simulacra of the past, "postmodern" implying neither a future nor a true continuity with the past, since the emblems—the revived jazz clubs, the "nouvelle ethnic" restaurants, the seaport "markets" selling Italian knit sweaters rather than fish—are a substitute for connection with the people who used to live in the emblematic sites. It would seem that a city of artificial differences could hardly offer balm for the wounds of race or class; it is itself a wound inflicted on the small communities where once the disadvantaged in society at least were not dispossessed of their own space. And yet this ersatz public realm of consumption might somehow be connected to the grave and dignified work of creating difference in time which appears in an essay like Baldwin's.

Palpable fakes arouse a sense of irony in those who view them. In Greek plays, the *eiron* was the figure who appeared in order to announce that another character's speech or what just had happened on stage could be seen in an opposite way: he was not a figure who announced that the characters had lied or that the action was deceptive, only that the spectator might view it in other terms than the characters themselves did. To call "the new Harlem" fake is not to speak as the Greeks spoke of irony, but rather to see through the illusion by knowing its reality in time.

What if one credited this fake as nonetheless possessed of some value, since some people in the city like it just for what it is, a safe copy? I'm not thinking of the aesthetics of kitsch, the curiously intellectual celebration of popular culture as a duty. Rather, I'm looking at these fake places in the city as the Greeks might have looked at a play, once the *eiron* had entered: here is life, but it is also otherwise. Once kasha was eaten by Russians here, once collard greens by people whose grandparents were slaves. The eye turns inward, after some years living in a city: what passes on the streets also passes within one's head—rapidly shifting scenes, to which one gives partial attention because the scenes are not entirely real or compelling. The 9th Avenue apparent to the eye is replaced by inner scenes of rage, love, or need, these inner scenes which one also views somewhat distractedly because, like all city dwellers, one is always on the way somewhere else and always running a little late. To come to view one's passions as slightly ridiculous might be to make oneself a great gift.

An ironical temper will find it easier to experience difference than a deadly self-serious one; even if the smile hurts a little one is free to look and listen. "I will love you forever, if only you are not too long." This "I" is so much stronger, so much more *engaged* than the deadly "I" who can name and complete itself, its loving or politicking or work ever so serious, the deadly "I" obsessed with achieving catharsis.

The poets of Baldwin's generation, "New York School" poets of the postwar years, found in the very arbitrary character of the city—streets filled with tourists photographing one another, the kind of New York parties where people become instant best friends without learning each other's names, or kosher Chinese delis— some stimulation for an ironical engagement in life on these terms.

The gift of self-mockery marks the poetry of Frank O'Hara, for instance. His street-smarts made him suspicious of himself whenever he was feeling particularly poetic, the same powers of irony which he used to deadly effect in his "Answer to Voznesensky & Yevtushenko," the two Russian poets having declared on a visit that the "soul" of New York lay in black culture. O'Hara's answer begins:

> We are tired of your tiresome imitations of Mayakovsky
> we are tired
>   of your dreary tourist ideas of our Negro selves
> our selves are in far worse condition than the obviousness
> of your color sense.[2]

Much of O'Hara's work shows an awareness of Baudelaire's Paris poems. O'Hara knows himself a lesser poet, but also inhabiting a different city, oddly a more hospitable city in its contrasts and turnings. Ordinary urban experience he puts to poetic use in contriving a voice which finally achieves a comfort in belonging to the city through little acts of questioning and through suspending his own passions.

That ironic voice has found a form, and a classical one, in works like John Ashbery's long and great poem "Litany," which consists of two columns of different text, printed parallel to one another on the page. The author writes that "the two columns of 'Litany' are meant to be read as simultaneous but independent monologues." The poem thus begins:

<table>
<tr><td>

For someone like me
The simple things
Like having toast or
Going to church are
Kept in one place.

Like having wine and cheese
The parents of the town
Pissing elegantly escape knowledge
Once and for all. The
Snapdragons consumed in a wind
Of fire and rage far over
The streets as they end.

</td><td>

So this must be hole
Of cloud
Mandate or trap
But haze that casts
The milk of enchantment

Over the whole town,
Its scenery, whatever
Could be happening
Behind tall hedges
Of dark, lissome
   knowledge.
The brown lines persist
In explicit sex.[3]

</td></tr>
</table>

The poem presents a profane monologue on the left, a more "poetic" monologue on the right, but not for long. The voices will switch sides suddenly, or mimic one another, or argue, or ignore one another for pages until the reader wonders if they have, in the end, been printed together, and then suddenly there will be another leap across, and the meaning of an "independent" voice, as the poet first announces it, becomes clear. An independent voice exists in relation to another voice, rather than in isolation. In form, that was the function of the *eiron* on the Greek stage: to establish the independence of the characters, showing that their views belonged to them as particular human beings, by establishing a simultaneous alternative.

Irony is taken to be one of the marks of modern consciousness in general, and in general, as general things are, it is a rather watery mark. The critic Wayne Booth discerns no less than seventy-eight modern synonyms for "irony" in his *A Rhetoric of Irony*.[4] The prevalence of so many ironic forms may be due in part to its power: this mode penetrates, delegitimates, unmasks. As a political act of imagination, the poet Czeslaw Milosz once took ironic speech to task in the following words: "Yes, I know that man uses irony to cope with evil. . . . We should not forget, however, that irony is an ambivalent and sometimes dangerous weapon, often corroding the hand which wields it. From what is a desperate protest masked with a smile to nihilistic acquiescence is but one step."[5]

And this brings us back to the subject of race, the gravamen for a humane language of belonging. A poem like Ashbery's is not dialectical, one experience giving way to its opposite, which in turns leads to some higher state combining and transmuting the two. There is no higher "family of man," but instead a "we" contained in the separateness, the static crossings, the lack of resolution recognized as something like a litany.

It may be objected that the ironic voices heard among the white New York poets who happened to be Baldwin's age share nothing, in their lightness and seeming abhorrence of politically serious issues, with the pain, passion, and rhetorical pounding of the black writer. And yet irony in the formal sense is what Baldwin's essay accomplishes, by prose means. He installs himself in the world, in putting a distance between himself and the completion of his journey from black preacher to Black Muslim; he creates this distance by prose means, by a narrative in which at the crucial moment he displaced a personal story to look outward.

In the flurry of interview and commentary over the latest racial killing in New York, none of the interlocutors asked, "How long have you been Italian?" Nor in disputes over housing integration in Brooklyn are those who resist asked, "How intensely Jewish does a community have to be for outsiders to be illegitimate in its midst?" The answer could only be an ironic demotion of the word "we." Baldwin asked himself identity questions at crucial moments in his life, and found he could give no personal answer, he whose skin should have furnished the answer in one word. There is no narrative denouement a person can give to ethnicity, any more than to race. Instead, there is only the contemplation of irony's end: multiplicity.

Baldwin was a remarkable man who conducted a lifelong interrogation of himself on the subject of his race. I don't imagine that large numbers of people will spontaneously generate for themselves questions like "When did you first become Italian?"—questions which prohibit an answer about the past, and even more, a guide to the future. The problem in our political life is precisely that those who suffer from or oppose symbolic ethnicity never challenge its rhetorical construction. There seems something almost impolite about challenging another person's ethnicity; yet without that challenge, a person caught in its rhetorical triangle has lost the opportunity to find it leads literally nowhere: no sense of "how I shall or should live" from this passive, backward construction of "us"; no chance, in being asked to tell the story of ethnicity in the active voice, to realize it is a story which cannot be finished.

The rhetoric of ethnic identity is built upon the sentiment of loss. It seldom speaks in the active voice, or confronts its own subjects: "the past," "we," "community." That work of self-confrontation has, however, occurred in art; I have invoked James Baldwin, because of the pressing connection between race and ethnicity. One could have equally invoked Philip Roth, who stages this battle with himself in his "Zuckerman" quartet of novels. The sense of "us," the act of mutual recognition occurs, in their writings, when people cease looking for reflections, when "us" no longer denotes something in common—no more replicated selves. Instead, "we" becomes a bond amongst people who have transcended the accounting of likeness and difference. Liberal piety hoped for this "we" to appear simply as an act of goodwill. The piety is both naive and unworthy of the struggle involved in learning to think fraternally about those one does not resemble. Baldwin and Roth give us a clear idea of the nature of that struggle. It is a struggle to think about one's identity in the world as an active story, to recognize that, at the climactic moment, the story will disappear—if only one forces oneself to continue speaking in that active voice. The active voice is ironic in tone. An artist might force himself or herself to do that work out of sheer love of storytelling. In ordinary social life, that work has to be done through discourse, discourse in which we challenge each other's identities. The result of this active discourse would be a truly modern social bond, a bond acknowledging otherness. The city, in its very complexity, should be the natural site for this challenging, curiously humane self-deprecation.

Notes

Notes

Bender and Wellbery: Rhetoricality

1. Søren Kierkegaard, *Repetition*, trans. Walter Lowrie (New York: Harper & Row, 1941). Gilles Deleuze, *Différence et Répétition* (Paris: P.U.F., 1968).

2. Throughout this essay we generally use the terms "modernism" and "postmodernism" in conjunction or synonymously. This usage seems appropriate here in view of the large-scale historical articulation we attempt. Of course, we realize that a more fine-grained analysis would distinguish between these terms. For our purposes, however, it seems most practical to consider postmodernism as the radicalization of tendencies already present in modernism. After this essay had been composed we learned of Renato Barilli, *Rhetoric*, trans. Giuliana Menozzi (Minneapolis: University of Minnesota Press, 1989), which develops a construction of the history of rhetoric that in several aspects runs parallel to our own.

3. Umberto Eco, *A Theory of Semiotics* (Bloomington: Indiana University Press, 1976), pp. 134, 276–88.

4. Aristotle, *Rhetorica*, with an English translation by John Henry Freese, Loeb Classical Library vol. 193 (Cambridge, Mass.: Harvard University Press, 1975), pp. xii–xiii. On the important role of the Sophists see Barilli, *Rhetoric*, chap. 1.

5. On the shift from stratificational to functional differentiation, see Niklas Luhmann, *The Differentiation of Society*, trans. Steven Holmes and Charles Larmore (New York: Columbia University Press, 1982).

6. *The Works of Francis Bacon*, ed. Basil Montagu (London: 1825), 1:281 and 254.

7. Max Horkheimer and Theodor W. Adorno, *Dialectic of Enlightenment*, trans. John Cumming (New York: Seabury, 1972), chap. 1.

8. Galileo Galilei, *Discoveries and Opinions of Galileo*, trans. Stillman Drake (New York: Doubleday Anchor, 1957), pp. 24–25.

9. *The Philosophical Works of Descartes*, trans. Elizabeth S. Haldane and G. R. T. Ross (New York: Dover, 1955), 1:85.

10. See John Bender, *Imagining the Penitentiary* (Chicago: University

of Chicago Press, 1987), chap. 6; John H. Langbein, "The Criminal Trial before the Lawyers," *University of Chicago Law Review* 45 (1978): 280–81, and "Shaping the Eighteenth-Century Criminal Trial: A View from the Ryder Sources," *University of Chicago Law Review* 50 (1983): 55–83; Alexander Welsh, "The Evidence of Things Not Seen: Justice Stephen and Bishop Butler," *Representations* 22 (1988): 60–88.

11. Welsh, "Evidence of Things Not Seen," pp. 69–70, 74–75. On probabilistic thinking, see also Ian Hacking, *The Emergence of Probability* (Cambridge: Cambridge University Press, 1975); Barbara J. Shapiro, *Probability and Certainty in Seventeenth-Century England: A Study of the Relationships Between Natural Science, Religion, History, Law, and Literature* (Princeton, N.J.: Princeton University Press, 1983); Douglas Lane Patey, *Probability and Literary Form: Philosophical Theory and Literary Practice in the Augustan Age* (Cambridge: Cambridge University Press, 1984), pp. 3–74.

12. Antoine Arnauld and Pierre Nicole, *The Art of Thinking. Port-Royal Logic*, trans. James Dickoff and Patricia James (Indianapolis, Ind.: Bobbs-Merrill, 1964); Thomas Hobbes, *The Art of Rhetorick; with a Discourse of the Laws of England* (London: Printed for William Crooke, 1681).

13. Immanuel Kant, "What Is Enlightenment?" in Immanuel Kant, *On History*, ed. and trans. Lewis White Beck (Indianapolis, Ind.: Bobbs-Merrill, 1957), pp. 3–10. It is notable in this connection that the most powerful and influential antirhetoric on the current scene, the transcendental pragmatics of Habermas, is a redaction of this Enlightenment model. See Jürgen Habermas, *Communication and the Evolution of Society*, trans. Thomas McCarthy (Boston: Beacon, 1979), pp. 1–64.

14. Robert Darnton, *The Business of Enlightenment: A Publishing History of the Encyclopédie 1775–1800* (Cambridge, Mass.: Harvard University Press, 1979), p. 23.

15. See René Wellek, "The Name and Nature of Comparative Literature," in his *Discriminations: Further Concepts of Criticism* (New Haven, Conn.: Yale University Press, 1970), pp. 1–36.

16. Ernst Robert Curtius, *European Literature and the Latin Middle Ages*, trans. Willard R. Trask (New York: Pantheon, 1953).

17. Michel Foucault, "What Is an Author?" in *The Foucault Reader*, ed. Paul Rabinow (New York: Pantheon, 1984), pp. 101–20.

18. We have taken these data from Heinrich Bosse's excellent study *Autorschaft ist Werkherrschaft: Über die Entstehung des Urheberrechts aus dem Geist der Goethezeit* (Paderborn: F. Schöningh, 1981), pp. 8–9. See also Mark Rose, "The Author as Proprietor: Donaldson v. Becket and the Genealogy of Modern Authorship," *Representations* 23 (1988): 51–85.

19. Johann Wolfgang von Goethe, *Sämtliche Werke nach Epochen seines Schaffens*, ed. Karl Richter with Herbert G. Göpfert, Norbert Miller, and Gerhard Sauder, vol. 1, pt. 2 (Munich: Hanser, 1987), p. 364, our translation.

20. Heinrich Bosse, "Dichter Kann man nicht bilden. Zur Veränderung der Schulrhetorik nach 1770," *Jahrbuch für Internationale Germanistik* 2 (1976): 81–125.

Notes to Pages 17–28

21. Robert S. Leventhal, "The Emergence of Philological Discourse in the German States, 1770–1810," *Isis* 77 (June 1986): 243–60.
22. David E. Wellbery, *Lessing's Laocoön* (Cambridge: Cambridge University Press, 1984), chap. 2.
23. Michael Fried, *Absorption and Theatricality* (Berkeley: University of California Press, 1980).
24. Immanuel Kant, *Critique of Judgment*, trans. J. H. Barnard (New York: Harper, 1951), p. 171.
25. Mikhail Bakhtin, *The Dialogic Imagination*, ed. and trans. Michael Holquist and Caryl Emerson (Austin: University of Texas Press, 1981), p. 3.
26. On free indirect discourse see Dorrit C. Cohn, *Transparent Minds: Narrative Modes for Presenting Consciousness in Fiction* (Princeton, N.J.: Princeton University Press, 1978). For arguments on the specifically written character of free indirect discourse see Ann Banfield, *Unspeakable Sentences: Narration and Representation in the Language of Fiction* (Boston: Routledge & Kegan Paul, 1982).
27. See Manfred Fuhrmann, *Rhetorik und öffentliche Rede* (Konstanz: Universitätsverlag, 1983).
28. Philippe Lacoue-Labarthe, "Le détour," *Poétique* 5 (1971): 53–76. For a further development of the interpretation of Nietzsche sketched in the following paragraphs, see David E. Wellbery, "Nietzsche—Art—Postmodernism," *Stanford Italian Review* 6 (1986): 77–104.
29. Of course, the classical rhetoric we have been speaking of here descends from Plato and Aristotle through Quintilian and the Neoplatonists to a medieval and Renaissance tradition that remained vital into the Enlightenment. One could also construct a pre-Nietzschean history of rhetoric beginning with the Sophists and including such figures as Machiavelli and Vico. The aspect of Nietzsche's thought that we have sought to capture here with the notion of rhetoricality, in other words, has certain precursors. The fact remains, however, that only under the social and cultural conditions of modernity could the category of rhetoricality assume the operative force disclosed by Nietzsche.
30. Roland Barthes, "The Old Rhetoric: An Aide-memoire," in his *The Semiotic Challenge* (New York: Hill and Wang, 1988), pp. 11–94.
31. Heinrich Lausberg, *Handbuch der literarischen Rhetorik, Eine Grundlegung der Literaturwissenschaft*, 2 vols. (Munich: Hueber, 1960).
32. Thomas S. Kuhn, *The Structure of Scientific Revolutions* (Chicago: University of Chicago Press, 1962).
33. Paul K. Feyerabend, *Against Method: Outline of an Anarchistic Theory of Knowledge* (rev. ed.; London: Verso, 1988).
34. Ian Hacking, *Representing and Intervening: Introductory Topics in the Philosophy of Natural Science* (Cambridge: Cambridge University Press, 1983).
35. Nelson Goodman, *Ways of Worldmaking* (Indianapolis, Ind.: Hackett, 1978).
36. See Peter Galison, *How Experiments End* (Chicago: University of

Chicago Press, 1987); Bruno Latour, *Science in Action* (Cambridge, Mass.: Harvard University Press, 1987).

37. Hayden White, *Metahistory: The Historical Imagination in Nineteenth-Century Europe* (Baltimore, Md.: Johns Hopkins University Press, 1973).

38. Clifford Geertz, *Works and Lives: The Anthropologist as Author* (Stanford, Calif.: Stanford University Press, 1988). The University of Wisconsin Press is publishing a series of books on rhetoric in various disciplines. See, for example, Donald N. McCloskey, *The Rhetoric of Economics* (Madison: University of Wisconsin Press, 1985).

39. Roman Jakobson, "Two Aspects of Language and Two Types of Aphasic Disturbances," in his *Fundamentals of Language* (The Hague: Mouton, 1956), reprinted in Roman Jakobson, *Language in Literature*, ed. Krystyna Pomorska and Stephen Rudy (Cambridge, Mass.: Harvard University Press, 1987), pp. 95–119.

40. Jacques Dubois et al., *A General Rhetoric*, trans. Paul B. Burrell and Edgar M. Slotkin (Baltimore, Md.: Johns Hopkins University Press, 1981); Paolo Valesio, *Novantiqua: Rhetorics as a Contemporary Theory* (Bloomington: Indiana University Press, 1980).

41. Jean Laplanche, *Life and Death in Psychoanalysis* (Baltimore, Md.: Johns Hopkins University Press, 1976).

42. Nicolas Abraham and Marie Torok, *L'écorce et le noyau* (Paris: Aubier-Flammarion, 1978), esp. pp. 203–28.

43. Erving Goffmann, *Forms of Talk* (Philadelphia: University of Pennsylvania Press, 1981), and *The Presentation of Self in Everyday Life* (New York: Anchor, 1959).

44. Dan Sperber and Deirdre Wilson, *Relevance: Communication and Cognition* (Cambridge, Mass.: Harvard University Press, 1986), p. 237.

45. Marvin Minsky, "A Framework for Representing Knowledge," in *The Psychology of Computer Vision*, ed. Patrick Henry Winston (New York: McGraw-Hill, 1975); Roger Shank, "The Structure of Episodes in Memory," in Daniel G. Bobrow and Allen Collins, eds., *Representation and Understanding* (New York: Academic Press, 1975).

46. George Lakoff and Mark Johnson, *Metaphors We Live By* (Chicago: University of Chicago Press, 1980).

47. Kenneth Burke, "Symbolic Action in a Poem by Keats," in his *A Grammar of Motives* (Berkeley: University of California Press, 1969), pp. 447–64; Kenneth Burke, "Goethe's *Faust*, Part I," in his *Language as Symbolic Action* (Berkeley: University of California Press, 1966), pp. 139–62.

48. Kenneth Burke, *A Rhetoric of Motives* (Berkeley: University of California Press, 1969), and *The Rhetoric of Religion, Studies in Logology* (Berkeley: University of California Press, 1970).

49. Burke's own "definition of man" (explicated in the essay by that title) reads: "Man is the symbol-using (symbol-making, symbol-misusing) animal, inventor of the negative (or moralized by the negative), separated from his natural condition by instruments of his own making, goaded by

the spirit of hierarchy (or moved by the sense of order), and rotten with perfection" (*Language as Symbolic Action*, p. 16).

50. Julia Kristeva, *Desire and Language*, ed. Leon S. Roudiez, tr. Thomas Gora et al. (New York: Columbia University Press, 1980).

51. See R. S. Crane et al., *Critics and Criticism, Ancient and Modern* (Chicago: University of Chicago Press, 1952).

Nagy: The Crisis of Performance

1. A. B. Lord, *The Singer of Tales* (Cambridge, Mass.: Harvard University Press, 1960).

2. J. L. Austin, *How to Do Things with Words* (Cambridge, Mass.: Harvard University Press, 1962).

3. Barbara Johnson, *The Critical Difference: Essays in the Contemporary Rhetoric of Reading* (Baltimore, Md.: The Johns Hopkins University Press, 1980), p. 56. On the term "shifter," referring to forms in which the referent can be determined only from the standpoint of the interlocutors, see Roman Jakobson, "Shifters, Verbal Categories and the Russian Verb," in his *Selected Writings II* (The Hague: Mouton, 1971), pp. 130–47.

4. Quoted in B. Johnson, *Critical Difference*, p. 56, from Emile Benveniste, *Problèmes de linguistique générale* (Paris: Gallimard, 1966), p. 274.

5. Plato, *Ion* 533d–536d. References to passages from classical authors follow the editions cited in *The Oxford Classical Dictionary*, ed. N. G. L. Hammond and H. H. Scullard (Oxford: Oxford University Press, 1970). All translations of these passages are my own.

6. Quoted in Laura Boulton, *The Eskimos of Hudson Bay and Alaska* (New York: Folkways Records, Album Notes for FE4444, 1954), pp. 4–5.

7. I suggest that we may achieve a more balanced formulation from the vantage point of anthropology. Cf. Alan P. Merriam, *The Anthropology of Music* (Evanston, Ill.: Northwestern University Press, 1964), pp. 312–13, who observes that, whereas innovation in oral traditions may be initiated by individuals, the cultural background has to *allow* it (for example, by way of collaboration of effort, expectation of change, and the like).

8. *Shāhnāma* 6.136.18, quoted in Olga M. Davidson, "The Crown-Bestower in the Iranian Book of Kings," in *Acta Iranica, Hommages et Opera Minora*, vol. 10, *Papers in Honour of Professor Mary Boyce* (Leiden: Brill, 1985), p. 110; cf. also in general pp. 103–42. Textual references to the *Shāhnāma* follow the volume and page numbers of A. Y. Bertel's, *Ferdowsi: Shāhnāma* 1–9 (Moscow: Akademija Nauk S.S.S.R., 1966–71).

9. *Shāhnāma* 3.6.9, quoted in Davidson, "Crown-Bestower," p. 109.

10. In Homeric poetry, the *aoidos*, "singer," belongs to the category of the *dēmiourgoi*, "artisans in the district [*dēmos*]" (*Odyssey* 17.381–85). Other professions that belong to this category are the *mantis*, "seer"; the *iātēr*, "physician"; the *tektōn*, "carpenter"; and the *kērux*, "herald" (ibid., 17.381–85 and 19.135). In Hesiod, *Works and Days* 25–26, the *aoidos* is juxtaposed with the *tektōn* and the *kerameus*, "potter." The *dēmiourgoi*

are socially mobile, being juridically immune as they travel from one district (*dēmos*) to another. For an example of a cognate institution, I cite the Old Irish "people of the craft [*cerd*]," the designation for artisans, including poets, who were, again, juridically immune as they traveled from one tribe (*tuath*) to another. In fact, two of the most basic metaphors for the art of poetry in the Greek art of poetry are the crafts of carpentry (as in Pindar, *Pythian* 3.113; cf. Pausanias 10.5.8) and weaving (as in Bacchylides 5.9–10 and 19.8).

11. Claude Lévi-Strauss, *La voie des masques* (Paris: Plon, 1979), pp. 153–63.

12. Cf. Marcel Detienne, *Les maîtres de vérité dans la Grèce archaïque* (Paris: Maspero, 1973), pp. 22–27.

13. Roman Jakobson, "Signe zéro," in his *Selected Writings II*, p. 136; I have omitted the final part of Jakobson's working definition, which is: "and is used chiefly, but not exclusively, to indicate the absence of A" (ibid.).

14. For discussion and bibliography see Linda R. Waugh, "Marked and Unmarked: A Choice between Unequals in Semiotic Structure," *Semiotica* 38 (1982): 299–318.

15. The pertinent passages are discussed in Gregory Nagy, "Sēma and Noēsis: Some Illustrations," *Arethusa* 16 (1983): 44. This expression *oude me/se/he lēthei*," it does not escape my/your/his-her mind," implies a synchronic understanding of the word *alētheia* as a compound consisting of privative *a-* and the root *lēth-*. In the formulation of Thomas Cole, "Archaic Truth," *Quaderni Urbinati* 13 (1983): 12, the reference of *alētheia* is "not simply to non-omission of pieces of information . . . but also to not forgetting from one minute to the next what was said a few minutes before, and not letting anything, said or unsaid, slip by without being mindful of its consequences and implications." (For a critique of Heidegger's celebrated explanation of *alētheia*, see Cole, "Archaic Truth," pp. 7–8.)

16. I cite again Hesiod, *Theogony* 53–55 and 98–103.

17. Anya P. Royce, *The Anthropology of Dance* (Bloomington: Indiana University Press, 1977), p. 104, points out, with reference to traditions of dance, that rigid structures can suffer "abrupt confrontation and loss."

18. The threat of "abrupt confrontation and loss," to use the expression quoted above in n. 17, could of course help promote an impetus for recording by way of writing.

19. We may well ask, how does the local perspective contribute to the Panhellenic, and to what degree does the Panhellenic perspective recognize the local? From the standpoint of the local tradition, the best chance for self-assertion is a process of self-selection that accommodates the Panhellenic tradition. Note the discussion by Royce, *Anthropology of Dance*, p. 164, of the repertory of some ninety sones (dances) among the Zapotec of the Isthmus of Tehuantepec: in asserting their identity to outsiders, the Zapotec tend to select just three of these ninety sones. Royce notes (ibid.) that "these three are the dances that any non-Zapotec would name if asked about 'typical' dances of the Isthmus," and that it is these three dances

that are synthesized by the Ballet Folklórico in its suite "Wedding in Tehuantepec."

20. For a history of the usage of "canon" to designate a selective listing of authors and works, see Rudolf Pfeiffer, *History of Classical Scholarship: From the Beginnings to the End of the Hellenistic Age* (Oxford: Oxford University Press, 1968), p. 207.

21. For an introduction to the era of Alexandrian scholarship, see ibid., pp. 87–233.

22. For a survey of this usage, see ibid., p. 117. There is a blurring of distinction between *krisis* of authors and *krisis* within the oeuvre of an author.

23. See ibid., pp. 89, 242.

24. Ibid., pp. 206–7. Cf. Horace, *Odes* 1.1.35, and the comments of Pfeiffer, *History*, p. 206.

25. Pfeiffer, *History*, p. 207. The canon as conceived by the Alexandrian scholars is not to be confused with the actual collection of works housed in the great library of the Museum at Alexandria. The *Pinakes*, or "Tables," of Callimachus, in 120 books, was intended not as a selection but as a complete catalogue of the holdings of the Museum, generally organized along the lines of formal criteria, including meter. For an informative discussion, see James E. G. Zetzel, "Re-creating the Canon: Augustan Poetry and the Alexandrian Past," *Critical Inquiry* 10 (1983): 98–100, who stresses that the Alexandrian system of classification was "eminently suitable for describing the literature of pre-Alexandrian Greece" (p. 99).

26. On the principles of selection from Aristotle to the Alexandrians, see Pfeiffer, *History*, pp. 117, 205. This is not to assume that there was an ongoing process of actual selecting of classical (as opposed to current) authors in the period of Alexandrian scholarship; I cite D. L. Page, "Corinna," *The Society for the Promotion of Hellenic Studies Supplementary Paper* 6 (1953): 68, who doubts that "any ancient lyrical poet whose works were in circulation up to the Alexandrian era was omitted by the Alexandrian editors from their collection." In the case of epic, Quintilian, *Institutio Oratoria* 10.1.55, notes explicitly that the Alexandrian editors Aristophanes and Aristarchus included no contemporary poets into the *ordo*, or canon, barring even Apollonius of Rhodes.

27. For the wording, see, e.g., the description in Plato, *Laws* 659ab.

28. First we had the "works"; now we have the "days."

29. M. L. West, ed., *Hesiod: Works and Days* (Oxford: Clarendon Press, 1978), p. 351.

30. For the apparent exception in the island of Keos, see the passages quoted by West, p. 351.

31. In the *Odyssey*, the new moon is the context for a festival of Apollo (14.162–19.307; 20.156, 276–78; 21.258).

32. For example, Aphrodite was specially worshipped on this day.

33. The seventh was the most important holy day of Apollo.

34. For example, the eighth at Athens was the day for honoring Poseidon and Theseus.

35. For example, the ninth at Athens inaugurated the City Dionysia.

36. That is, they may be holy days, but they are not necessarily holidays. This hedge suggests that the eighth and the ninth are less "Panhellenic" than the first, fourth, and seventh.

37. The waxing and waning of the day are in symmetry with the waxing and waning of the moon.

38. That is, the ant. Cf. the cicada at l. 582. Note the Aesop fable "The Grasshopper and the Ant," which is really "The Cicada and the Ant" (no. 373 in *Aesopica*, ed. B. E. Perry (Urbana: University of Illinois Press, 1952).

39. The "stealthy relations" may include sexually suggestive sweet talk. The features enumerated here are characteristic of a traditional persona such as Perses, or such as portrayed in the poetry of Archilochus.

40. See n. 37 above.

41. The characterization seems to suit the persona of Hesiod himself.

42. The Hesiodic name "thrice-nine" would be the Panhellenic designation, as implied by the word *alēthēs*. We may note the earlier observations about *alētheia* in the context of l. 768. Local designations of this day may have been subject to tabu. The number thrice-nine is particularly sacred: see the references collected by West, *Works and Days*, p. 361.

43. This interpretation differs from what is found in the standard editions.

44. Note again the periphrasis, as in the case of thrice-nine at l. 814.

45. Here we see the localized perspective.

46. Here we see the Panhellenic perspective. "Know" here has the sense that we have seen at l. 792.

47. This riddle can be better understood by reading Georges Dumézil, *Camillus: A Study of Indo-European Religion as Roman History* (Berkeley: University of California Press, 1980).

48. "'Truth', which itinerant, would-be oral poets are 'unwilling' to tell because of their need for survival [*Odyssey* 14.124–25], is 'willingly' conferred by the Muses ['whenever we are willing' at *Theogony* 28]. We see here what can be taken as a manifesto of Panhellenic poetry, in that the poet Hesiod is to be freed from being a mere 'belly'—one who owes his survival to his local audience with its local traditions: all such local traditions are 'lies' in face of the 'true things' that the Muses impart specially to Hesiod. The conceit inherent in the Panhellenic poetry of Hesiod is that this overarching tradition is capable of achieving something that is beyond the reach of individual local traditions." (Gregory Nagy, "Hesiod," in *Ancient Writers*, ed. T. J. Luce [New York: Scribner's, 1982], p. 48).

49. Nagy, "Hesiod," pp. 48–49.

50. Ibid.

51. Ibid., pp. 47–49. The phrase *alēthea gērūsasthai*, "announce things that are true [*alēthea*]," at Hesiod, *Theogony* 28, is one of a set of variants, including *alēthea mūthēsasthai*, "tell [verb *mūtheomai*] things that are true" at Homer, *Iliad* 6.382, *Homeric Hymn to Demeter* 121, etc. (also attested as a textual variant at *Theogony* 28), and *etētuma mūthēsasthai*, "tell [verb *mūtheomai*] things that are real [*etētuma*]" at *Homeric Hymn to Demeter* 44. I suggest that these variations result from a chain of

differentiations setting off a marked Panhellenic version from unmarked versions that are ostensibly local or at least more local. The variant *gērū-sasthai*, "announce," represents a differentiation of marked *gērūsasthai*, "announce," from unmarked *mūthēsasthai*, "tell"; also, the variant *al-ēthea*, "things that are true [*alēthea*]," represents a differentiation of marked *alēthea*, "things that are true," from unmarked *etētuma*, "things that are real." In each case, I further suggest, the marked member differentiates a concept that is Panhellenic from an earlier concept that is perceived as obsolete with reference to the new marked member. At each stage of differentiation, we must allow for the possibility that the unmarked member of the opposition had once been the marked member in earlier sets of opposition.

52. That is, *kharis* personified. I interpret *kharis* as "pleasurable compensation, by the song of poetry, for a deed deserving of glory."

53. I am following here the formulation of David Young, whose article on this passage is forthcoming.

54. See Andrew Miller, "Phthonos and Parphasis: Nemean 8.19−34," *Greek Roman and Byzantine Studies* 23 (1982): 114.

55. On *nostos* as both "homecoming" and "song about homecoming," see Gregory Nagy, *The Best of the Achaeans: Concepts of the Hero in Archaic Greek Poetry* (Baltimore, Md.: Johns Hopkins University Press, 1979), par. 6n2.

56. See again Miller, "Phthonos and Parphasis," p. 114.

57. Cf. Nagy, *Best*, p. 98. Telemachus is "wrong" in not understanding that the myth applies to the situation in the here and now. For him, the "newness" of the song has the surface meaning of mere novelty (cf. the interpretation in Plato, *Republic* 424bc). But he is "right" in insisting that the singing proceed. This way, the *nostos* sung by the singer may ultimately be fulfilled in the *nostos* of Odysseus, which is the "novelty" of the *Odyssey*—the "news," as it were, of what finally happened in the *Odyssey*. Penelope, by contrast, is "right" in understanding that song applies to the present, but she is "wrong" in how she interprets it at this particular moment in the overall narrative of the *Odyssey*. What is absolutely right, not wrong, can emerge only from the overall narrative in progress.

58. The Ionic form *apodexis* in the usage of Herodotus, guaranteed by the testimony of inscriptions written in the Ionic dialect, may reflect a conflation of *apo-deik-numai*, "make public," and *apo-dek-omai*, "accept or approve a tradition"; cf. Herodotus, *Histories* 6.43. The conflation of *apodeixis* and *apodexis* is not just a sporadic event in Herodotus's mind: it is a linguistic fact of the Ionic dialect, as we see immediately from the epigraphical evidence. For further details see Gregory Nagy, "Herodotus the Logios," *Arethusa* 20 (1987): 175−84, 209−10.

59. As in Homer, *Iliad* 2.486, 11.227.

60. Thucydides 1.22.4.

61. Aristophanes, *Frogs* 93, 766, 770, 780, 786, 793, 811, 831, 850, 939, 961, 973, 1369, 1495.

62. John Herington, *Poetry into Drama: Early Tragedy and the Greek Poetic Tradition* (Berkeley: University of California Press, 1985), p. 106.

63. Thus Euripides cannot even be a runner-up to Aeschylus: that honor is reserved for Sophocles (Aristophanes, *Frogs* 787–94, 1515–19).

64. Aristophanes, *Frogs* 785, 867, 873, 882.

65. Richard Seaford, "The 'Hyporchema' of Pratinas," *Maia* 29 (1977–78): 86.

66. Aristophanes, *Frogs* 785; *krisis* and its verb *krīnō* are also at 779, 805, 873, 1467, 1473.

67. For the wording, see again the description in Plato, *Laws* 659ab.

68. Cf. Helene P. Foley, *Ritual Irony: Poetry and Sacrifice in Euripides* (Ithaca, N.Y.: Cornell University Press, 1985), pp. 205–58. Note *Euripides: Cyclops*, ed. Richard Seaford (New York: Oxford University Press, 1984), p. 43, on the affinities of the *Bacchae* with the Dionysiac theme of the captivity and liberation of satyrs.

69. Foley, *Ritual Irony*, p. 215.

70. E. R. Dodds, ed., *Euripides Bacchae* (Oxford: Oxford University Press, 1960), p. 159.

71. Such self-reference, commonly known as "aetiology," should not be taken as evidence for the notion that myth exists in order to explain ritual. It would be more accurate to say that ritual motivates myth as much as myth motivates ritual. In another context, I have offered the following additional observations on the Greek term *aition*, "cause," in the sense of "a myth that *traditionally* motivates an institution, such as a ritual": "I stress 'traditionally' because the myth may be a tradition *parallel to* the ritual, not *derivative from* it. Unless we have evidence otherwise, we cannot assume in any particular instance that an aetiological myth was an *untraditional* fabrication intended simply to explain a given ritual. The factor of *motivating*—as distinct from *explaining*—is itself a traditional function in religion, parallel to the traditional function of ritual. It is only when the traditions of religion become obsolescent that rituals may become so obscure as to invite explanations of a purely literary nature" (Nagy, *Best*, p. 279, par. 2n2).

72. Pierre Chantraine, *Dictionnaire étymologique de la langue grecque* (Paris: Klincksieck, 1968–80), p. 17. Note the usage of *sun-agō* in Euripides, *Bacchae* 563 and 564, in the context of Orpheus as he plays the *kithara*.

73. E.g., Pindar, *Pythian* 10.30.

74. E.g., Pindar, *Olympian* 9.90.

75. Cf. *agōnismos*, "rivalry," in Thucydides 7.70.

76. As in *Homeric Hymn* 6.19–20. On *agōn* as a festival of contests in athletics *and* in poetry, song, and dance, see *Homeric Hymn to Apollo* 149–50 and Thucydides 3.10.3/5. Note too the following three subjects of the verb *agōnizomai*, "compete, engage in an *agōn*," in Herodotus: athletes (e.g., 2.160.3–4), warriors (e.g., 1.76.4), and *rhapsōidoi*, "rhapsodes" (5.67.1).

77. E.g., Demosthenes 18.33.

78. Mark Griffith, "Personality in Hesiod," *Classical Antiquity* 2 (1983): 58 n. 82, suggests that I do deny this notion in Nagy, *Best*, pp. 5–6, 296–97.

79. Griffith, "Personality," p. 58 n. 82, again, suggests that I do so argue in Nagy, *Best*, pp. 5–6, 296–97.

80. On categories of ownership of song and dance, see Merriam, *Anthropology of Music*, p. 83.

81. This is what occurs in Rwanda praise poetry, with memorization and remembering of the "original" composer by name; see Ruth Finnegan, *Oral Poetry: Its Nature, Significance, and Social Context* (Cambridge: Cambridge University Press, 1977), p. 79; cf. also p. 75. In Somali poetry, "a poet's composition . . . becomes his own property, under his own name, and another poet reciting them has to acknowledge from whom he has learnt them" (ibid., p. 74). For a possible trace of this type of attribution in the South Slavic traditions, see Lord, *Singer of Tales*, pp. 19–20.

82. For Rwanda and Somali examples see Finnegan, *Oral Poetry*, p. 83. Cf. Merriam, *Anthropology of Music*, p. 83, on the ownership of songs by kinship groups.

Parker: Metaphor and Catachresis

1. Quintilian, *Institutio oratoria*, trans. H. Rackham (Cambridge, Mass.: Harvard University Press, 1935), 8.6.35–36. All translations of Quintilian in this essay are from this edition unless otherwise indicated.

2. Joannes Susenbrotus, *Epitome troporum ac schematum et grammaticorum et rhetorum* (Zurich, 1541), p. 10.

3. Richard Lanham, *A Handlist of Rhetorical Terms* (Berkeley, Los Angeles, London: University of California Press, 1968), p. 21.

4. Northrop Frye, *Anatomy of Criticism* (1957; reprint, New York: Atheneum, 1966), p. 281; *Princeton Encyclopedia*, s.v. "catachresis."

5. César Chesneau Dumarsais, *Les tropes de Dumarsais, avec un commentaire raisonné par M. Fontanier*, ed. Gérard Genette, 2 vols. (1729 [Dumarsais] and 1818 [Fontanier]; reprint, Geneva: Slatkine Reprints, 1967), 1:157. I have explored some of the gothic possibilities in this neoclassical tradition's figure of the room or "house" and its definition of metaphor as an "alien" that usurps a place not its own, in an essay entitled "The Metaphorical Plot," whose full version appears in *Metaphor: Problems and Perspectives*, ed. David S. Miall (Sussex, England: Harvester, 1982).

6. George Puttenham, *The Arte of English Poesie* (1589), ed. Baxter Hathaway (1906; reprint, Kent, Ohio: Kent State University Press, 1970), pp. 188–91; my emphasis.

7. Pierre Fontanier, *Les figures du discours* (1821–27), ed. G. Genette (Paris: Flammarion, 1977). For Fontanier's *Commentaire* see the edition of *Les tropes* cited above in n. 5. All translations from Fontanier in the text are my own.

8. Dumarsais, *Les tropes*, 1:52; this and all other translations of Dumarsais in the essay are mine. The original of the passage just quoted is as follows: "Les langues les plus riches n'ont point un assez grand nombre de mots pour exprimer chaque idée particulière, par un terme qui ne soit que le signe propre de cette idée; ainsi l'on est souvent obligé d'emprunter le mot propre de quelqu'autre idée, qui a le plus de rapport à celle qu'on veut exprimer." Dumarsais begins in *Les tropes*—as Beauzée in his subsequent article for the *Encyclopédie* makes clear and as Fontanier will at

length point out—by rejecting the notion of the origin of tropes in necessity, but increasingly relies on it, in the description of catachresis cited here, in the later article devoted to "La métaphore" ("cette disète de mots a doné lieu à plusieurs métaphores," *Les tropes*, 1:160), and, most strikingly, at the end of the whole second part of *Les tropes*, devoted to "tropes in particular" ("La catachrèse est la première espèce de métaphore. On a recours à la catachrèse part nécessité, quand on ne trouve point de mot propre pour exprimer ce qu'on veut dire," ibid., 1:249).

9. See, for example, Fontanier, *Commentaire*, in Dumarsais, *Les tropes*, 2:84, together with his citation of d'Alembert in 2:384n.

10. Jacques Derrida, "La mythologie blanche," in *Poétique*, 5 (1971); translated as "White Mythology" by F. C. T. Moore, *New Literary History* 6, no. 1 (Autumn 1974): 5–74.

11. Cicero, *De oratore*, trans. H. Rackham, Loeb Classical Library (Cambridge, Mass.: Harvard University Press, 1942), 3.38.155. All translations of Cicero in this essay are from this edition, except where indicated otherwise.

12. Dudley Fenner, *The Artes of Logike and Rethorike* (1584), s.v. "Metaphor." I have discussed the gender implications of this passage's "shamefast" and "maydenly" in *Literary Fat Ladies: Rhetoric, Gender, Property* (London and New York: Methuen, 1987), p. 108.

13. John Hoskins, *Directions for Speech and Style* (1589).

14. Hugh Blair, *Lectures on Rhetoric and Belles Lettres*, ed. Harold F. Harding, 2 vols. (Carbondale and Edwardsville: Southern Illinois University Press, 1965), 1:289. All subsequent references to Blair are to this edition.

15. On the reversal of natural and ornamental, primitive and secondary, as a motif running through descriptions of metaphor, see Jonathan Culler, "The Turns of Metaphor," in his *Pursuit of Signs* (Ithaca, N.Y.: Cornell University Press, 1981), pp. 202–3.

16. Paul de Man, "Autobiography as De-Facement," in his *The Rhetoric of Romanticism* (New York: Columbia University Press, 1984), pp. 79–80. What de Man has suggested elsewhere as a kind of gothic plot for metaphor (see "The Epistemology of Metaphor," in *On Metaphor*, ed. Sheldon Sacks [Chicago: University of Chicago Press, 1979], pp. 19–21) might be extended into the range of mutual echoings between discussions of figuration in the period from Blair to Fontanier and developments in gothic fiction and in the poetics of Romanticism or, before it, what used to be called its "pre-Romantic" prefigurings. It is, for example, the posited element of freedom in metaphor, as opposed to compulsion or lack of control in catachresis, that Fontanier will later underscore when he speaks of metaphor as the taking of words "in a sense that one gives them *for the moment* and that is *merely borrowed*" (*Les figures*, p. 66). The stress on "for the moment" and "merely borrowed" here is such as to suggest that it is also fueled by an anxiety about its opposite—a transport or transference that is more than merely temporary, and less than free or voluntarily controlled. Fontanier's description of the "freedom" of metaphor in contrast to the transports of catachresis may recall to some ears the more gothic overtones of Coleridge's description of that "willing suspension of disbelief *for*

the moment, which constitutes poetic faith," a passage whose insistence on temporariness suggests as its anxious opposite the possibility of a transport from which there may be no return. One way of approaching the link between eighteenth-century discussions of metaphor—with their delight in its controlled errancy and their concern with less simply delightful wandering would be to note Blair's citation, in the midst of the discussion of figurative language as "an instrument of the most delicate and refined luxury" (*Lectures,* 1 : 289), of Addison's passage on the advantages of being "entertained with pleasing shows and apparitions" rather than seeing things only "in their proper figures and motions"—a passage that offers a kind of condensed "Belle Dame sans Merci": "In short, our souls are . . . delightfully lost, and bewildered in a pleasing delusion; and we walk about, like the enchanted hero of a romance. . . . But, upon the finishing of some secret spell, the fantastic scene breaks up, and the disconsolate knight finds himself on a barren heath, or in a solitary desert" (*Spectator* 413, quoted in Blair, *Lectures,* 1 : 290). What is here cited by Blair as a masterful use of language by a writer "whose imagination is, at once remarkably rich, and remarkably correct and chaste" (1 : 289), becomes in its context a pre-Romantic romance of figuration itself, a kind of darker stand-in for Cicero's description, echoed elsewhere in Blair, of metaphor as allowing one's thoughts to be "led to something else . . . without going astray" (*De oratore* 3.39.160).

17. Gérard Genette points to this element of conscious transfer in his introduction to the Dumarsais-Fontanier *Les tropes*: "Il ne peut y avoir figure en général, et trope en particulier, que si le locuteur a conscience de substituer à l'expression propre une expression figurée qui fait *écart.*"

18. See Fontanier's *Commentaire,* in Dumarsais, *Les tropes,* 2 : 383, and the distinction between "tropes figures" and "tropes catachreses" in 2 : 392n: "Les uns sont employés librement et par choix, par gout, pour l'ornement du discours . . . les autres sont employés forcement et par necessité, pour subvenir aux besoins de la langue, et suppléer au defaut des mots propres qui lui manquent."

19. "Le *sens tropologique* est, ou *figuré,* ou purement *extensif,* selon que la nouvelle signification à laquelle il est du, a été donnée au mot librement et comme par jeu, ou qu'elle en est devenue *propre* comme la signification primitive" (Fontanier, *Les figures,* p. 75).

20. "Devenues à la longue familières, habituelles, ou meme fixes, invariables, [ils] ont fini par perdre tout-à-fait leur caractere d'emprunt, et par être regardées à-peu-pres comme autant de significations propres" (ibid., p. 159).

Goldberg: On the One Hand . . .

1. Jacques Derrida, *Of Grammatology,* trans. Gayatri Chakravorty Spivak (Baltimore, Md.: Johns Hopkins University Press, 1976), p. 87. All translated quotations of foreign works in this essay are from the editions cited unless otherwise noted.

2. Jacques Derrida, "Freud and the Scene of Writing," in his *Writing*

and Difference, trans. Alan Bass (Chicago: University of Chicago Press, 1978), pp. 230–31.

3. The interview appears on p. 24 of *Le Monde*; English translation by Linda Coverdale in Roland Barthes, *The Grain of the Voice* (New York: Hill and Wang, 1985), p. 177.

4. Roland Barthes, *The Responsibility of Forms*, trans. Richard Howard (New York: Hill and Wang, 1985), p. 116.

5. Roland Barthes, *Roland Barthes*, trans. Richard Howard (New York: Hill and Wang, 1977), p. 97.

6. I do not mean this literally; the French reads "dans ce qu'il écrit, chacun défend sa sexualité" (Roland Barthes, *Roland Barthes* [Paris: Seuil, 1975], p. 159). Nonetheless, to regard the writing surface as a defensive structure is at once to protect and to project sexuality onto writing.

7. Roland Barthes, *The Empire of Signs*, trans. Richard Howard (New York: Hill and Wang, 1982), p. 85.

8. See Jerome Christensen, "Setting Byron Straight: Class, Sexuality, and the Poet," in *Literature and the Body*, ed. Elaine Scarry (Baltimore, Md.: Johns Hopkins University Press, 1988).

9. Jacques Derrida, "*Geschlecht*: Sexual Difference, Ontological Difference," *Research in Phenomenology* 13 (1983): 65–83, and "*Geschlecht* II: Heidegger's Hand," in *Deconstruction and Philosophy*, ed. John Sallis (Chicago: University of Chicago Press, 1987), pp. 161–96.

10. Martin Heidegger, *Parmenides* (Frankfurt am Main: Vittorio Klostermann, 1982), p. 119.

11. See Eve Kosofsky Sedgwick, *Between Men: English Literature and Male Homosocial Desire* (New York: Columbia University Press, 1985).

12. Martin Heidegger, *Was Heisst Denken?*, trans. as *What Is Called Thinking?* by Fred D. Wieck and J. Glenn Gray (New York: Harper & Row, 1972), p. 16.

13. See Frank Lentricchia, *After the New Criticism* (Chicago: University of Chicago Press, 1980), pp. 85–88, for a discussion that mine frequently parallels.

14. Martin Heidegger, *Being and Time*, trans. John Macquarrie and Edward Robinson (New York: Harper & Row, 1962), p. 104.

15. G. Wundt, quoted in Sigmund Freud, *The Psychopathology of Everyday Life*, trans. Alan Tyson (New York: Norton, 1965), p. 131.

16. Melanie Klein, *Love, Guilt and Reparation and Other Works, 1921–1945* (New York: Delta, 1975), p. 64.

17. Erasmus, trans. A. S. Osley, in *Scribes and Sources* (Boston: David R. Godine, 1980), pp. 34–35.

18. Jacques Derrida, *The Post Card: From Socrates to Freud and Beyond*, trans. Alan Bass (Chicago: University of Chicago Press, 1987), p. 105. The epigraph to this paper appears on p. 191.

Hertz: Lurid Figures

1. Paul de Man, *The Rhetoric of Romanticism* (New York: Columbia University Press, 1984), pp. 288–90. Henceforth this volume will be cited

as *RR*. Three other volumes of Paul de Man's writings will be similarly cited by abbreviations. They are *Blindness and Insight: Essays in the Rhetoric of Contemporary Criticism* (New York: Oxford University Press, 1971), cited as *BI*; *Allegories of Reading: Figural Language in Rousseau, Nietzsche, Rilke, and Proust* (New Haven, Conn.: Yale University Press, 1979), cited as *AR*; and *The Resistance to Theory*, edited and with an introduction by Wlad Godzich (Minneapolis: University of Minnesota Press, 1986), cited as *RT*.

2. According to Tom Keenan, who is responsible for the bibliography of de Man's writings in *RT*, the reissue never appeared, so "Wordsworth and the Victorians" was published for the first time in *RR*. Judging from its placement in that volume, between "Autobiography as De-Facement" and "Shelley Disfigured," and from the concerns and idiom it shares with those essays, it was probably written during the same year, 1979.

3. Both papers, written in the early 1980's, will be included in a collection of de Man's essays on philosophical texts edited by Andrzej Warminski, *Aesthetic Ideology* (Minneapolis: University of Minnesota Press, 1990). "Phenomenality and Materiality in Kant" was first published in *Hermeneutics: Questions and Prospects*, ed. G. Shapiro and A. Sica (Amherst: University of Massachusetts Press, 1984), pp. 121–44.

4. "Sheer" adds a note of admiring insistence to the various nouns that designate the unanalyzable, disruptive instance at work in a particular text or at a particular point in de Man's argument. For example, from "Hypogram and Inscription": "Do these readings cope with the sheer strength of figuration, that is to say master [tropes'] power to confer, to usurp, and to take away significance from grammatical universals?" (*RT*, p. 45). Cf. also "sheer metonymic enumeration" (*AR*, p. 152), "sheer imposition" (*RR*, p. 118), etc. Sometimes the rhyme "mere" will serve the same function, particularly where unexpected aleatory effects ("mere chance," "mere coincidence," *AR*, pp. 288–89) are operating to undo the intelligibility of a text.

5. Cf. Wordsworth's "And in the sheltered and the sheltering grove / A perfect stillness" (1850 *Prelude* 1.69–70). In "Phenomenality and Materiality in Kant," de Man makes a distinction between the "sheltering" sky of Wordsworth and Heidegger, under which man can "dwell," and a figure of the sky in Kant's Third Critique that is not "associated in any way with shelter." That would be, although de Man doesn't use the term here, an instance of "sheer sky." The two "sh-" words are brought together effectively in the last sentences of "Wordsworth and the Victorians": "It would be naive to believe that we could ever face Wordsworth, a poet of sheer language, outright. But it would be more naive still to think that we can take shelter from what he knew by means of the very evasions which this knowledge renders impossible" (*RR*, p. 92).

6. See Paul de Man, "Hegel on the Sublime," in *Displacement: Derrida and After*, ed. Mark Krupnick (Bloomington: Indiana University Press, 1983), pp. 139–53. Here the characterization of the "American interpretation of Romanticism" as a "closely familial romance" (p. 144) is followed by a comment on Hegel's rejection of a genetic or "familial" reading of the *fiat lux* (p. 146).

7. See in particular "Autobiography as De-Facement," in *RR*, pp. 70–71.

8. See Julia Kristeva, *Histoires d'Amour* (Paris: Denoël, 1984), esp. pp. 27–58, and the chapter entitled "Something to Be Scared Of," in Kristeva's *Powers of Horror: An Essay on Abjection*, trans. Léon S. Roudiez (New York: Columbia University Press, 1982), pp. 32–55.

9. The reference to Mallarmé alludes to a discussion in an earlier chapter of de Man's dissertation, one never published. Hérodiade is described as turning away from the "element of natural, maternal affection": "The heroine rejects it with all the determination of one who knows its seductiveness" (Paul de Man, *Mallarmé, Yeats and the Post-Romantic Predicament*, Ph.D. diss., Harvard University, May 1960, p. 23). My thanks to Barbara Johnson for supplying me with a photocopy of these chapters, and to the Harvard University Library for allowing her to.

10. *RR*, p. 70. On the "seductions of identification" see Minae Mizumura, "Renunciation," in *The Lesson of Paul de Man*, ed. Peter Brooks et al., Yale French Studies, vol. 69 (New Haven, Conn.: Yale University Press, 1985), pp. 91–97.

11. On the same page on which de Man notes Hérodiade's rejection of the seductiveness of the maternal (see n. 9 above) one can find a similar fending-off of psychoanalysis. Commenting on Mallarmé's revising an early poem, changing an apostrophic "Notre *Père*" to "Notre *Dame*," he writes: "This change adds a world of meaning (of which psychoanalytic criticism has eagerly and all too literally taken advantage)." The allusion, a footnote indicates, is to Charles Mauron's work.

12. Illuminating discussions of de Man's forcing of his texts can be found in Hans-Jost Frey's "Undecidability," in Brooks et al., *The Lesson of Paul de Man*, pp. 124–33, and in Rodolphe Gasché's contribution to *Reading de Man Reading*, ed. Lindsay Waters and Wlad Godzich (Minneapolis: University of Minnesota Press, 1989), pp. 259–94. The most notorious instance, de Man's reading of Rousseau's story of Marion and the purloined ribbon (*AR*, pp. 278–301), is discussed below. But one could look, too, at the last essay in *The Rhetoric of Romanticism*, in which the sequence of anecdotes in Kleist's text on puppets is read in jumbled fashion, as though the discussion of marionettes were the culminating, rather than the first, episode. One effect of this rearrangement is a puzzling symmetry: *Allegories of Reading* concludes with "Marion," *The Rhetoric of Romanticism* with "marionettes." Moreover the two nouns are brought together at a critical juncture of the earlier essay, where de Man is considering Rousseau's claim that the lie he told about Marion was not voluntary but rather the *effet machinal* of his embarrassment: "The machinelike quality of the text of the lie is more remarkable still when, as in the Marion episode, the disproportion between the crime that is to be confessed and the crime performed by the lie adds a delirious element to the situation. By saying that the excuse is not only a fiction but also a machine one adds to the connotations of referential detachment, of gratuitous improvisation, that of the implacable repetition of a preordained pattern. Like Kleist's marionettes, the machine is both 'anti-grav', the anamorphosis of a form detached from

meaning and capable of taking on any structure whatever, yet entirely ruthless in its inability to modify its own structural design for nonstructural reasons" (*AR*, p. 294). The conceptual articulation de Man is proposing here—between the "referential detachment" of fiction and the "implacable repetition" of formal patterns—is allegorically read out of two lurid episodes, that of Marion, the disfigured victim of Rousseau's lie, and that of the marionettes, "suspended in dead passivity." I believe de Man would acknowledge the appearance of such figures in his own writing as involuntary illustrations of his thesis—that one is "bound to repeat the disfiguration of metaphor . . . in what appears to be a more violent mode" (*RR*, p. 120). This formulation is considered at greater length below.

13. The most haunting exemplification of this theme comes in de Man's reading of the Rilke poem "Quai du Rosaire" (*AR*, pp. 40–43), which focuses on the "seductive but funereal image" of houses reflected, upside down, in the canals of Bruges while, above, the sounds of a carillon can be heard, "suspended in the skies." Rilke's characteristic "synthesis of rising and falling" is alluded to in de Man's discussion of Kleist's marionettes, "hanging and suspended like dead bodies" (*RR*, p. 287).

14. Shelley, "The Triumph of Life," variorum text ed. Donald H. Reiman, in Reiman, *Shelley's "The Triumph of Life": A Critical Study* (Urbana: University of Illinois Press, 1965), pp. 192–95. The lines quoted are 410–15 and 424–36.

15. For especially lucid discussions of the problem of "face," in Wordsworth and in de Man, see Catherine Caruth, "Past Recognition: Narrative Origins in Wordsworth and Freud," *MLN* 100 (Dec. 1985), pp. 935–48, and Cynthia Chase, "Giving a Face to a Name: De Man's Figures," in her *Decomposing Figures: Rhetorical Readings in the Romantic Tradition* (Baltimore, Md.: Johns Hopkins University Press, 1986), pp. 82–112. This is a good place to acknowledge a longstanding debt to Cynthia Chase, whose writings and conversation have been a challenge and a source of encouragement.

16. Reiman (*Shelley's "Triumph"*, p. 60) takes the "shape all light" as an allusion to Julie; de Man, I believe, would not quarrel with that, although in other respects his reading of *The Triumph of Life* is at odds with Reiman's. De Man's persistent reference to Rousseau's *Julie, ou la Nouvelle Héloïse* is, as he liked to say, well-known: it can be documented in the indexes to *BI*, *AR*, *RR*, and *RT*.

17. In the concluding sentences of de Man's "The Resistance to Theory," written two or three years after "Shelley Disfigured," that "going under" itself surfaces, this time as a way of characterizing the weirdly persistent life-in-death of a quasipersonified "literary theory": "The loftier the aims and the better the methods of literary theory, the less possible it becomes. Yet literary theory is not in danger of going under; it cannot help but flourish, and the more it is resisted, the more it flourishes, since the language it speaks is the language of self-resistance. What remains impossible to decide is whether this flourishing is a triumph or a fall" (*RT*, pp. 19–20).

18. A sustained and acute reading of the movement of these pages can be found in Werner Hamacher's remarkable essay "LECTIO: De Man's Imperative," in *Reading De Man Reading*, pp. 171–201.

19. On obsession as a mode of intelligibility, see de Man's pairing of Baudelaire's sonnets "Correspondances" and "Obsession" in "Anthropomorphism and Trope in the Lyric" (*RR*, pp. 252–62).

20. See Barbara Johnson's "Gender Theory and The Yale School," in *Rhetoric and Form: Deconstruction at Yale*, ed. Robert Con Davis and Ronald Schleifer (Norman: University of Oklahoma Press, 1985), pp. 101–12, and Cynthia Chase's "The Witty Butcher's Wife: Freud, Lacan, and the Conversion of Resistance to Theory," *MLN* 102 (Dec. 1987), pp. 989–1013.

21. For a brief but exemplary reading of these pages, see William Ray's fine study *Literary Meaning: From Phenomenology to Deconstruction* (Oxford: Basil Blackwell, 1984), pp. 198–205.

22. This essay was written in 1986, before the discovery of the newspaper articles and reviews now collected under the title *Wartime Journalism, 1939–1943. By Paul de Man*, ed. Werner Hamacher, Neil Hertz, and Thomas Keenan (Lincoln: University of Nebraska Press, 1988), a discovery that adds another set of lurid themes, figures, and circumstances to those taken up in these pages. Can an account of them be articulated with the interpretation of de Man's later writings offered here? I believe so, but I am certain that the relation between what Paul de Man did and wrote during the Second World War and what he did and wrote thereafter is not a simple one. A continuation of "Lurid Figures," entitled "More Lurid Figures," will appear in a forthcoming issue of *Diacritics*; meanwhile, I prefer to leave this discussion of lurid figures dated but unrevised.

Borch-Jacobsen: Analytic Speech

1. Martin Heidegger, *Unterwegs zur Sprache* (Pfüllingen: Neske, 1959), p. 206.

2. Paul Ricoeur, *La métaphore vive* (Paris: Le Seuil, 1975).

3. Roland Barthes, "L'ancienne rhétorique," *Communications* 16 (1970): 194–95; Gérard Genette, "La rhétorique restreinte," *Communications* 16 (1970): 158–59; Ricoeur, *Métaphore*, pp. 13–14 and 63–66; Tzvetan Todorov, *Théories du symbole* (Paris: Le Seuil, 1977), chaps. 2 and 3. The quoted term is from Ricoeur, *Métaphore*, p. 14.

4. G. A. Kennedy, *Classical Rhetoric and Its Christian and Secular Tradition from Ancient to Modern Times* (Chapel Hill: University of North Carolina Press, 1980), pp. 4–6.

5. V. Florescu, *La retorica nel suo sviluppo storico* (Bologna: Il Mulino, 1971). On that (very classical) opposition between "art of persuasion" and "art of speaking well" cf. also C. Perelman and L. Olbrechts-Tyteca, *Rhétorique et philosophie* (Paris: Presses Universitaires de France, 1952), pp. 15–16; A. Kibédi Varga, *Rhétorique et littérature* (Paris: Didier, 1970), p. 20; and, not forgetting Kant, *The Critique of Judgment*, trans. James Creed Meredith (Oxford: Clarendon Press, 1952), p. 192: "Rhetoric, so far as this is taken to mean the art of persuasion, i.e. the art of deluding by

means of a fair semblance (as *arts oratoria*), and not merely excellence of speech (eloquence and style), is a dialectic, which borrows from poetry only so much as is necessary to win over men's minds to the side of the speaker before they have weighed the matter, and to rob their verdict of its freedom."

6. Emile Benveniste, "Remarques sur la fonction du langage dans la découverte freudienne," in his *Eléments de linguistique générale* (Paris: Gallimard, 1966); Roman Jakobson, "Two Aspects of Language and Two Types of Aphasia Disturbances," in his *Fundamentals of Language* (The Hague: Mouton, 1956); Jacques Lacan, "L'instance de la lettre dans l'inconscient," in his *Ecrits* (Paris: Le Seuil, 1966).

7. J.-Fr. Lyotard, *Discours, figure* (Paris: Klincksieck, 1971), especially the chapters "Le travail du rêve ne pense pas" and "Connivences du désir avec le figural"; Todorov, *Théories*, chap. 8 ("La rhétorique de Freud"); Genette, "La rhétorique," p. 162, n. 1; Nícolas Abraham and M. Torok, *L'écorce et le noyau* (Paris: Aubier-Flammarion, 1978), the chapter "L'écorce et le noyau."

8. Sigmund Freud, "Psychical (or Mental) Treatment," in *Standard Edition of the Complete Psychological Works of Sigmund Freud*, James Strachey gen. ed. (London: Hogarth Press, 1953), 7:283. All Freud quotations in this essay are from the *Standard Edition*, henceforth abbreviated *SE*.

9. Friedrich Nietzsche, *Course of Rhetoric* 3, quoted by Philippe Lacoue-Labarthe, *Le sujet de la philosophie* (Paris: Aubier-Flammarion, 1979), p. 48 (English translation from the French by D. Brick).

10. Freud, "Preface to the Translation of Bernheim's *Suggestion*," *SE*, 1:82.

11. Freud, *Totem and Taboo*, *SE*, 13, chap. 3 ("Animism, Magic and the Omnipotence of Thoughts").

12. Plato, *Phaedrus* 261a. *Collected Dialogues*, ed. Edith Hamilton and Huntington Cairns, trans. R. Hackforth (Princeton, N.J.: Princeton University Press, 1961), p. 506 (translation altered).

13. Freud, *Beyond the Pleasure Principle*, *SE*, 18:18.

14. Freud, "Remembering, Repeating and Working-Through. Further Recommendations on the Technique of Psychoanalysis II," *SE*, 12:148–49.

15. Freud, *Group Psychology and the Analysis of the Ego*, *SE*, 18:115.

16. Freud, "On Psychotherapy," *SE*, 7:258: "A factor dependent on the psychical disposition of the patient contributes, without any intention on our part, to the effect of every therapeutic process initiated by a physician. . . . We have learned to use the word 'suggestion' for this phenomenon . . . it is a disadvantage, however, to leave the mental factor in our treatment so completely in the patient's hands. Thus it is impossible to keep a check on it, to administer it in doses or to intensify it. Is it not then a justifiable endeavor on the part of the physician to seek to obtain command of this factor, to use it with a purpose, and to direct and strengthen it? This and nothing else is what *scientific* psychotherapy proposes" (my emphasis).

17. Lacan, *Ecrits*, p. 106 (psychoanalytic dialogue discussed in relation to the "failure of verbal dialectic" in the *Republic*); p. 128 (in relation to the exclusion of rhetoric in *Gorgias*); p. 192 (in relation to *Parmenides*); p. 292 (in relation to "the dialectic of consciousness-of-self, such as it is realized from Socrates to Hegel"); p. 852 (in relation to "Socrates, precursor to the analyst"). See also Maurice Blanchot, "La parole analytique," in his *L'entretien infini* (Paris: Gallimard, 1969), pp. 343–44 (psychoanalytic dialogue discussed in relation to the substitution of "dialectic" for the "magic" of hypnosis).

18. See, among a thousand other passages, "Intervention sur le transfert," in Lacan, *Ecrits*, pp. 215–26.

19. Freud, "Remembering and Repeating," p. 156: "From a theoretical point of view one may correlate it [analytic treatment] with the 'abreacting' of the quotas of affect strangulated by repression—an abreaction without which hypnotic treatment remained ineffective."

20. Freud, "The Unconscious," *SE*, 14:166: "It is of course only as something conscious that we know it [the unconscious], after it has undergone transformation or translation into something conscious."

21. Freud, *Beyond the Pleasure Principle*, p. 60.

22. "Metaphor of the Subject" is the title of the *Annexe* II of Lacan's *Ecrits*, devoted to a discussion of the works of C. Perelman (*Traité de l'argumentation* [Paris: Presses Universitaires de France, 1958], vol. 2).

23. Freud, "An Autobiographical Study," *SE*, 20:42.

24. Freud, *Group Psychology*, p. 107. (Freud takes identification with the symptom to be a model for collective hysteria: "One ego has perceived a significant analogy with another upon one point—in our example upon openness to a similar emotion; an identification is thereupon constructed on this point, and, under the influence of the pathogenic situation, is displaced onto the symptom which the one ego has produced" (ibid.).

25. For a fuller discussion, see my *The Freudian Subject*, trans. Catherine Porter (Stanford, Calif.: Stanford University Press, 1988), "The Primal Band," pp. 127–239.

Sperber and Wilson: Rhetoric and Relevance

1. Samuel Taylor Coleridge, *Biographia literaria*, ed. J. Shawcross (London: Oxford University Press, 1907), 2:115.

2. I. A. Richards, *The Philosophy of Rhetoric* (London: Oxford University Press, 1936), p. 11.

3. Jonathan Culler, *The Pursuit of Signs: Semiotics, Literature, Deconstruction* (Ithaca, N.Y.: Cornell University Press, 1981), p. 209.

4. Victor Hugo, *Oeuvres complètes: Poésie II* (Paris: Robert Laffont, 1985), p. 265.

5. For an elaboration, see Dan Sperber, *On Anthropological Knowledge* (Cambridge: Cambridge University Press, 1985), chap. 1.

6. See Dan Sperber and Deirdre Wilson, *Relevance: Communication and Cognition* (Cambridge, Mass.: Harvard University Press, and Oxford: Blackwell, 1986). For a more detailed account of looseness and metaphor,

see our "Loose Talk," *Proceedings of the Aristotelian Society* n.s. 86 (1986): 153–71. For a more detailed account of irony, see our "Irony and the Use-Mention Distinction," in *Radical Pragmatics*, ed. Peter Cole (New York: Academic Press, 1981), pp. 295–318.

7. Samuel Taylor Coleridge, *The Collected Works*, vol. 5-II, *Lectures 1808–1819 on Literature* (Princeton, N.J.: Princeton University Press, 1987), pp. 527–28.

8. See Deirdre Wilson and Dan Sperber, "Mood and the Analysis of Non-declarative Sentences," in *Human Agency: Language, Duty, and Value*, eds. Jonathan Dancy, J. M. E. Moravcsik, and C. C. W. Taylor (Stanford, Calif.: Stanford University Press, 1988), pp. 77–101.

9. D. C. Muecke, *Irony* (London: Methuen, 1970), p. 63.

10. Wayne C. Booth, *A Rhetoric of Irony* (Chicago: University of Chicago Press, 1974), p. 42.

Zimmerli: The Emancipation of Rhetorical Elements in Art

1. Hans-Georg Gadamer, "Rhetorik, Hermeneutik und Ideologiekritik. Metakritische Erörterungen zu *Wahrheit und Methode*," in K.-O. Apel et al., *Hermeneutik und Ideologiekritik* (Frankfurt am Main: Suhrkamp, 1971), pp. 63–64. All translations of foreign texts cited in this essay are mine.

2. Cf. C. P. Snow, *The Two Cultures* (London, 1959); Walther Ch. Zimmerli, "Einheit oder Vielheit der Kulturen? Geistes- und Naturwissenschaften in einer technologischen Welt," *Physikalische Blätter* 44, no. 3 (March 1988): 57–62.

3. Hans-Georg Gadamer, "Philosophie oder Wissenschaftstheorie?" in *Interdisziplinär*, ed. H. Holzhey, *Philosophie aktuell* vol. 2 (Basel and Stuttgart: Schwabe, 1974), p. 101.

4. See Walther Ch. Zimmerli, "Das antiplatonische Experiment. Bemerkungen zu technologischen Postmoderne," in *Technologisches Zeitalter oder Postmoderne?*, ed. W. Ch. Zimmerli (Munich: Fink, 1988), pp. 13–35, esp. pp. 19 ff.

5. J. J. Beckmann, *Anleitung zur Technologie* (Göttingen, 1777), p. 17, and his *Entwurf der allgemeinen Technologie* (Göttingen, 1806).

6. See, e.g., Wolfgang Welsch, *Unsere postmoderne Moderne* (Weinheim: VCH Acta humaniora, 1987); *Wege aus der Moderne, Schlüsseltexte der Postmoderne-Diskussion*, ed. W. Welsch (Weinheim: VCH Acta humaniora, 1988).

7. Cf. Jürgen Habermas, *Kleine politsche Schriften* (Frankfurt am Main: Suhrkamp, 1981), pp. 444 ff., and his *Die neue Unübersichtlichkeit* (Frankfurt am Main: Suhrkamp, 1985), esp. pp. 47 ff.

8. Ilya Prigogine, *From Being to Becoming—Time and Complexity in Physical Sciences* (San Francisco: Freeman, 1979); Erich Jantsch, *Die Selbstorganisation des Universums* (Munich: dtv, 1979).

9. See Friedrich Nietzsche, "Über Wahrheit und Lüge im aussermoralischen Sinne" (1873), in his *Sämtliche Werke: Kritische Studienausgabe*, vol. 1 (Berlin: De Gruyter, 1980), pp. 880–90.

10. Still one of the best ones is Umberto Eco, *Einführung in die Semiotik* (Munich: Fink, 1971).

11. Ovid, *Metamorphoses* 11.90 ff.; cf. Walther Ch. Zimmerli, "How Autonomous Can Art Be? Philosophical Remarks on Photo-Realism and Post-Modern Aesthetics," *Man and World* 21 (1988): 191–211, esp. pp. 195 ff. ("The theorem of Midas").

12. An early version of this analysis has been published in Walther Ch. Zimmerli, "Die ästhetisch-semiotische Relation und das Problem einer philosophischen Literaturästhetik," *Studia Philosophica* 43 (1984): 173–89, esp. pp. 178 ff.

13. See S. Shoemaker, "Verkörperung und Verhalten" (1976), in *Identität der Person*, ed. L. Siep (Basel and Stuttgart: Schwabe, 1983), pp. 96–126.

14. See K. Cramer, "'Erlebnis'. Thesen zu Hegels Theorie des Selbstbewusstseins mit Rücksicht auf die Aporien eines Grundbegriffs nachhegelscher Philosophie," in *Stuttgarter Hegel-Tage 1971*, ed. Hans-Georg Gadamer, Hegel-Studien Beiheft 11 (Bonn, 1974), pp. 573–603.

15. Ch. Morris, "Ästhetik und Zeichentheorie" (1939), reprinted in *Ästhetik*, ed. W. Henckmann, *Wege der Forschung* 31 (Darmstadt: WBG, 1979), pp. 269–93, esp. p. 278.

16. Cf. Eco, *Einführung*, p. 146.

17. Umberto Eco, *Das offene Kunstwerk* (1962) (Frankfurt am Main: Suhrkamp, 1972), p. 148.

18. See Charles Jencks, *Language of Postmodern Architecture* (New York: Rizzoli, 1977); Welsch, *Unsere postmoderne Moderne*, esp. pp. 87 ff.

19. Habermas, *Kleine politische Schriften*, esp. pp. 444 ff. ("Die Moderne—ein unvollendetes Projekt").

20. T. W. Adorno, "Funktionalismus heute," in his *Gesammelte Schriften*, vol. 10, part 1 (Frankfurt am Main: Suhrkamp, 1977), pp. 375 ff.; cf. again Habermas, *Die neue Unübersichtlichkeit*, esp. pp. 11 ff. ("Moderne und postmoderne Architektur").

21. See H. Schlüter, *Grundkurs der Rhetorik* (Munich, 1974), esp. pp. 61 ff., with respect to the rhetoric of advertisement; for the classical background see H. Lausberg, *Elemente der literarischen Rhetorik* (Munich: Hueber, 1963).

Bercovitch: The Ends of American Puritan Rhetoric

1. Cotton Mather, *Magnalia Christi Americana; or, the Ecclesiastical History of New England*, Books 1 and 2, ed. Kenneth B. Murdock (Cambridge, Mass.: Harvard University Press, 1977), pp. 118, 119, 93, 121, 123.

2. John Foxe, quoted in William Haller, *Foxe's "Book of Martyrs" and the Elect Nation* (London: The Trinity Press, 1963), p. 110.

3. Larzer Ziff, "Upon What Pretext? The Book and Literary History," *Proceedings of the American Antiquarian Society* 95 (1985): 308.

4. John Winthrop, "A Model of Christian Charity" (1630), in *Puritan Political Ideas, 1558–1794*, ed. Edmund S. Morgan (New York: Bobbs-

Merrill, 1965), pp. 90–99; Perry Miller, *Errand into the Wilderness* (Cambridge, Mass.: Harvard University Press, 1958), p. 16.

5. Michael Wigglesworth, "God's Controversy," in *The Puritans: A Sourcebook of Their Writings*, ed. Perry Miller and Thomas H. Johnson, 2 vols. (New York: Harper and Row, 1963), 2:616; Nathaniel Hawthorne, *The Scarlet Letter*, ed. Millicent Bell (New York: The Library of America, 1983), pp. 332–33.

6. Cotton Mather, *Theopolis Americana: An Essay on the Golden Street of the Holy City* (Boston: B. Green, 1710), p. 9.

7. John Cotton, *God's Promise to His Plantations* (London, 1630), in *Old South Leaflets* (Boston: Directors of the Old South Work [1896]), vol. 3, no. 53, p. 17.

8. John Danforth, *A Brief Recognition of New England's Errand into the Wilderness*, in *The Wall and the Garden: Selected Massachusetts Election Sermons*, ed. A. William Plumstead (Minneapolis: University of Minnesota Press, 1968), pp. 57–62.

9. Herman Melville, *White-Jacket, or, The World in a Man-of-War*, ed. C. Thomas Tanselle (New York: Library of America, 1983), p. 506; John Adams to Thomas Jefferson, Oct. 9, 1818, in *The Adams-Jefferson Correspondence*, ed. Lester J. Cappon (New York and Chapel Hill, N.C.: University of North Carolina Press, 1959), p. xliv; Thomas Paine, *Representative Selections*, ed. Harry H. Clark (New York: Hill and Wang, 1961), p. 61; John Louis O'Sullivan, "The Great Nation of Futurity," *United States Magazine and Democratic Review* 6 (1839): 427, 430; Ronald Reagan, "Closing Statement [to televised presidential debate]," *The New York Times*, Sept. 22, 1980, p. B7.

10. Henry David Thoreau, *Walden; or Life in the Woods*, ed. Robert F. Sayre (New York: Library of America, 1985), p. 486; W. E. B. Du Bois, "Patriotism," *Crisis* 17, no. 1 (1918): 10; Langston Hughes, quoted in Coretta Scott King, "King's Dream of Equality, Brotherhood Is Really the American Dream," *Atlanta Journal and Constitution*, Jan. 5, 1986, p. 7.

Sennett: The Rhetoric of Ethnic Identity

1. James Baldwin, *The Price of the Ticket: Collected Nonfiction, 1945–1985* (New York: St. Martin's Press, 1985), p. 334. Hereafter citations are given in parentheses after quotations and are shortened to *Collected Nonfiction*.

2. *The Selected Poems of Frank O'Hara*, ed. Donald Allen (New York: Vintage, 1974), pp. 198–99.

3. John Ashbery, "Litany," in his collection *As We Know* (New York: Viking, 1979), author's note p. 2; poem p. 3.

4. Wayne C. Booth, *A Rhetoric of Irony* (Chicago: University of Chicago Press, 1974).

5. Czeslaw Milosz, quoted in D. J. Enright, *The Alluring Problem: An Essay on Irony* (Oxford: Oxford University Press, 1986), p. 20.

Index

Index

Abraham, Nicolas, 32
Adams, John, 187
Addison, J., 22
Adorno, T. W., 166
Aeschylus, 55
Aesop, 216
Alembert, J. L. R., 14
Arbuthnot, J., 149
Archilochus, 216
Aristophanes, 55–56
Aristotle, 6, 38, 48, 56, 68, 90, 132, 134, 166, 211
Arnauld, Antoine, 13
Ashbery, John, 204f
Attis, 109–11, 116
Austin, J. L., 43

Bacon, Francis, 6, 8
Bakhtin, Mikhail, 19–20, 37
Baldwin, James, 192–97, 200–206 passim
Bally, Charles, 29
Banfield, Ann, 211
Baraka, Amiri (LeRoi Jones), 194
Barilli, Renato, 209
Barthes, Roland, 27, 77–85, 90–91, 93f, 99, 127–28
Baudelaire, C.-P., 24
Baumgarten, Alexander, 18
Beckett, Samuel, 24
Beckmann, Johann J., 159
Bender, John, 3–39, 209
Benveniste, Emile, 43, 129, 134
Benjamin, Walter, 24, 105 ff, 109, 124
Bercovitch, Sacvan, 171–90
Bernheim, Hippolyte, 130 ff

Blair, Hugh, 68–71, 73, 220–21
Blanchot, Maurice, 24, 228
Booth, Wayne, 153
Borch-Jacobsen, Mikkel, 127–39, 228
Bosse, Heinrich, 210
Brick, Douglas, 127 n
Burke, Kenneth, 36–37, 106, 212–13
Byron, G. G., Lord, 83

Calvin, John, 185
Caruth, Catherine, 225
Chase, Cynthia, 123, 225
Chomsky, Noam, 31
Cicero, 7, 17, 60–61, 62, 66–70, 71, 73
Cohn, Dorrit C., 211
Cole, Thomas, 214
Coleridge, Samuel Taylor, 20–21, 141, 149
Corax, 7
Cosimo II de Medici, 9–10
Cotton, John, 182f
Cromwell, Oliver, 177, 179
Culler, Jonathan, 142, 220
Curtius, Ernst Robert, 15–16

Danforth, John, 186
Daqiqi, 44–45
Defoe, Daniel, 20
Delboeuf, Joseph, 132
Deleuze, Gilles, 4
Derrida, Jacques, 36, 65, 77–99, 122, 199, 220, 221–22
Descartes, René, 11 ff, 19, 23, 87, 134
Diderot, Denis, 14, 101

235

Index

Du Bois, W. E. B., 187
Dumarsais, César Chesneau, 63–71
  passim, 219–20, 221
Dumézil, Georges, 216
Dwight, Timothy, 175

Eco, Umberto, 7, 166f
Ellison, Ralph, 199
Emerson, Ralph Waldo, 187
Empson, William, 35, 111–12
Engels, Friedrich, 87
Erasmus, 98–99
Euripides, 55–57

Ferdowsi, 44
Feyerabend, Paul K., 28
Fichte, J. G., 11
Fielding, Henry, 20
Florescu, V., 128, 226
Fontanier, Pierre, 63ff, 71–73, 140,
  219–20, 220–21
Foucault, Michel, 13, 16, 28
Foxe, John, 174, 185, 188
Freud, Sigmund, 31, 33, 73, 77,
  81–82, 83, 90–99, 129–39, 199,
  227–28
Frey, Hans-Jost, 224
Fried, Michael, 18
Frye, Northrop, 36, 61

Gadamer, Hans-Georg, 156–57, 160,
  165
Galilei, Galileo, 9–11, 28
Galsworthy, John, 95
Gasché, Rodolphe, 224
Geertz, Clifford, 28
Genette, Gérard, 127, 221
Gide, André, 83
Gödel, K., 23
Goethe, J. W. von, 17, 21, 36
Goffman, Erving, 34
Goldberg, Jonathan, 77–99
Goodman, Nelson, 23, 28
Griffith, Mark, 218

Habermas, Jürgen, 160, 166, 210
Hacking, Ian, 28
Hamacher, Werner, 225–26
Hawthorne, Nathaniel, 182, 188–89
Hegel, G. W. F., 11, 79, 86f, 134, 177,
  223
Heidegger, Martin, 24, 34, 77, 84–91,

93–99 *passim*, 107, 127, 158, 161,
  165, 199, 223
Heisenberg, W. K., 23
Herder, J. G. von, 14
Herodotus, 48, 54–55, 217
Hertz, Neil, 100–124, 226
Hesiod, 46, 49–53, 213–14, 216–17
Heyne, Christian Gottlob, 17
Hill, Christopher, 190
Hobbes, Thomas, 13
Homer, 44f, 54f, 213–14
Hughes, Langston, 187
Hugo, Victor, 142

Jakobson, Roman, 29–30, 31, 46,
  129, 134, 213f
Janet, Pierre, 132
Jencks, Charles, 166
Johnson, Barbara, 43, 224
Johnson, Edward, 182
Johnson, Mark, 35

Kafka, Franz, 24
Kant, Immanuel, 11, 13, 18–19, 101,
  226–27
Keats, John, 36
Keenan, Thomas, 223, 226
Kennedy, G. A., 128
Kierkegaard, Søren, 4
King, Martin Luther, 172
Kingston, Maxine Hong, 199
Klein, Calvin, 33
Klein, Melanie, 97–98, 99
Kleist, H. von, 100ff, 105, 111, 224f
Kluckhohn, Clyde, 191
Kristeva, Julia, 37, 108, 122
Kuhn, Thomas S., 28

Lacan, Jacques, 31, 33, 73, 98, 122,
  129–35 *passim*, 228
Lacoue-Labarthe, Philippe, 26
Lakoff, George, 35
Lanham, Richard, 61
Laplanche, Jean, 31–32
Lausberg, Heinrich, 27
Le Bon, Gustave, 136–37
Leibniz, G. W., 14
Lentricchia, Frank, 86
Lévi-Strauss, Claude, 45, 48
Locke, John, 13–14
Lord, Albert B., 43
Loti, Pierre, 83

Luhmann, Niklas, 209
Luther, Martin, 177, 185
Lyotard, J.-Fr., 129, 227

Machiavelli, N., 211
Mayhew, Edward, 198
Mallarmé, Stéphane, 24, 109, 224
Man, Paul de, 36, 70, 100–124,
   220–21, 222–26
Marx, Karl, 79, 82, 177
Mather, Cotton, 172–73, 174–75,
   181, 185, 187–89
Mauron, Charles, 224
McDougall, William, 136
McLuhan, Marshall, 173
Melville, Herman, 187
Merriam, Alan P., 213, 219
Michelangelo, 80
Miller, Perry, 179
Milosz, Czeslaw, 204–5
Milton, John, 177
Minsky, Marvin, 35
Morris, Charles, 163
Morrison, Toni, 199
Muecke, D. C., 152
Muhammed, Elijah, 195–96
Myers, F. W. H., 101

Nagy, Gregory, 43–59, 214, 218
Nicole, Pierre, 13
Nietzsche, F. W., 26–27, 33, 37, 107,
   131, 160–61, 195, 211, 227

Oedipus, 95–96
O'Hara, Frank, 203
Olbrechts-Tyteca, L., 226
O'Sullivan, John, 187

Page, D. L., 215
Paine, Thomas, 175
Parker, Patricia, 60–73, 220
Pausanias, 47
Perelman, C., 226
Pfeiffer, Rudolf, 215
Pindar, 49, 53–54
Plato, 6, 44f, 89f, 131, 133–34, 139,
   158, 211, 217
Pope, Alexander, 149
Puttenham, George, 63–64, 219

Quintilian, 60–64, 68–73 *passim*,
   140, 211, 215

Reagan, Ronald, 33, 187
Reiman, Donald H., 225
Richards, I. A., 35, 152
Richardson, S., 20
Ricoeur, Paul, 127
Rilke, Rainer Maria, 225
Roth, Philip, 199, 206
Rousseau, Jean-Jacques, 84, 107, 112,
   115, 120f, 122–23, 224–25
Royce, Anya P., 214–15
Rwanda, 219

Sachs, Hanns, 95
Saussure, F. de, 29f, 73
Schiller, J. C. F. von, 100
Schubert, Franz, 21
Schumann, Robert, 21
Sedgwick, Eve Kosofsky, 84
Sennett, Richard, 191–206
Sewall, Samuel, 188
Shakespeare, William, 149, 153–54
Shank, Roger, 35
Shelley, Percy Bysshe, 101, 105,
   112–16, 120f, 223
Sherwood, Samuel, 175
Smith, Adam, 14
Smith, Sir Thomas, 12
Socrates, 44, 89, 132f, 139, 152
Sollers, Philippe, 78–79
Sperber, Dan, 34, 140–55, 228–29

Tacitus, 17
Tarde, Gabriel, 136
Tate, Allen, 35
Telemachus, 217
Thoreau, Henry David, 187
Thucydides, 55
Tisias, 7
Todorov, Tzvetan, 127

Valesio, Paolo, 30
Vico, G., 211
Virgil, 188

Wellbery, David E., 3–39, 211
Welsh, Alexander, 13
West, M. L., 215
White, Hayden, 28
Wigglesworth, Michael, 182
Wilson, Deirdre, 34, 140–55, 228–29
Winthrop, John, 178–80, 182
Wittgenstein, L. J. J., 34

Wolf, Hugo, 21
Wordsworth, William, 20, 101–124,
  223
Wundt, G., 93–94

Yeats, William Butler, 108–11, 116
Young, David, 217

Znaniecki, Florian, 198
Zimmerli, Walther Ch., 156–67

Library of Congress Cataloging-in-Publication Data

The Ends of rhetoric : history, theory, practice / edited by John Bender
and David E. Wellbery.
    p.   cm.
ISBN 0-8047-1817-2 (alk. paper)
ISBN 0-8047-1818-0 (pbk. : alk. paper)
    1. Rhetoric.   I. Bender, John B.   II. Wellbery, David E.
P301.E55   1990
808—dc20   90-9518
                                                                    CIP

⊛   This book is printed on acid-free paper